PRESIDENTS' SECRETS

MARY GRAHAM

Presidents' Secrets

THE USE AND ABUSE OF HIDDEN POWER

Yale

UNIVERSITY PRESS

NEW HAVEN AND LONDON

Published with assistance from the foundation established in memory of
Calvin Chapin of the class of 1788, Yale College.

Yale University Press books may be purchased in quantity for educational,
business, or promotional use. For information, please e-mail sales.press@yale.
edu (U.S. office) or sales@yaleup.co.uk (U.K. office).

Set in Time Roman type by IDS Infotech Ltd., Chandigarh, India.
Printed in the United States of America.

ISBN 978-0-300-22374-3
Library of Congress Control Number 2016950309
A catalogue record for this book is available from the British Library.

This paper meets the requirements of ANSI/NISO Z39.48-1992
(Permanence of Paper).

10 9 8 7 6 5 4 3 2 1

CONTENTS

ACKNOWLEDGMENTS

MANY PEOPLE HAVE HELPED MAKE THIS BOOK possible. I owe a special debt of gratitude to Senator Daniel Patrick Moynihan, who provided the inspiration for much of my work over the past twenty years. When I began to write about the politics of public information in the late 1990s, Senator Moynihan introduced me to eminent scholars and led impromptu seminars for me and my research assistants. The report of the Commission on Protecting and Reducing Government Secrecy, which he chaired, and his 1998 book *Secrecy* informed our work at Harvard's Kennedy School of Government and provided a starting point for this book. Beginning in my college days, he and his wife Liz provided wise counsel, intellectual challenge, good humor, and hospitality as they did for so many students. I am grateful for Liz's continuing friendship.

I am grateful to another early teacher, Edward C. Banfield, professor of government at Harvard, with whom I studied and for whom I worked most college summers. Ed never gave up trying to teach his students to think skeptically and write clearly, despite our shortcomings.

I would not have had the temerity to begin this book or to complete it if it had not been for the encouragement and advice of presidential historian Michael Beschloss. His encyclopedic knowledge of presidents' lives and deeds is unparalleled, as is his patience.

Jim and Kate Lehrer read the full manuscript at an early stage, gave me detailed comments, helped answer countless questions, and remained optimistic that I would someday finish this project. When I thought I had completed the manuscript, Bob Samuelson, who has been one of my best critics since our days as college journalists, suggested that I take more time to revise it. I learned a great deal from that extra year, and I hope the revisions have resulted in a clearer, more cohesive story.

Corby Kummer, senior editor of the *Atlantic* and editor-in-chief of *Ideas: The Magazine of the Aspen Institute,* edited multiple versions of the manuscript with his usual high standards, good humor, and exceptional tolerance of an author's foibles. I have learned more about writing from Corby than from anyone else. When I was tempted to give up an endeavor that was more difficult than I expected, it was Corby who said "you can't."

At Yale University Press I am grateful to executive editor Bill Frucht, consulting editor Steve Wasserman, and manuscript editor Phillip King. My agents, Katherine Flynn and Ike Williams, shepherded the book through the publishing process. Michael Rudell and Eric Brown provided exceptional support and legal advice.

I am grateful to the historians, journalists, and scholars who took the time to read and comment on some or all of the manuscript. They include Jill Abramson, Michael Beschloss, John Milton Cooper, Jr., Chris DeMuth, Jack Fuller, Archon Fung, Alonzo Hamby, Bo Jones, Marjorie Scardino, Geoffrey Stone, and David Weil. Michael Schudson, who reviewed the manuscript for Yale University Press, offered many insights that helped to improve the final product.

Family and friends who provided helpful comments included Will Graham, Molly Graham, Don Graham, Liz Moynihan, and Laura and Tim O'Shaughnessy. I am grateful to John Auerbach, Afsaneh Beschloss, Sara Lawrence-Lightfoot, Walter Pincus, and Bob Woodward for their interest and support.

I have had the great pleasure of working with two exceptional researchers. We aimed to rely on primary sources and original documents whenever possible, supplemented by the accounts of participants, and by the interpretations of leading historians. Hilary McClellen worked with me on the Cold War chapters and on the particularly difficult task of understanding and documenting the emergence of twenty-first-century secrecy and openness. Her precision, good judgment, and unfailing "can-do" spirit made this a much better book. Terri Saint-Amour, then a reference librarian at Harvard Law School, constructed a remarkable database of original documents tracing the founders' views of secrecy and openness and those of the nation's first president, including debates, correspondence, and contemporary newspapers. She also helped me reconstruct from primary sources the complexities of Woodrow Wilson's presidency and his illness.

I am grateful to the many archivists at presidential libraries who helped answer research questions. They include Claudia Anderson, Sarah Cunningham, and Jennifer Cuddeback at the Lyndon Baines Johnson Presidential Library; Randy Sowell at the Harry S. Truman Library; Jeremy Schmidt and Elizabeth Druga at the Gerald R. Ford Presidential Library; Jon Fletcher at the Richard Nixon Presidential Library; Ira Pemstein at the Ronald Reagan Presidential Library; Keith Shuler at the Jimmy Carter Presidential Library; Jason Kaplan at the William J. Clinton Presidential Library; and Brandon Zogg at the George W. Bush Presidential Library.

Others who assisted with research questions included Betty Koed, associate historian, United States Senate; Brian McLaughlin at the Senate library; Bruce Bustard and Abigail Myrick at the National Archives and Records Administration; Julie Thomas, a librarian at California State University, Sacramento; Amy Fitch, an archivist at the Rockefeller Archive Center; and Rachel Scheer, a publicist at *Scientific American.*

I was also assisted by scholars David M. Barrett, John Feerick, Jeffrey A. Engel, Beverly Gage, Joel K. Goldstein, Thomas J. Knock, Michael R. Lemov, Christopher E. Manning, and Garrison Nelson.

Cambridge colleagues Archon Fung and David Weil have provided fifteen years of learning and collaboration at the Transparency Policy Project as we have tried to understand the politics of public information, and their friendship has enriched my life. It has been a great pleasure to work with Elena Fagotto, who not only directed research at the project but also handled daily demands and supervised research assistants while I was writing.

I am grateful to friends and neighbors Royal Kennedy Rodgers, Jessica Roth, and the Bosco family in Washington, D.C., and to Edna and Peter Collom, Susan and Chip Morse, Karen and Tom Tierney, Judy and Phil Richardson, Katie Westfall Tharp and Eugene Mirman, Ann Dvorak Warner, and Annalisa Eisen in Woods Hole, Massachusetts.

I learned a great deal from accounts by participants in the administrations of the presidents I have focused on. The participants are too numerous to name but their books and articles were extremely valuable in providing diverse perspectives and lively detail. I especially want to acknowledge the accounts of members of the intelligence community who have taken the time to explain the importance of protecting essential secrets in an open government.

I remain in awe of biographers and historians who have spent years chronicling the life of one president or the events of one historical period. To mention a few of those whose work was particularly important to this book: Michael Beschloss, Douglas Brinkley, James MacGregor Burns, James Cannon, Robert A. Caro, Ron Chernow, John Milton Cooper, Jr., Robert Dallek, John Lewis Gaddis, Jack Goldsmith, David M. Kennedy, William E. Leuchtenburg, Arthur Link, Robert H. Ferrell, Alonzo Hamby, Pauline Maier, Harold Relyea, Richard Rhodes, Geoffrey R. Stone, and Gordon S. Wood.

Among the journalists who broke difficult and controversial stories or painstakingly pieced together accounts of twenty-first-century leaders' actions behind closed doors are Jonathan Alter, Peter Baker, Bart Gellman, Bradley Graham, Sy Hersh, Eric Lichtblau, David Maraniss, Dana Priest and William M. Arkin, Walter Pincus, David Remnick, James Risen, David E. Sanger, Charlie Savage, Scott Shane, Bob Woodward, and Lawrence Wright.

I benefited from early opportunities to work in two of the three branches of government. While in law school, I worked for the chief judge of the D.C. Circuit Court of Appeals. Later, I worked in the Office of Management and Budget and the Department of Transportation. I observed the struggles between the media and government when my husband Don Graham served as an executive at the Washington Post Company. Proceeds from this book will be donated to the National Archives Foundation, which works to improve appreciation of the nation's heritage and encourage citizen engagement in democracy.

Finally, I am grateful to my children and grandchildren, Liza, Laura, Will, Molly, Tim, Peter, Charlotte, and Lucy. They add joy to all my days.

PRESIDENTS' SECRETS

Introduction

THE TERRORIST ATTACKS OF SEPTEMBER 11, 2001, which shattered the nation's prevailing notions of national security, also called into question a generation of limitations on presidents' secrets. Threats from elusive networks of extremists created an urgent need for secret intelligence in order to locate terrorists before they attacked. But those threats also created an urgent need for public information so that citizens could understand the new challenges, protect themselves and their communities, guard their rights, and grant their consent to new policies.

New threats and advances in digital technology meant that old bargains didn't work anymore. In the years that followed, presidents could no longer protect the nation's vital secrets. Nor did they provide the openness that Americans now expected.

Uncertainty bred confusion and suspicion. Fewer than a quarter of Americans trusted the federal government most of the time, close to an all-time low since the 1950s. Nearly all of those polled said that they had lost control of their personal information. Most believed they were being watched as they went about their daily lives. Growing distrust deprived leaders' actions of legitimacy and kept the nation from responding with its full strength to new crises.[1]

In this time of rapid change, the aims and instincts of the first two presidents of the twenty-first century took on unusual importance. Determined to prevent the next attack and intent on demonstrating executive authority, George W. Bush circled around settled law and practice. His new programs of stealth detention, interrogation, and surveillance tested the limits of presidents' secret, unilateral actions. Eight years later, Barack Obama revealed some of those programs, anchored anti-terrorism policies in national and international law, and made a bold promise that the president's secret actions would always be accompanied by oversight from Congress and the courts. However, secretive oversight of secretive programs no longer worked. Citizens no longer trusted Congress, and they expected open debate about presidents' proposals that affected their rights or their safety. When information leaked out about surveillance, armed drones, and cyberattacks, the president demonstrated belatedly that it was possible to have a productive debate about security measures without revealing operational secrets.

Amid presidents' steps and missteps, partisan rancor, media hype, and changing threats, the nation is seeking an accommodation between openness and secrecy for the digital age. Far from being helpless, ordinary citizens have a leading role to play in deciding what the new bargain will be.

Three times in the past, Americans have recalibrated the role of secrecy in open government when confronted with new threats and advancing technology. Change was never part of a grand plan and often was not even recognized while it was taking place. Instead, new accommodations emerged from political conflict, personal power struggles, and presidents' ad hoc efforts to solve pressing problems. Each time, however, recalibrating the role of secrecy led to lasting changes in American democracy.

From the start, the nation's founders recognized that a measure of secrecy was essential to democratic governance but that excessive secrecy represented its greatest danger. The delegates to the Constitutional Convention and the nation's first president designed the initial balance between openness and secrecy in response to a national emergency. The Constitution divided authority among the president, Congress, and the courts in order to guard against tyranny. Shared power meant shared information. Government by the people required an informed public.

The first Congress added the amendments that became the Bill of Rights. At a time when Britain and Spain conspired to seize territory and bankrupt farmers were rioting, the nation's leaders deemed it particularly important to protect against unreasonable searches, arbitrary detention, and press censorship.

At the same time, there was an understanding that secrecy was essential to military operations, successful diplomacy, and confidential deliberations. The

Constitutional Convention itself met behind closed doors in an effort to avoid the passions of the moment and encourage delegates to freely change their views.

George Washington, as the nation's first president, translated these parchment promises into a culture of open government and bounded secrecy that endured for more than a hundred years. As crisis followed crisis, Congress demanded that he disclose confidential papers—everything from correspondence about a military contractor's misdeeds to proposed payments to the Barbary pirates. Washington agonized over each request, acutely aware that he was setting precedents. He sought advice from his department heads, who often disagreed among themselves. Struggling to find workable arrangements that allowed public scrutiny without sacrificing security, he became the master of the middle ground. He supported the principle of congressional oversight, provided confidential correspondence but limited access to it, and handed over papers but deleted sensitive sections. Washington's example endured. Secrecy would be circumscribed for more than a hundred years.

Two well-meaning presidents, Woodrow Wilson and Harry Truman, became the chief architects of a new reckoning that grew out of the long struggle against communism. By the beginning of the twentieth century, trade, travel, and technology brought new prosperity and also new vulnerabilities. Peacetime intelligence gathering and protection of secrets became a necessity when armed conflicts did not end threats to security. But these presidents made fateful choices to give officials new hidden powers without constructing limits to keep covert activities, investigations, and surveillance from encroaching on enduring values. As a result, the uses, misuses, and abuses of secrecy flourished during the Cold War.

President Wilson laid a foundation for peacetime secrecy without accountability. When the Bolsheviks seized power in Russia in 1917, fears of communist aggression created new imperatives to learn Soviet secrets, hide American plans, and find an invisible enemy hidden in American communities, and perhaps in the government itself. Wilson stirred up those fears by suggesting conspiracies among communists, immigrants, striking workers, and violent anarchists. Responding to real and imagined threats, his administration sponsored mail-opening, tapped telegraph lines, instituted loyalty investigations of government employees, and championed a vaguely worded espionage act. His secrecy about his own incapacitating stroke left the nation without a working president and freed zealots within his administration to detain immigrants, radicals, labor organizers, and other suspicious persons on hidden charges.

After World War II, President Truman built on Wilson's foundation a collection of powerful agencies that grew in the dark. In a Cold War that lasted longer than anyone expected, agents took on dangerous assignments and provided critical intelligence. But they also spied on ordinary Americans and conducted stealth operations that violated U.S. and foreign laws, creating a double standard that presidents and other leaders secretly endorsed. These agencies were designed to avoid checks by Congress and the courts. The Central Intelligence Agency (CIA), which engaged in election-fixing, bribery, and paramilitary activities, was exempted from budget reviews and congressional questioning. The National Security Agency (NSA), its very existence classified, was authorized to operate outside of usual controls. J. Edgar Hoover, the nation's Federal Bureau of Intelligence (FBI) director for forty-eight years, cast a wide net to spy on politicians, civil rights activists, and suspicious persons.

No president intended the ramshackle edifice of peacetime agencies and stratified secrets that grew out of the Cold War. Instead, impromptu measures created single-mission organizations that made their own rules because no one was watching. Secrecy walled off decisions from the tug and pull of competing priorities and midcourse corrections.

Ordinary men, serving in the nation's highest office and facing challenges they never expected, had to act quickly to address new and unfamiliar threats. They did not have the luxury of pondering questions of openness, secrecy, and accountability at their leisure. And they usually did not consider the distant consequences of their immediate actions. Instead, they responded to the urgency of events, constrained by limited knowledge, confronted with conflicting advice, and harassed by political opponents. With little guidance about the limits of secrecy, they reacted to the politics of the moment with their varied experience or inexperience, their understanding of history and the Constitution, and their inclination to seek advice or to avoid debate.

Along the way, Cold War secrecy became a habit, "a characteristic mode of governance," as Senator Daniel Patrick Moynihan observed in *Secrecy,* his landmark book published in 1998. Presidents expanded surveillance in order to catch spies and uncover enemies' secrets. But they also hid their mental or physical illnesses, their ethical lapses, their intrusions into the privacy of ordinary citizens, and their illicit efforts to weaken their political opponents.

Competing sleuths hid information from each other, from Congress, and some-times from the president himself. Each new president inherited a jumble of hidden executive orders, memos, legal opinions, guidelines, and overgrown institutions that no one had designed and that the American people had never approved.

Then chance events brought decades of abuses out into the open, engaged congressional leaders, and began a long process of embedding presidents' secret actions in constitutional checks. Congress first tried to counter Cold War secrecy with the Freedom of Information Act in 1966, but the public right to government information was weakened by President Lyndon Johnson's polit-ical maneuvering. Then, in the early 1970s, investigative reporting suggested links between Republican president Richard Nixon's White House and a bungled burglary of Democratic headquarters in Washington's Watergate office complex. Reporting triggered congressional scrutiny. Scrutiny uncovered evidence of CIA involvement in the burglary as well as a taping system in the Oval Office. Tapes indicated that the president had lied under oath and had interfered with the FBI's investigation of the burglary. After Nixon resigned and Gerald Ford was inaugurated as president, an investigation by a new CIA director revealed hundreds of other questionable activities since the agency's creation in 1947.

The result was a patchwork of new laws, resolutions, executive orders, and court decisions that limited presidents' secrecy, protected citizens' privacy rights, and strengthened the public's right to examine government documents. Officials who had done what earlier presidents asked, in violation of the law, were suddenly blamed for those actions. There were flaws and gaps in these reforms, and Cold War habits proved hard to break. But the nation gradually returned to the founding idea that the president was responsible to the people and their representatives for his secret actions, even in times of trouble.

Congress imposed three kinds of limits on presidents' secret activities. Some laws banned such activities altogether. The CIA was forbidden to participate in assassination plans. Both the CIA and NSA were barred from engaging in domestic surveillance. Other laws required advance approval of secret activi-ties and after-the-fact oversight by Congress and the courts. Covert actions required presidential approval and congressional briefing. FBI wiretaps required the attorney general's signoff. Still others created new institutions to reconcile the need for both openness and secrecy. Strengthened inspectors general, embedded in government agencies, investigated secret policies and practices, and reported to Congress. A foreign intelligence surveillance court replaced warrantless searches with required court approval. New congressional intelligence committees had to be informed of covert activities and other security initiatives. In amendments to the Freedom of Information Act, Congress fortified the public's right to examine government files, and authorized judges to question presidents' security secrets. One characteristic of these accommodations, however, was that oversight itself was often conducted behind closed doors.

Then came the terrorist attacks of September 11, 2001. President George W. Bush tested twenty-five years of legislated restraints on secrecy. Like some other conservative leaders, he believed that the reforms of the 1970s had gone too far in limiting executive authority. They tangled a president's initiatives in a labyrinth of reviews by agency lawyers, Congress, and the courts when the president needed to act quickly and decisively to protect the nation. Bush inaugurated new kinds of military commissions, secret programs to detain and interrogate terrorist suspects, domestic surveillance by the NSA, the use of armed drones, and the development of offensive cyberweapons, all without congressional or public debate.

But secrecy no longer worked as it had during the Cold War. In the environment of growing accountability fostered by 1970s reforms, more watchdogs within and outside of government stalked each decision. Domestic and foreign media searched for clues. Troubled officials, trained to follow a generation of restraining rules, and investigative reporters, made skeptical by earlier abuses, revealed some of Bush's actions. Members of Congress, who had become accustomed to scrutinizing the president's actions, rejected some of his plans and amended others. Courts, too, had become more active in protecting individual rights and questioning security measures. The Supreme Court brought the president's detention of terrorist suspects back within the bounds of U.S. and international law. A national emergency does not give a president a blank check, Justice Sandra Day O'Connor wrote in one opinion.

In his first national security address in May 2009, President Obama promised openness when it was possible, and oversight by Congress and the courts when it was not. He rejected some of President Bush's stealth policies, anchored others in national and international law, and issued new orders for government transparency. But by trying unsuccessfully to keep secret ground rules for drone strikes, cyberattacks, and the surveillance of Americans, Obama missed opportunities for leadership, ceded initiative to troubled officials and the media, and inflamed debate.

Out of these controversies came elements of a new accommodation between openness and secrecy. The enormous growth of stealth enterprises, supported both by presidents and by Congress, was accompanied by steps toward oversight that was more open, independent, and fair. Secrecy about new programs that altered Americans' rights or expectations no longer served the interests of the president, the Congress, or the public. Under duress, Obama had shown that it was possible to openly debate and improve such programs without sacrificing security. The nation began adapting to the digital age the idea that more secrecy could be matched by more openness.

But much depended on the actions of future leaders. Challenges included providing intelligence agents with safe spaces to do their work, assuring allies that sensitive negotiations and shared intelligence would remain confidential, and sweeping out remaining remnants of Cold War secrecy. Congress had not yet found ways to carry out more open and active oversight. And courts had not yet developed standards for reviewing complex security issues. As Justice Stephen Breyer wrote in *The Court and the World:* "If the Court is no longer prepared to give the President a blank check [in national emergencies], just what kind of check is it prepared to give him?"[2]

Americans are right to continue to worry about presidents' secrets. Congress cannot challenge policies that secretive presidents do not reveal. Courts cannot protect the rule of law if presidents are inclined to hide injustices. Citizens cannot judge how well their government is doing if leaders are lying. Genuine accountability is impossible if people cannot know what the government is accountable for. Secrecy nurtures arbitrary power and squelches debate. New policies gain lasting legitimacy only if an informed public approves of them.

Americans should also care about responsible openness. Presidents cannot keep the nation safe unless they can guard nuclear codes, the specifics of military operations and weapons technologies, intelligence agents' identities and locations, and confidential negotiations. Excessive secrecy threatens security, but so does the theft of gigabytes of government documents.

I began this work during the presidency of George W. Bush. After the terrorist attacks of 2001, I wrote a report for the *Atlantic,* "The Information Wars," puzzling over the sudden disappearance from government websites of information that might be useful to terrorists but that Americans also needed to protect their health and safety. Under White House direction, officials had deleted information about the risks to communities from accidents at chemical plants, the safety of water reservoirs, and the location of oil and gas pipelines. I had co-founded with David Weil and Archon Fung a project at Harvard University's John F. Kennedy School of Government to examine more closely issues of government secrecy and openness. When controversial leaks of classified information in 2005 and 2006 revealed some of President Bush's extraordinary measures and sparked an acrimonious debate, I wanted to know what ground rules earlier presidents had observed for secrecy and openness during these long periods of foreign and domestic threats, the troubled peace that has characterized much of the nation's history.[3]

I have focused mainly on one kind of government secrecy, presidents' actions at times when their choices changed American democracy. I have focused on presidents because they have unique power to keep hidden important decisions. I have not written about congressional or judicial secrecy, both formidable topics. I have not compared the United States' experience with that of other democracies, or explored broader topics of information access or executive authority.

In American politics, secrecy, the purposeful withholding of known plans, deeds, or factual information, has proven to be a malleable practice. The circle of those in the know may be small or large. Those excluded may be insiders or outsiders: presidents' advisers, members of Congress, judges, or the public at large. Secrecy may last for days, weeks, months, or decades. In a democracy, it cannot last forever. In the United States, secrecy is always an exception to the public's right to open information and deliberations, grounded in the Constitution's insistence on a government by the people and embodied in federal and state laws.

The attention here to presidents' varied inclinations toward secrecy is not meant to belittle their accomplishments. President Wilson supported the creation of the Federal Reserve System, the Federal Trade Commission, tariff reform, antitrust legislation, and a plan for a league of nations to prevent future wars. President Truman supported the efforts of free peoples everywhere to counter communist takeover. He proposed the Marshall Plan to revive European nations devastated by war, created civilian control of the armed forces and atomic energy, and outlawed racial discrimination in the armed forces and in interstate transportation. President Johnson championed civil rights legislation, Medicare and Medicaid, and other progressive reforms. President George W. Bush sought to improve public education, cut taxes, and reform Medicare and Social Security. President Obama managed the nation's recovery from a dreadful financial crisis, expanded health care, opened relations with Cuba, and worked to improve immigration laws and gun control.

I have focused on the three periods when presidents' choices made lasting changes to the role of secrecy in open government, concluding with the nation's current dilemmas. The first two chapters describe the struggles of the nation's founders to create a lasting culture of open government. The next two chapters follow Woodrow Wilson and Harry Truman as they confronted communist aggression, creating secretive institutions and practices that expanded during the Cold War. Then, secrecy itself came under attack. Two chapters track Lyndon Johnson's resistance to increasing openness, his credibility gap as he tried to manage the politics of information in an unwinnable war, and his stealth effort to cripple a robust public information law. By contrast, Gerald Ford's measured responses helped to construct limits to secrecy's future misuse. The final two chapters chronicle George W. Bush's unsuccessful efforts to defy those limits after the terrorist attacks of 2001, and the controversies surrounding Barack Obama's steps and missteps in adapting openness and secrecy to the digital age.

This search for understanding has taken me to unexpected places. To a hot, dark, fly-infested room in Philadelphia 225 years ago, for the most important secret deliberation in the nation's history. To President Washington's home in Philadelphia, where an unruly mob protested his attempt to keep secret the terms of a proposed treaty with Britain while the Senate debated it behind closed doors. To President Wilson's darkened bedroom, where the most harrowing story of hidden presidential incapacity unfolded in ways that altered the nation's future. To the White House lunch room, where President Truman celebrated the launch of the Central Intelligence Group by handing out black capes and fake mustaches. To President Johnson's ranch, where he pondered whether to sign a public information law he despised. To the House chamber, where President Ford tried unsuccessfully to persuade members of Congress that it would be catastrophic to reveal past intelligence abuses. And finally to the Oval Office, as the first two presidents of the twenty-first century wrestled with the dual challenges of terrorism and digital technology.

The Constitutional Convention:
The President's Limited Power

George Washington presided over the nation's most important secret meeting, the meeting that created the government he would lead as the nation's first president. Faced with domestic and foreign threats to the nation's survival, the delegates to the Constitutional Convention and the first Congress nonetheless created a government based on shared power and shared information, and explicitly protected privacy and freedom of expression. At the same time, they introduced the idea that secret deliberations had a place in open government. Closing the doors of the Convention itself encouraged delegates to speak candidly and reach constructive compromises. But secrecy also produced leaks, misinformation, and charges of conspiracy that nearly defeated their efforts.

"I KNOW NOT WHOSE PAPER IT IS, but there it is, let him who owns it take it," George Washington thundered. He threw the papers down on the table in front of him and strode from the room. Someone had broken the vow of secrecy.

The three dozen men facing him were alarmed. Their leader was usually a silent and benevolent presence. But as they prepared to adjourn for the day, his anger vanquished his usual self-control. "I am sorry to find that some Member of this Body, has been so neglectful of the secrets of the Convention as to drop in the State House a copy of their proceedings, which by accident was picked up and delivered to me this Morning. I must entreat Gentlemen to be more careful, lest our transactions get into the News Papers, and disturb the public repose by premature speculations."

William Pierce, the delegate who later described this scene, put his hand in his coat pocket as the president spoke and was shocked to find his own copy of the papers missing. Approaching the president's table with trepidation, he was relieved to find that the abandoned copy included notes that were not in his handwriting. When he returned to the Indian Queen, the boarding house where he and many others were staying, he was relieved to find his copy in the pocket of a coat he had pulled off that morning.

No one ever claimed the dropped papers.[1]

Washington's outburst reflected the desperation of the moment. The delegates to the Constitutional Convention of 1787 were engaged in a high-risk enterprise to remake the new nation's government. It was not what they had been assigned to do. Washington feared that if word leaked out, the meeting's failure would mean civil war or foreign occupation.

The four-year-old government had failed. The Continental Congress, the sole governing body, did not have the authority to collect revenue, regulate trade, or settle states' disputes over boundaries and tariffs. Meanwhile, Britain and Spain schemed to pick off vulnerable frontier territory, and economic turmoil triggered farmers' rebellions.

Instead of strengthening the Articles of Confederation as Congress and their state legislatures had instructed them to do, the delegates were debating an entirely new plan of government. It was an illicit enterprise with a seemingly impossible goal. There were too many competing interests—small versus large states, the south versus the north, the frontier versus the eastern seaboard, and national needs versus state and local autonomy. Only a secret meeting had a chance of creating a lasting representative government.

Over the next four months, the words and actions of these men, meeting behind closed doors in Philadelphia's stifling summer heat, embedded in American governance two competing ideas. The first was that the government would be accountable to the American people. It would derive its legitimacy from the consent of the governed. The second was that secrecy had a legitimate place in an open government.

The delegates created an open government at a time of national emergency. The thirteen colonies had won the Revolutionary War but had not yet secured the peace. After the treaty of 1783 that secured the nation's independence, the British, who still controlled Canada, continued to give military support to hostile Indian tribes, block exports to the West Indies, negotiate separate trade agreements with individual states, and occupy forts in American territory. Spain barred trade through New Orleans, effectively cutting off commerce on the Mississippi River, and bribed frontier politicians in attempts to sever Appalachian lands and attach them to the Spanish empire. Washington feared that western settlers would be driven into the arms of these foreigners.[2]

Writing to Thomas Jefferson soon after he arrived in Philadelphia, Washington warned that "the general government, if it can be called a government, is shaken to its foundation, and liable to be overturned by every blast. In a word, it is at an end; and, unless a remedy is soon applied, anarchy and confusion will inevitably ensue." The fifty-five-year-old general had come out of retirement reluctantly to risk his reputation on the success of these secret sessions because he viewed them as the last hope to save the nation. He had served in the French and Indian War, commanded the army in the Revolutionary War, and served in the Virginia House of Burgesses and the First Continental Congress, and now the Convention had unanimously elected him its leader. But he craved a respite from public service. This was not the kind of gathering he felt comfortable leading. A man of action with less formal education than many of the delegates, he was not in his element debating about the structure of government.[3]

Nor was there peace among the states and territories. They made conflicting foreign policies, maintained their own navies, and fought over borders. Western migrants decreed a new state called Franklin in what later became eastern Tennessee. Connecticut claimed Pennsylvania's Wyoming Valley. Vermont claimed parts of New York and New Hampshire, and threatened to secede from the union. New York imposed heavy fees on New Jersey and Connecticut vessels using its ports. South Carolina, New York, and Pennsylvania taxed the goods of competing states.

In letters and in their debates, the delegates often referred to the breakdown of law and order and the impotence of the Continental Congress. Four months before the Convention convened, 1,100 debt-ridden farmers, threatened with imprisonment for failing to pay their creditors, marched on the Springfield, Massachusetts, courthouse and arsenal in what became known as Shays' Rebellion. With no authority or funding to send in troops, Congress stood by helplessly.

It was these fears that emboldened the delegates to defy Congress's orders. The Convention was to meet "for the sole and express purpose of revising the

Articles of Confederation." Secrecy would prevent the members of Congress who had authorized their meeting and the state legislators who had paid for their attendance from knowing that the delegates were not following their instructions.[4]

The delegates had not planned to meet behind closed doors. On a rainy Friday, May 25, their first meeting day, they named three of their number to serve as the Convention's Rules Committee. George Wythe of Virginia, senior in age and stature, served as the committee's chair. Respected for his honesty, integrity, and legal learning, Wythe, who was sixty-one, had helped organize Virginia's government. He had served as speaker of that state's House of Delegates, and as a member of Congress. He had taught future presidents Thomas Jefferson and James Monroe, and future Supreme Court justice John Marshall, at the College of William and Mary. He was joined on the committee by Alexander Hamilton, a generation younger at thirty-two, Washington's aide during the Revolutionary War and a member of Congress from New York, and Charles Pinckney, thirty, of South Carolina, who had served in both Congress and his state legislature.

When the delegates reconvened after the weekend, the committee's report did not include a recommendation of secrecy. Wythe explained that each state delegation would have one vote, and that delegates of seven states had to be present for a quorum. In an effort to counter legislative multitasking, apparently already endemic, he warned that while a delegate was speaking, "none shall hold discourse with another, or read a book, pamphlet or paper, printed or manuscript." But at the end of the day, Pierce Butler of South Carolina made a motion that the rules also forbid "licentious publications of their proceedings."[5]

By the next morning, Tuesday, May 29, the committee had broadened Butler's suggestion into three sweeping rules that closed all of the Convention's deliberations:

> That no copy be taken of any entry on the journal during the sitting of the House without leave of the House.
>
> That members only be permitted to inspect the journal.
>
> That nothing spoken in the House be printed, or otherwise published, or communicated without leave.

Sitting alone at the president's table, a sober Washington immediately stopped entering the day's deliberations in his personal diary. At the end of the

Convention's first week he wrote: "No minutes of the proceedings has been, or will be inserted in this diary."[6]

The decision was controversial at a time when open deliberations had become a prevailing practice. Colonial legislatures generally recorded their proceedings. The Articles of Confederation required that Congress publish its journal, even during the Revolutionary War, providing for a secret journal for sensitive matters. The constitutions of Pennsylvania and New York explicitly required open legislative sessions. In Britain, parliamentary debates were officially reported beginning with the reign of George III in 1760. Often legislative journals included only actions and votes. Open doors came later.[7]

Respected leaders pointed out the virtues of publicity. Open debate would lead to better decisions that would benefit from a diversity of views from leaders outside the meeting room. Such decisions were likely to more accurately reflect the will of the people. And open proceedings would promote free discussion among the delegates themselves both in the assembly room and in the boarding houses and taverns where they spent leisure hours.

Informed by James Madison about the rule, Thomas Jefferson, who was serving as minister to France, wrote to John Adams: "I am sorry they began their deliberations by so abominable a precedent as that of tying up the tongues of their members. Nothing can justify this example but the innocence of their intentions, & ignorance of the value of public discussions."[8]

Delegate Luther Martin of Maryland protested that "so far did this rule extend that we were thereby prevented from corresponding with the gentlemen in different States upon the subjects under our discussion. . . . I had no idea, that all the wisdom, integrity, and virtue of this State, or of the others, were centred in the convention. I wished to have corresponded freely and confidentially with eminent political characters in my own and other States . . . to give their sentiments due weight and consideration. . . . The members *were prohibited even from taking copies of resolutions on which the convention were deliberating, or extracts of any kind from the journals, without formally moving for, and obtaining permission . . . thereby precluding even the members themselves from the necessary means of information and deliberation* on the *important business in which they were engaged*" (emphasis in the original).[9]

Patrick Henry, the acclaimed orator who had served four terms as Virginia's governor but who had declined to serve as a delegate, asked at the state's ratification convention: What dangers of "such awful magnitude" warranted such a fundamental change in government? "What right had they to say *We, the people?* . . . The people gave them no power to use their name."[10]

The *Pennsylvania Herald* reported that "such circumspection and secrecy mark the proceedings of the federal convention, that the members find it difficult to acquire the habit of communication even among themselves, and are so cautious in defeating the curiosity of the public, that all debate is suspended upon the entrance of their own inferior officers."[11]

However, to the delegates, there were compelling reasons why the Convention represented a legitimate exception to the emerging idea of open deliberations. Secrecy would make it easier for delegates to alter their stands on issues, compromise, and quickly reach agreement. Furthermore, the Constitution was only a proposal. Secrecy would last only four months. After that, the results of their deliberations would be revealed and representatives chosen by the voters of each state would decide whether to approve the new government. Finally, their efforts could be obstructed by popular passions. When Washington berated the delegates for not being careful enough with their papers, he was concerned that revelations would "disturb the public repose by premature speculations." The Convention's work would inevitably disturb the public repose, but only after the proposed Constitution was printed and circulated in September.

It is significant that the delegates voted to close their doors on the same day that Edmund Randolph, governor of Virginia and an influential leader, proposed that they consider an entirely new national government. It would consist of a president, a two-chamber legislature with the power to veto state laws, and an independent judiciary. The proposal became known as the Virginia plan. Most of the delegates had come to consider only modest changes in the Articles of Confederation. Many were passionately committed to preserving state sovereignty and deeply suspicious of concentrating power in a national government. Suddenly, they were being asked to consider an entirely new and powerful president and legislature.

Washington himself had a pragmatic view of the enterprise. His close friend Henry Knox had warned him that the Convention might be considered an illegal gathering, even a conspiracy. "The legality of this Convention I do not mean to discuss," he responded. "That which takes the shortest course to obtain [needed federal powers] will, in my opinion, under present circumstances, be found best." All attempts to alter or amend the Articles of Confederation would be like "the propping of a house which is ready to fall."[12]

The next morning, May 30, only their third day of meeting and their first behind closed doors, the proponents of the Virginia plan boldly asked the delegates to vote on the general idea that "a national government ought to be established consisting of a supreme Legislative, Executive and Judiciary." Surprisingly, and no doubt in part because the meeting was then closed, six of the eight states then attending voted to support that principle. Connecticut voted no and New York did not record a vote because its delegates could not agree.

Closing the Convention's doors was only one of several decisions the delegates made to limit the openness of their deliberations. They recorded only state votes, rejecting the recommendation of Wythe's committee that they include individual votes in the journal. Alexander Hamilton had strongly favored the recording of individual votes. He was in an impossible position, advocating a strong central government but knowing that he would be outvoted on each issue by the other two New York delegates, who wanted to preserve the dominant power of the states. But most agreed with George Mason of Virginia, who argued that recording individual votes would discourage the delegates from changing their minds, and would "furnish handles to the adversaries" of the new Constitution. Delegates also worked much of the time as a committee of the whole, meaning that votes represented merely recommendations, not final decisions. And they simply skipped over difficult topics when they reached stalemates, assigning them to committees that met separately and whose proceedings were not recorded. The delegates approached the issues of the president's selection, tenure, and powers at least three separate times, unable to reach agreement. Finally, the issues seemed so intractable that they were assigned to the aptly named Committee on Postponed Parts.[13]

The Convention's confidential deliberations did have benefits. They encouraged candid debate, made it easier to ignore Congress's limited mandate, and produced an enduring agreement. Had the debate been publicized, the Convention would almost certainly have been aborted. Hamilton judged that "had the deliberations been open while going on, the clamors of factions would have prevented any satisfactory result."[14] James Madison wrote to James Monroe that "the [secrecy] rule was a prudent one not only as it will effectually secure the requisite freedom of discussion." He added, too optimistically, "it will save both the Convention and the Community from a thousand erroneous and perhaps mischievous reports."[15]

But the Convention also provided a preview of secrecy's costs in a representative government. Closed doors deprived the delegates of diverse ideas and perspectives, and insulated them from popular sentiment. Their failure to include explicit protection of citizens' privacy and freedom of expression from government intrusion nearly doomed their efforts. On September 12, as the delegates were completing their work, Elbridge Gerry moved that the Convention consider including a bill of rights similar to the declarations found in many state constitutions. The idea was quickly voted down. The Constitution gained approval by the states only after Madison promised during ratification debates to combine such protections in a Bill of Rights that the first Congress approved.[16]

One of the delegates' arguments had been that secrecy would make it possible to avoid politics. But the Convention was of course all about politics, just limited to resolving conflicts among the factions that were represented in the room. The decisions to avoid the issue of slavery, to create a two-chamber Congress with equal representation for small states in one chamber, and to set up checks and balances among three independent branches of government were all political compromises between north and south, big states and small, frontier communities and the eastern seaboard.

Secrecy also gave undue influence to the accounts of individual delegates, both in the ratification debates and in later years. Individual delegates' accounts became even more important because the Convention's secretary, William Jackson, who was charged with keeping an official journal, took little care with his responsibilities. A politically ambitious lawyer, Jackson often recorded votes on loose slips of paper without reference to what was voted on. When the Convention ended, he burned many of his notes. The remaining jumbled papers created two centuries of confusion.[17]

Robert Yates, one of the two anti Federalist delegates from New York who soon left the Convention, wrote to his uncle on June 1 that the debates were being held in secrecy but that he was keeping private notes. Rufus King of Massachusetts, James McHenry of Maryland, William Pierce of Georgia, William Paterson of New Jersey, Alexander Hamilton of New York, and George Mason of Virginia all took personal notes that survive.

James Madison, of course, took the most detailed notes in order to provide a historical record of the proceedings. By his own account, he "chose a seat in front of the presiding member . . . [and] in this favorable position for hearing all that passed I noted . . . what was read from the Chair or spoken by the members," never missing a day and working on his notes every evening. Congress bought his notes from his widow, Dolley Madison, after his death in 1836 and published them in 1840—more than half a century after the Convention had taken place.[18]

In an effort to encourage New York's ratification, Hamilton, Madison, and John Jay provided their interpretations of the proposed Constitution in essays that became known as the Federalist Papers. They wrote using pseudonyms for fear of being accused of breaking the Convention's vow of secrecy. Appearing initially as newspaper articles, the essays were widely circulated and appeared in book form early in 1788.

Concealment created a vacuum that was quickly filled by speculation, rumor, leaks to the press, and politically motivated misinformation—consequences that would remain familiar two centuries later. As Madison had written to Jefferson, closed deliberations encouraged "unbiased discussion within doors, and . . . misconceptions & misconstructions without."[19]

Delegates had been hopeful that secrecy would keep the press in check. Alexander Martin of North Carolina wrote to governor Richard Caswell that secrecy "was thought prudent, lest unfavourable Representations might be made by imprudent printers of the many crude matters & things daily uttered & produced in this Body, which are unavoidable, & which in their unfinished state might make an undue impression on the too credulous and unthinking Mobility."[20]

But New York's *Daily Advertiser* reported that the Convention was considering the establishment of a monarchy. And the *Pennsylvania Journal* joined that speculation. In New York, opponents of a strong federal government claimed that the Convention aimed to install George III's son as king.[21]

In the absence of an open record, political opponents reinterpreted facts—or ignored them entirely. As the Convention completed its work, Abraham Yates, Jr., the son of Robert Yates, one of the New York delegates who had walked out of the Convention in early July, wrote that the Convention was far from agreeing and that Massachusetts refused to join in its recommendations. In an eighteenth-century version of deniability, Yates noted that "these are Information I have Picked up from the Members of Congress. . . . You had better not make this public as coming from me." In 1808, Edmond Genet, a former minister from France, pieced together fragments of Yates's notes to paint James Madison, then a candidate for president, as advocating the elimination of state governments during the Convention.[22]

Delegates also leaked information. They resided at boarding houses, dined at Philadelphia's taverns, and accepted the hospitality of local citizens. And the temptation to write confidential letters to friends and relatives proved irresistible.

Some leaks occurred by mistake. Manasseh Cutler of Ipswich, Massachusetts, stopping in Philadelphia while the Convention was meeting, reported a near leak by the oldest delegate, eighty-one-year-old Benjamin Franklin. Finding Franklin under a mulberry tree in his garden with several gentlemen and ladies, Cutler listened to him tell a humorous story about the day's events at the Convention, "for he seemed to forget that everything in Convention was to be kept a profound secret." When one of his visitors reminded him about the secrecy rule, he stopped mid-story.[23]

In other instances, delegates just couldn't resist telling someone what they knew. Richard Henry Lee wrote to his brother in early July that he "found the Convention at Phila. very busy & very secret," but he surmised that the government would be composed of an executive and a two-house legislature.[24]

Nicholas Gilman of New Hampshire wrote to a relative on July 31, "As secrecy is not otherwise enjoined than as prudence may dictate to each individual . . . I gave him [his brother John] a hint respecting the general principles of the plan of national Government."[25]

Leaks and rumors sparked a public debate short on facts and long on passion. Fear and suspicion dominated newspaper articles that warned that the national government or foreign powers would overpower the states. "Vermont, Canada, the Indian Nations, etc. will join their forces to the monster rebellion and drive you head-long, into the pit of political damnation," a writer for the *New York Daily Advertiser* warned.[26]

Madison remained confident that fear for the nation's survival would lead the people to accept whatever the Convention offered. Ten days before the Convention adjourned, he wrote Thomas Jefferson that "the public mind will now or in a very little time receive anything that promise stability to the public Councils & security to private right."[27]

Against this backdrop, the delegates set about creating a government of divided authority that relied on open debate. They limited the president's power and made his actions accountable to the American people, even in the dire emergency that the nation then faced. In doing so, they were not motivated by a lofty view of human nature or by optimism about political behavior. Instead, they drew on the mixed results of their own experiments in representative government during the past decade, and the slightly more distant memories of colonial rule in which they had no voice.

They had to resolve seemingly impossible contradictions. The government needed sufficient authority to settle disputes among states, maintain order, quell economic turmoil, and stand up to European powers. But it had to maintain a measure of state autonomy, avoid autocracy, and remain responsible to the American people.

Madison's meticulous study of earlier republics had convinced him that neither "parchment barriers" nor public opinion would stop officials from abusing their power. Instead, each branch of government must be given "the constitutional means and personal motives to resist encroachments of the others. . . . Ambition must be made to counteract ambition," he explained.[28]

The president had to govern by persuasion. To get anything done, he had to convince Congress, and ultimately the voters, of the wisdom and necessity of his actions. He commanded the nation's military forces and managed its diplomacy. But Congress made the laws, provided the funding, and set limits on military action. The Senate confirmed appointments of ambassadors, judges, and other senior officials, and approved proposed treaties.

There was a general understanding that presidential secrecy had a limited role in meetings with advisers, diplomatic negotiations, and military operations, although the Constitution itself said nothing about it. It stated only that the president would provide Congress with information about the state of the union from time to time.[29]

Even the acclaimed orator Patrick Henry, who opposed a strong central government, noted in Virginia's ratification debate that he was "not an advocate for divulging indiscriminately all the operations of government. . . . Such transactions as relate to military operations or affairs of great consequence, the immediate promulgation of which might defeat the interests of the community, I would not wish to be published." John Marshall, the future chief justice of the Supreme Court, assured Henry that "in this plan, secrecy is only used when it would be fatal and pernicious to publish the schemes of government."[30]

The delegates' early debates about the presidency showed how unsettled were their views about this new office. Their recent experience had been with purely legislative rule under the Articles of Confederation, with weak executives under most state constitutions, and with abuses of power by colonial governors and King George III. They often referred to their fear of a return to tyranny.

A single executive seemed an invitation to autocracy. But a triumvirate would not place sufficient responsibility on one individual. If elected by the national legislature, the president would be too dependent on that body. But if elected by state legislatures or by the people directly, he might not be the best candidate for the job. If serving for one long term, he might amass too much power. But if serving for two or more shorter terms, he might be too beholden to those who elected him. If given veto power, he might constrain the democratic excesses of the legislature, but he might also go too far in ignoring the will of the people. If easily removed from office by the legislature for misdeeds, he would find it difficult to take unpopular stands. But if too difficult to remove, he could lead the country to ruin.

Three months later, when most other issues were settled, the delegates were still debating the presidency. Would the president be a despicable tyrant, or might he truly represent the people? Would he be a creature of the legislature, or provide a healthy check on its power? Would he represent northern interests over southern, large states over small? Finally, on August 31, little more than two weeks before they would adjourn, the delegates decided to send these perplexing issues to the Committee on Postponed Parts. It was composed of one member chosen by each state delegation.

It was that committee that came up with the compromises that limited the president's power while providing him independence from the legislature. He would be accountable to the people by election, and chosen indirectly by the voters for a term of four years by electors. Increasingly worried about the concentrated power of the Senate, the committee gave the president the authority to make treaties, and to appoint ambassadors, Supreme Court justices, and other officers, with the Senate's advice and consent. At the last minute the Convention also gave the president, rather than the Senate, the power to appoint the nation's treasurer. The president could be removed from office, but only if impeached by the House of Representatives and convicted by the Senate of high crimes or misdemeanors.

"There is no indication that the delegates foresaw the possibility of presidential attempts to withhold from Congress any information it might need to perform its constitutional functions," Daniel N. Hoffman wrote in *Governmental Secrecy and the Founding Fathers*. It would have been self-evident that "a system that requires the sharing of power necessarily requires the sharing of information as well."[31]

In the Convention's final days, secrecy created issues of legitimacy that broke apart its fellowship and threatened the Constitution's approval by the states. Madison wrote to Thomas Jefferson in Paris: "Nothing can exceed the universal anxiety for the event of the meeting here. Reports and conjectures abound concerning the nature of the plan which is to be proposed" as people are "certainly in the dark." But, he noted, "the Convention is equally in the dark as to the reception which may be given to it."[32]

On Saturday, September 15, the Convention's last day of deliberation, the delegates finally turned to the details of how to present their radical proposal to the American people. It was three in the afternoon, the usual time of adjournment. The delegates had already agreed on an unconventional ratification process. Instead of submitting the Constitution to state legislatures, it would be ratified by special state conventions elected directly by the voters.[33]

Governor Randolph of Virginia proposed that states be permitted to offer amendments to the proposal and that a second convention then vote on those amendments. His fellow Virginia delegate, George Mason, agreed. Widely respected for his knowledge of governance, Mason had drafted the Virginia constitution and bill of rights that became models for the governing documents of other states. He pointed out that "this Constitution had been formed without the knowledge or idea of the people. A second Convention will know more of the sense of the people, and be able to provide a system more consonant to it. It was improper to say to the people, take this or nothing."

Elbridge Gerry of Massachusetts joined Randolph and Mason. Raised in his father's cod-shipping business, Gerry had chaired the group that had resolved the Convention's thorniest issue—how the House and Senate would be chosen. He was one of the delegates who feared tyranny, and he had introduced a motion to include a bill of rights. A second convention would provide an opportunity for public sentiment to insist on such a provision.

The price of secrecy was suddenly escalating. Mason, Randolph, and Gerry said that they could not sign the Constitution without a commitment to a second convention. They might oppose its ratification as well. All would sign if the delegates approved the idea.

Their distressed colleagues tried persuasion. Such dissension could threaten the Constitution's chance of acceptance. "A few characters of consequence . . . by refusing to sign the Constitution, might do infinite mischief by kindling the latent sparks which lurk under an enthusiasm in favor of the Convention," Alexander Hamilton warned. Three states—Rhode Island, Delaware, and New York—had already opted out of the Convention because it was working toward a national government that could overpower the states. What would happen if three prominent delegates—of the remaining forty-two—refused to sign the Constitution and even lobbied against it? At around 6:00 p.m., Washington called for a vote. It was the Convention's longest day. The idea of a second convention was voted down.[34]

Washington now feared that the Constitution itself would be rejected by the states. The delegates' refusal to sign the document would alarm the people. Its adversaries would be more active than its supporters in the ratification debates. He had long believed that if the Convention failed, it would mean the end of national government.[35]

On Monday, September 17, the delegates met together for the last time. Again they tried to persuade Randolph, Mason, and Gerry to join them in signing the document they had worked all summer to create. Franklin appealed directly to Randolph: "I hope that you will lay aside your objections, and, by concurring with your brethren, prevent the great mischief which the refusal of your name may produce." Randolph rose again to say that in refusing to sign he took the "most awful" step of his life, but he remained convinced that presenting it as the only alternative to the people after a secret convention "would produce . . . anarchy and civil convulsions."

The one remaining item of business related to the secrecy of the proceedings. Just as the Convention began by committing the delegates to silence, it ended by considering what to do with the official journal kept by its secretary, Major Jackson. Rufus King of Massachusetts suggested that the journal should be either destroyed or placed in the custody of the Convention's president, because if the papers were made public "a bad use . . . [would] be made of them by those who would wish to prevent the adoption of the Constitution." The delegates decided that Washington should keep the journal and other papers, subject to an order from Congress, "if ever formed under the Constitution."

The delegates, except for Randolph, Mason, and Gerry, then filed to the front of the room by state to sign the proposed Constitution. Franklin made the remark that became famous: after wondering throughout the Convention about the sun carved on the back of Washington's chair, he said, "Now at length I have the happiness to know that it is a rising and not a setting sun."[36]

Washington noted in his diary: "The business being thus closed, the delegates adjourned to the City Tavern, dined together and took a cordial leave of each other." When he returned to Robert Morris's home, where he was lodging, he received a note from Jackson, the Convention's secretary. Jackson said that he had already burned "all the loose scraps of paper that belonged to the Convention" but would bring Washington the remaining journal. Washington received the journal. Then, he wrote in his diary, he "retired to meditate on the momentous wk. which had been executed."[37]

The document's 4,543 words of plain English were already set in type. Each delegate received a printed copy. Jackson set off for New York to deliver the document to Congress. Within weeks the radical proposal was reprinted in the newspapers of every state.

It remained for Washington to explain to members of Congress why the delegates had departed from Congress's instructions. In a letter accompanying the Constitution, Washington explained that under the Articles of Confederation, Congress exercised unchecked power—with no strong or independent executive to counter it. But if the national government was to have new authority to tax, declare war, and regulate commerce, "the impropriety of delegating such extensive trust to one body of men is evident—Hence results the necessity of a different organization." He acknowledged that the new Constitution was the product of political compromise—of "mutual deference and concession"—and expressed his ardent wish that it would "promote the lasting welfare of that country so dear to us all, and secure her freedom and happiness." Congress debated for two days whether to censure the Convention's delegates for violating Congress's orders but in the end took no action, simply transmitting the Constitution to the states without expressing either support or disapproval.[38]

As the proposed plan of government became public, its official journal remained secret and was nearly lost altogether. Washington left Philadelphia before noon on September 18 in a carriage drawn by two horses, carrying the journal with him to Mount Vernon. The carriage had new glass panes, brass plates, cushions, and carpet. But near the head of Maryland's Elk River (now

Elkton, Maryland), an old bridge collapsed in high water. Washington and his companion, John Blair, another Virginia delegate, had gotten out, perhaps sensing danger. One horse slid off, nearly plunging the carriage, including the journal, into the river, Ron Chernow wrote in *Washington*. Mill workers nearby came to the rescue, removed the fallen horse from its harness, and saved the carriage. Washington arrived at Mount Vernon—with the Convention's journal—at sunset four days later.[39]

There followed a ten-month battle that provided reminders of the cost of closed deliberations. The secrecy of the Convention's proceedings spawned scurrilous rumors about the delegates' motives. In state ratifying conventions held in the fall of 1787 and the spring of 1788, opponents of the Constitution argued that it represented a conspiracy by a small group of propertied men to further their commercial interests. Patrick Henry proclaimed that such "dangerous powers" would not have been approved if the proceedings "had not been concealed from the public eye."[40]

During New York's convention, John Lansing, Jr., one of the delegates who had left the Convention in protest, accused Alexander Hamilton of proposing in the closed sessions to abolish the states. Rumors that Hamilton had tried to persuade the Convention to adopt a monarchy persisted even when he served as Washington's secretary of the treasury two years later, "a subject of extraordinary curiosity," John Quincy Adams noted.[41]

Many respected leaders objected to the delegates' high-handed decision to present the Constitution to the people on a take-it-or-leave-it basis. It was this controversy that came to dominate ratification debates and threatened to defeat the entire effort. How much voice should the people have to alter a proposal drafted in secret?

By late September, the delegates realized that their decision not to allow amendments meant that ratification might fail. Hamilton took stock in late September and concluded that the Constitution's fate was uncertain. It would depend entirely on "the incalculable fluctuations of the human passions." Failure would lead to civil war, monarchies in some parts of the nation, and possible reunion with Britain. Washington worked behind the scenes, quashing false rumors and encouraging Madison and other colleagues. He, too, believed that failure would mean the end of national government.[42]

Shenanigans in Pennsylvania presaged trouble. When the Constitution was read to the legislative assembly on September 28, nineteen members failed to come back for the afternoon session in order to prevent the convening of a ratification convention. As Pauline Maier relates the story in *Ratification,* the sergeant of arms, sent to find the absent members and bring them back, located nearly all of them at a local boarding house. When they refused to return, the assembly lacked a quorum and had to adjourn. The next morning, the sergeant of arms—now with a helper—located some of the members on the street, but one took flight, turned a corner, and disappeared. Two then appeared in the chamber, providing exactly the quorum needed. But one tried to leave again. There followed a debate about whether this member could be held against his will. As he bolted for the door amid shouts of "stop him," a crowd of spectators blocked his path. Having thwarted his escape, the assembly voted to convene a ratification convention and adjourned.[43]

The first state votes suggested unanimity that turned out to be deceptive. Delaware ratified the Constitution on December 12 with a unanimous vote of delegates to the state convention. New Jersey and Georgia, in need of help defending against attacks by the Creek Indians, also voted approval unanimously. By January 1788, five states had ratified the Constitution, as Connecticut and Pennsylvania joined the first three.

But then, in February, the New Hampshire convention adjourned without approving the Constitution, and Rhode Island voted it down overwhelmingly in a public referendum. The state's Quakers were offended by the Constitution's failure to ban slavery, and debtors and creditors alike feared that the paper money the state had issued would become worthless under a new government.[44]

With popular sentiment silenced by secrecy, the delegates had misjudged it. In Massachusetts, the issue became whether to insist on amendments that protected individual rights before ratification or settle for recommended amendments to be considered later by Congress. In the end, the state voted narrowly for the Constitution, 187 to 168, with proposed amendments attached to the ratification document—but only after John Hancock, the convention's president, and other influential delegates promised to help secure the amendments' approval by Congress. In all, the state conventions proposed more than two hundred amendments.[45]

Approval by the crucial states of Virginia and New York still hung in the balance. Without them, the nation would be a checkerboard with missing pieces.

Virginia's convention—where George Mason, Patrick Henry, and future president James Monroe helped lead the opposition—debated for four weeks and narrowly approved the Constitution (89–79) later in June, with twenty recommended amendments that included a bill of rights that guaranteed "the freedom of the press, as one of the great bulwarks of liberty . . . ought not to be violated." Amid cannon salutes, George Washington joined in celebrating Virginia's ratification in Alexandria by dining at a local tavern.[46]

Even the proposed president's limited authority excited suspicion in New York. Hamilton, a champion of strong central government, argued fervently that the president could not possibly become an autocrat. Unlike the British king, he served only a four-year term, could be impeached, could not sustain a veto without the approval of two-thirds of Congress, and required Senate approval for treaties and the appointment of ambassadors. But Hamilton's two fellow delegates to the Constitutional Convention had departed in protest when the Convention considered a more powerful national government, and Hamilton himself was accused of monarchist tendencies. Ten months after the Constitutional Convention adjourned, New York ratified the Constitution by a margin of only three votes, with four reservations, thirty-two amendments, and a call for a second convention.[47]

It is noteworthy that states insisted on amendments to forbid government interference with citizens' rights at a time when the nation's security was threatened. Liberty was not to be compromised. Instead, it was taken to be especially important in turbulent times. States' insistence on the people's right to be secure in their persons, houses, papers, and effects against unreasonable searches and seizures, and on court approval of searches, was a reaction to British general warrants that allowed officials to barge into colonists' homes. Insistence that an individual accused of a crime could not be deprived of life, liberty, or property without due process of law evoked memories of the arrest and detention of colonial leaders, the denial of jury trials, and the quartering of soldiers on citizens' property.

In the Convention's last days, delegates had considered and nearly approved a guarantee that "the liberty of the Press shall be inviolably observed." It had been defeated by one vote. Delegate Roger Sherman of Connecticut explained that such a guarantee was not necessary since Congress's authority did not extend to the press. In a later speech, Charles Pinckney of South Carolina, who had introduced the proposal, reassured voters that the government had no power to take away the invaluable blessing of press freedom.[48]

When the first Congress convened in March 1791 in New York, James Madison, elected to the House of Representatives from Virginia, consolidated the states' proposals and urged their approval, casually referring to them as a bill of rights. He did so for pragmatic political reasons, according to his biographer Jack Rakove. Madison still worried that listing a few rights would suggest that the government could encroach on others that were not listed, and he didn't believe that "parchment barriers" would prevent abuses.[49] But approval of a bill of rights could increase support for the new Constitution. The ten amendments were ratified by three-quarters of the states by the end of the year.[50]

The Constitutional Convention's debates remained one of the nation's best-kept secrets for thirty years. On March 19, 1796, as he prepared to leave the presidency, Washington delivered the official journal to then secretary of state Timothy Pickering. It remained in the State Department in a small red box when the government moved from Philadelphia to the new capital on the Potomac, and through several of the department's moves among buildings. Pasted inside the box cover was a handwritten note: "This trunk contains the Journal of the Federal Convention of 1787, which framed the Constitution of the United States. . . . The Original Books and Papers were deposited in the Department of State in 1796, by President Washington."[51] Congress finally removed the injunction of secrecy in 1818, ordering that the journal "be published under the direction of the President" and one thousand copies printed.[52]

It then fell to the secretary of state, John Quincy Adams, to prepare the journal for publication. Only then did it become evident how deficient had been the work of the Convention's secretary, William Jackson. Secrecy had protected incompetence for thirty years. Seeing that the journal in fact consisted of disordered loose sheets of paper as well as a bound volume with the last two days missing altogether, Adams asked Jackson to come to his office and explain their condition. But Jackson "had no recollection of them which could remove the difficulties arising from their disorderly state," Adams wrote in his memoirs. Instead, Jackson wanted to talk about how he had sacrificed many thousands of dollars when Washington asked him not to publish the separate personal notes he had kept during the Convention.[53]

For the next six months, Adams plodded through the loose sheets of paper in his spare time, trying to make sense of how votes matched issues. "I dare not trust the task to anyone else," he wrote in his memoirs. At times there was "nothing to indicate upon what questions [the votes] were taken." He decided that the scribbled notes were "so imperfect, and in such disorder, that to have published them, as they were, would have given to the public a book useless and in many respects inexplicable." Any editor would recognize his dilemma: "I begin to think I shall spend too much time and descend too much to minutiae. . . . The longer I brood upon it the more protracted and unprofitable the toil becomes." A frustrated Adams bemoaned "the consumption of time in this petty research." The journal, as pieced together by Adams, was finally published in 1819. Today, it resides in the National Archives.[54]

Madison's notes, the Convention's most complete record, were not published for more than fifty years after the Convention met. When he left the presidency in 1817, Madison turned his attention to his notes, enlisting his wife's brother, John C. Payne, to copy them so they could be published after his death. After reviewing the Convention's official journal and delegate Yates's notes, Madison made some additions and corrections to his own notes and dictated others to Payne.

After Madison's death on June 28, 1836, his wife Dolley offered his papers to the government. By act of Congress of March 3, 1837, the government purchased the papers for $30,000 (equal to nearly $800,000 in 2015). She delivered them to Secretary of State John Forsyth on April 1. Congress then ordered that the papers be published. They were published in three volumes in 1840 and the printer's copy deposited with the Library of Congress, where they still reside.[55]

The secrecy of the Constitutional Convention, rarely revisited in view of the Convention's successful result, introduced the enduring dilemma of balancing openness and secrecy in a representative government. The Convention created a government based on shared power and shared information, even in times of trouble. The president could govern only by persuasion, and remained accountable to the people and their representatives. Some measure of confidential deliberation remained essential. But making controversial public decisions in closed-door sessions risked public rejection, as the ratification debates suggested.

In the Convention itself, secrecy promoted candor, made it easier for delegates to change their minds, and produced a Constitution that has stood the test of time. But closed doors limited the delegates' understanding of public opinion, and led to leaks, misinformation, and charges of conspiracy that nearly defeated their efforts. The delegates' claim that secrecy insulated the debates from the influence of factions represented a bit of political mythology. The Constitution remains the nation's most spectacular political compromise.

The real test, however, would be how the new government worked in practice. The Constitution's durability will not be ascertained until an actual trial reveals it, James Madison wrote in the Federalist Papers. George Washington's eight years as the nation's first president would determine if the Constitution could indeed enable the American people to "form a more perfect union, establish justice, insure domestic tranquility, provide for the common defence, promote the general welfare, and secure the blessings of liberty to ourselves and our posterity."[56]

George Washington: A Culture of Openness

As the nation's first president, George Washington established a lasting culture of government openness. Conscious that he was creating enduring precedents and concerned about overstepping his constitutional authority, Washington created cabinet government, cooperated with congressional investigations, invented ways to protect essential secrets while providing public accountability, and supported subsidies for the free press that so annoyed him. But his unsuccessful effort to keep secret the terms of a proposed treaty with Britain while the Senate debated it triggered the most serious crisis of his years in office.

IT WAS THE FLEDGLING NATION'S WORST military disaster. Half an army division had been wiped out in a sunrise Indian raid. Out of a force of fourteen hundred men, there were more than nine hundred casualties. Nearly all the officers had been killed. Gruesome accounts filtered back east. Indians scalped soldiers and filled their mouths with dirt to warn settlers off Indian land. Survivors abandoned the wounded, threw down their guns, left the artillery, and fled back to Fort Washington, their base camp on the Ohio River, named in honor of their new president.

General Arthur St. Clair's expedition was part of an effort to clear western lands for settlement. It was supposed to demonstrate to the American people and to predatory European rulers the nation's military strength. Instead, President Washington faced the unpleasant prospect of telling Congress about a humiliating defeat.

This military misadventure deep in the woods of the Northwest Territory, near present-day Fort Wayne, Indiana, would provide the first test of whether the president, acting as commander in chief, would be held accountable to the American people. As news spread through the temporary capital of Philadelphia, the secrecy needed for military operations clashed with the openness needed for congressional oversight. For the first time, Congress would seek to investigate the president's actions.

Would Washington provide the confidential documents leading up to the massacre so the people's representatives could determine what had gone wrong? The Constitution provided no answer. It created three independent branches of government but said little about how they would relate to one another. In the absence of any road map, the crisis tested the openness of the new government and the leadership of the new president.

Washington received the alarming news on Friday, December 9, 1791. Tobias Lear, his personal secretary, interrupted him as he was greeting ladies at one of his wife Martha's Friday evening receptions in his large brick home at 190 High Street in Philadelphia. A courier had brought news of the disaster. According to Lear's diary published many years later, Washington read the dispatches, then returned to the elegant second-floor drawing room, maintaining his legendary self-control. When the ladies left, however, he paced in front of the fire, fuming to Lear about the defeat.

On Monday morning, the president dutifully notified Congress: "It is with great concern that I communicate to you the information received from Major General St. Clair, of the misfortune which has befallen the troops under his command."[1]

For the first time in the new government, the House of Representatives voted to launch an investigation and formally asked the secretary of war, Henry Knox, to provide all the confidential correspondence related to the debacle. To reassure the president that confidential documents would be protected, the House adopted a new rule: whenever members received or debated such communications from the president, "the House shall be cleared of all persons except the members and the Clerk" during the reading of the communication and the debates that followed.[2]

Washington knew that every decision he made would establish a standard for the future. "There might be papers of so secret a nature as that they ought not to be given up," he told his department heads soon after taking office. "As the first of everything, in *our situation* will serve to establish a Precedent, it is devoutly wished on my part, that these precedents may be fixed on true principles."[3]

As had become his custom in making momentous decisions, he first called a meeting of his department heads, Alexander Hamilton, secretary of the treasury; Thomas Jefferson, secretary of state; Henry Knox, secretary of war; and Edmund Randolph, attorney general. He needed advice. This was a new issue and he "had not thought upon it."[4]

After considering the question for two days, the president and his advisers outlined four points that provided an accommodation between secrecy and openness. First, the House had a constitutional right to initiate investigations of executive branch actions. Second, during such investigations, the House might call for information, including confidential papers. Third, such requests should go directly to the president. Finally, the president "ought to communicate such papers as the public good would permit and ought to refuse those, the disclosure of which would injure the public." In this instance, "there was not a paper which might not be properly produced." On April 4, Washington directed Secretary Knox to provide all the requested papers.[5]

In a refrain that would become familiar in later military fiascos, the House investigation blamed the defeat on fatal mismanagement and neglect by the army's chief contractor, William Duer. He had provided arms totally unfit for use, equipment deficient in quantity and bad in quality, and insufficient food.

This early clash between openness and secrecy embedded three lasting ideas in the new government. One was that the president, even when acting as commander in chief in a military emergency, was accountable to the American people through legitimate congressional oversight. Congress's agreement to keep sensitive information confidential provided one way of accommodating both secrecy and accountability.

Another was that the president, on occasion, might find it necessary to withhold information from Congress. Washington's words rather than his action of full disclosure would often be cited by future presidents as the earliest precedent for what became known as executive privilege.[6]

Finally, it highlighted Washington's creation of cabinet government. The president would not make important decisions unilaterally, even in times of crisis. Instead, he would seek advice from his cabinet (even though these department heads were not yet called a cabinet), often as a group. The Constitution said nothing about whether and how the president would seek advice.

Washington had appointed seasoned leaders with strong opinions who were bound to disagree, and he invited debate. Hamilton believed that a strong central government was essential to the nation's survival, while Jefferson was increasingly wary of a strong executive and was a zealous supporter of individual liberties and the bill of rights. In time, their disagreements became so pronounced that they went on to form rival political parties.

Washington also sought the views of members of Congress. Madison, now a member of the House of Representatives, remained Washington's most trusted adviser in these early days, juggling multiple roles. Madison wrote a draft of Washington's inaugural address, then the official House of Representatives' reply to the president's address. After that, he wrote Washington's response to the House's reply and Washington's reply to the Senate. As the editors of Madison's papers noted, Madison was essentially in a dialogue with himself.[7]

Amid threats at home and abroad, the nation's first president built a foundation of openness and tolerance that would characterize the United States through most of its history. He gave life to the constitutional plan that envisioned a president of limited powers, accountable to the American people. He initiated cabinet government, inaugurated the president's obligation to explain to the public his important proposals, legitimized congressional oversight of the executive branch, and made himself personally available to citizens by touring the country, receiving callers, and answering his own mail.

It was of course a very different time and a very different public. In a population of nearly four million, about 700,000 Americans remained slaves. In general, only white males who owned property could vote. The slowness and uncertainty of communication enlarged differences and fueled distrust. Most postal roads ran north to south, and in smaller towns and more remote areas, letters were still conveyed by friends or relatives on horseback or by boat.

Since there was no path to follow, much depended on the president's character. Washington deliberated slowly, sought advice, worried about overstepping his constitutional authority, and was supremely conscious of the precedents he was setting. He became a master of the middle ground. Responding to congressional requests for information, he found ways to protect the nation's secrets while confirming the legitimacy of congressional oversight. His requests for confidentiality staked out narrow exceptions to information sharing in order to protect sensitive diplomatic negotiations and guard the safety of the government's agents abroad. As political rivalries hardened into opposing parties and a partisan press attacked his actions and his reputation, Washington nonetheless championed subsidies for newspapers and the privacy of the mails. But in this increasingly partisan atmosphere, even the president's temporary secrecy became suspect, and his effort to temporarily withhold the terms of a controversial treaty with Britain while the Senate debated it behind closed doors led to the worst crisis of his presidency.

Washington's creation of an open presidency remains all the more remarkable because he governed during a time of national emergency. The nation was not at war but was, rather, in the kind of cold war that would characterize much of its later history. Six years after the Revolutionary War ended, Britain still occupied forts on the frontier, barred trade with the West Indies, and gave assistance to hostile Indian tribes. Spain still controlled commerce on the Mississippi River, and kept trying to annex frontier territory. Huge federal and state war debts threatened to destroy a government that had no reliable revenue, no national currency, and no sources of credit. But Washington also governed at a time when citizens' only experience with a strong executive was with the abuses of the British king and his government that had triggered their rebellion. If the voters feared economic insecurity, domestic strife, and predatory foreign powers, any of which might suggest deference to a strong executive, they feared more an autocratic ruler who would ignore the rights of individuals and the priorities of state governments.

Washington's openness was tested by a citizenry and a Congress more unruly than those he and the delegates to the Constitutional Convention had anticipated. Four years before General St. Clair's defeat, Washington had presided over the Constitutional Convention, whose delegates envisioned orderly democratic processes. Informed voters would elect their representatives and then remain quiescent until the next election, while members of Congress engaged in civil discourse to determine policies that best served the general welfare. A responsible free press, now protected by the Constitution's First Amendment, would bind together the citizens of cities, towns, farms, and the frontier, with shared information.

Instead, citizens sought to influence government by organizing demonstrations, throwing rocks, and destroying property. In the House of Representatives, "three or four representatives would be on their feet at once, shouting invective, attacking individuals violently, telling private stories, and making irrelevant speeches," historian Gordon Wood wrote in *Empire of Liberty*. The sergeant-at-arms carried a mace in case fights broke out. Pickpockets roamed the public visitors' gallery. Meanwhile, an increasingly partisan press spread politically charged rumors, slander, and misinformation.[8]

Private stenographers and newspaper reporters published accounts of the debates in the House in local newspapers, supplementing the spare official journals of motions and votes. The Annals of Congress for the first eighteen Congresses, compiled many years later mainly from these newspaper accounts, were followed by a register of debates and finally by the more complete Congressional Record in 1873.[9]

The Senate, by contrast, met behind closed doors for another five years, three times voting down motions for the public sessions that Washington favored. Even members of the House were not allowed in. "Why they keep their doors shut, when acting in a Legislative capacity, I am unable to inform you," Washington wrote a friend soon after the Senate convened in April 1789, "unless it is because they think there is too much speaking to the Gallery in the other House, and business thereby retarded." Senators employed a doorkeeper to guard the entrance to the chamber.[10]

Inevitably, the Senate's secrecy suggested conspiracy. "It augurs an unfriendly disposition in a public body that wishes to *masque* its transactions—Upright intentions, and upright conduct are not afraid or ashamed of publicity," noted one newspaper commentator.[11]

At this formative moment, character and circumstance combined to give the new nation a president who was cautious about exercising power, embraced diverse points of view, and understood that he was building a framework for the future.

Humility was one of his character traits. Washington often wrote and spoke about his own limitations. While he excelled at leadership, he remained supremely conscious that he lacked the formal education of many of the nation's leaders. From the age of eleven, when his father died, he had had to create his own path to respectability. When his mother could not pay for the education his older brothers had received, he took a job as a wilderness surveyor in the Shenandoah Valley, and first led troops into battle when he was twenty-two.

Ambitious, disciplined, and deliberate, the self-made Washington would always seek advice, care about appearances, and guard his reputation.

When he took office in 1789, his first request for advice was about how open a democratic leader should be. He wrote his vice president, John Adams, a series of questions. How should he avoid total isolation if he could not be available to everyone? Would it prompt "impertinent applications" if he let it be known he would be available every morning at 8:00 a.m. to receive those who had business with him? Would one day each week be sufficient for receiving ceremonial visitors? Would it be proper for the president to visit the homes of friends and acquaintances? Should he travel to all of the states to better understand their leaders and circumstances?[12]

The way in which Washington answered these questions created an entirely new kind of relationship between the citizens and their leader. First, he decided to visit every state in the union in order to better understand the nation he was leading. With Congress adjourned, Washington set out for New England in October 1789 in an open carriage with only three aides. Braving rutted roads and inclement weather, he visited more than fifty cities and towns, skipping Rhode Island, which had not yet ratified the Constitution. Then in March of 1791 he made a three-month swing through Virginia, North and South Carolina, and Georgia with aides and his greyhound Cornwallis, named after the British general who surrendered at Yorktown. On these arduous journeys he met local officials, toured factories, went deep-sea fishing, discussed future public works, and endured countless balls, receptions, and parades.[13]

Back at his Cherry Street residence in lower Manhattan, where he worked in a first-floor office in the nation's temporary capital, Washington settled on a routine of public receptions on Tuesday afternoons, his wife Martha's receptions for ladies on Friday evening, and official dinners every other Thursday. He attended church at St. Paul's Chapel, viewed performances at the John Street Theatre, and frequently took horseback or carriage rides around town.[14]

One issue that the president did not feel obliged to be open about was incapacitating illness. Two months after his inauguration in 1789, he had surgery to remove a painful abscess from his left thigh, was bedridden for six weeks, "and couldn't even draft a letter," biographer Ron Chernow wrote. In 1790 a respiratory infection, perhaps an influenza that swept through Philadelphia, led to probable pneumonia that threatened his life. A specialist was brought in "under

conditions of extraordinary secrecy" so as not to alarm the public, though
rumors surfaced in private letters and in newspapers.[15]

In consequential confrontations with Congress over openness and secrecy,
Washington provided early examples of how the president could govern by
persuasion and information sharing. He invented ways to protect the nation's
essential secrets while also accommodating congressional oversight. But he
also learned how difficult it was for a president to keep controversial proposals
hidden, even for a short time.

Washington's most important exercise of open government involved the
government's pressing financial issues, issues that were inflamed by fears about
the power of the president and Congress over the states, and by the opposing
interests of states large and small, north and south. The creation of the Bank of
the United States showed that the new government could resolve contentious
issues through open debate. But it also raised questions about the government's
authority, set in motion the formation of opposing political parties, exposed a
struggle between the president's two most esteemed cabinet members, and
launched a virulent war of opposing partisan newspapers.

There was no disagreement about the urgency of the problem. The government
could not pay its bills. War debts totaled $50 million, $12 million of which was
owed to France, Spain, and private bankers in the Netherlands. The rest was owed
to American citizens, much of it to those who had served in the war and were
rewarded with government certificates. Revenues came mainly from tariffs on
imported goods. Because of its debt, the government could not attract new credit.[16]

When Congress asked Washington's thirty-three-year-old treasury secretary
to prepare a report on public credit in December 1790, Hamilton sent back a
radical proposal for a national bank. With it he sent a long report designed to
persuade legislators that the bank could provide financial stability. His report
was quickly printed, distributed to Congress, and provided to newspapers.[17]

The Senate debated the bank proposal for more than two weeks, and finally
approved it. But in the House, James Madison led the opposition. He feared that
the bank would concentrate federal power, and that it represented an alliance
between northern merchants and speculators. It might be part of a plan to anoint
a commercial aristocracy and perhaps reestablish a monarchy. He argued that
the government had no authority to charter a bank. Hamilton's proposal was
unconstitutional.

The next step revealed perhaps an excess of openness in Washington's cabinet government. After a heated debate, the House approved the bank by a margin of 39 to 20, and sent the legislation to Washington for his signature. But it turned out that Washington had allowed Hamilton to send his proposal to Congress without first considering whether he and the rest of his advisers supported it, or even thought it was legal. When the bill came to the president for his signature, he paused over Madison's constitutional arguments, and asked his cabinet secretaries to submit their views in writing. Secretary of State Jefferson and Attorney General Randolph echoed Madison's view that the bank was unconstitutional. The Constitution said nothing about creating a national bank. Like Madison, Jefferson feared that Hamilton's plan was to create a powerful national government that would threaten the primacy of the states and the liberties of the people. He too came from a culture of Virginia plantation owners who were traditionally suspicious of banks. In a practice that was already becoming common, the entire text of Jefferson's confidential advice to the president was leaked to the press. These developments left Washington with his cabinet members engaged in a very public dispute about whether the government's most important economic measure was constitutional.[18]

Washington himself remained perplexed. He asked Madison to meet with him privately, and even asked him to draft a veto message. He also asked Hamilton to respond to charges that the bank was unconstitutional, a 13,000-word rejoinder that was also published. Hamilton argued that the Constitution implied authority to create the bank because it was necessary in order to carry out its tax collection and trade regulation duties. Washington was finally persuaded, both by Hamilton's arguments and by the urgent need to create greater economic stability. He signed the bank bill into law, knowing it would create more trouble.[19]

The bank controversy also featured a battle between partisan newspapers, secretly financed by Jefferson and Hamilton, the president's opposing cabinet members. Three days after Washington signed the bank bill, Jefferson and Madison enlisted Philip Freneau, a well-known poet, journalist, former sea captain, and college roommate of Madison's, to come to Philadelphia in order to launch an opposition paper. They provided stealth financing. Jefferson gave Freneau a government job as a translator for the State Department at $250 a year, all the department's printing business, and access to his foreign correspondence. Since Jefferson and Madison had not been successful in convincing members of Congress and the public that Hamilton's ideas were dangerous, they needed a better vehicle of persuasion to reach state leaders and voters. The war within the president's cabinet was about to become a war in the newspapers as well, and the president himself would soon become a target.

Freneau's *National Gazette* accused Hamilton of promoting economic policies that favored speculators and ignored the welfare of ordinary Americans. Madison contributed essays arguing that Republicans were the true friends of the union. They protected liberty against those who viewed the people as "stupid, suspicious, licentious." Soon Freneau was also attacking Washington's monarchical tendencies.

Hamilton, in turn, financed a sympathetic press that was already in business, funneling to John Fenno and his *Gazette of the United States* all of the Senate's printing business as well as some from Hamilton's Treasury Department, and with his allies giving Fenno two thousand dollars. Fenno had launched his newspaper just before Washington's inauguration in New York, and had followed the president to the new temporary capital in Philadelphia. The thirty-eight-year-old former Boston teacher and sometime journalist lauded the president, tracked his travels, and covered public events lavishly. Now Hamilton added essays under pseudonyms defending his economic policies, accusing the Republicans of threatening the union, and attacking Jefferson personally.[20]

Jefferson accused Fenno's paper of promoting "doctrines of monarchy, aristocracy, and the exclusion of the influence of the people." Fenno called the administration's opponents villains, brawlers, and enemies of freedom, and accused Freneau of sedition.[21]

A third newspaper added to the Republican fervor. Benjamin Franklin's grandson Benjamin Franklin Bache had founded his anti-Federalist newspaper in Philadelphia in 1790 when Bache was twenty-one, using the printing press he inherited from his renowned grandfather. Educated in France and friendly with the French journalist-politicians who helped foment the French Revolution, Bache combined the instincts of an investigative reporter with the hot temper of a rabble-rouser. He longed for stories of "party disputes" or "private abuse" to "raise the printer's drooping spirits."[22]

Bache's *General Advertiser* (renamed the *Aurora*) sounded the republican theme that citizens were obliged to engage in politics and the press was obliged to provide a constitutional check upon the conduct of public servants. But his attacks on Washington became increasingly shrill until, when Washington left office, the *Aurora* rejoiced that "the name of WASHINGTON . . . ceases to give a currency to political iniquity; and to legalize corruption."[23]

Showing remarkable restraint, Washington not only bore these personal attacks but insisted on legislation to subsidize the distribution of all newspapers. Deeply hurt by personal accusations that threatened the reputation he worked so hard to protect, he complained only in private letters that "the publications in Franeau's and Beeche's [*sic*] papers are outrages on common decency." He despaired that the press war would "make it impossible . . . for any man living to manage the helm or to keep the machine together." He would rather be in his grave than in his present situation.[24]

But Washington managed to hold on to the idea that a free press was an essential complement to open government. The success of the republican experiment depended on an informed public. In a nation where travel was difficult and public issues controversial, newspapers provided an essential link between the national government and citizens who lived in distant cities, towns, farms, and frontier outposts.

He urged that newspapers be delivered through the mail postage-free to subscribers and to other publications that might want to share their content. He told Congress that "every valuable end of Government is best answered by the enlightened confidence of the people: And by teaching the people themselves to know and to value their own rights, to discern and provide against invasions of them; to distinguish between oppression and the necessary exercise of lawful authority."[25]

Newspaper distribution via expanded mail routes and postal roads would spread "a knowledge of the laws and proceedings of the government" to guard the people against "the effects of misrepresentation and misconception." Madison agreed. For such a large nation to thrive, the government should encourage road-building, a postal network, and "particularly *a circulation of newspapers through the entire body of the people*" (emphasis in the original).[26]

The Post Office Act of 1792 embedded these views in law, even as Federalists and Republicans battered each other in the press. It required the Post Office to subsidize the distribution of all newspapers. Subscribers would pay a token amount to ensure that papers actually reached their destination. The law also allowed newspapers to exchange free copies—the beginning of news networks, Paul Starr suggested in *The Creation of the Media*.[27]

The same law established the privacy of personal mail. Any post office employee who delayed or opened any letter could be fined up to three hundred dollars and sentenced up to six months in jail. It was an important milestone. Congress explicitly rejected the tradition of government surveillance of private mail that prevailed in Britain and had prevailed in the American colonies.[28]

The congressional elections of 1792 marked the emergence of partisan politics that inflamed issues of government openness and secrecy. The Senate still tilted toward the administration by a slim margin, 16 to 13. But opponents of Washington's government gained a slight edge in the House, 55 of 105 members. Presidential secrecy began to acquire a partisan cast that made Congress more belligerent in demanding information and less tolerant of the president's rare requests for confidentiality. And the free press—now the federally subsidized and often partisan free press—had political motives to print annoying and disruptive leaks that in effect limited secrecy.

Two political parties emerged, each accusing the other of hidden motives. Citizens suspicious of the national bank and concerned with states' rights joined together in a Republican opposition led by Madison and Jefferson. Supporters of Hamilton's policies began calling themselves Federalists. Jefferson believed that Hamilton was creating a strong national government that favored rich merchants and speculators with "the ultimate object . . . to prepare the way for a change from the present republican form of government to that of monarchy."[29] Hamilton believed that Jefferson was trying to cripple efforts to stabilize the economy and provide national unity. The parties divided merchants and farmers, northerners and southerners, those on the settled east coast and those eking out a living on the newly opened western lands, those who supported protection of trade with Britain and those who tilted toward friendlier relations with the new French republic.

Washington remained a unifying presence. Jefferson and Madison, now leaders of the Republican opposition, joined with Hamilton to persuade the president to run for a second term. He "was the only man in the U.S. who possessed the confidence of the whole . . . [and] the longer he remained, the stronger would become the habits of the people in submitting to the government and in thinking it a thing to be maintained," Jefferson told him. Hamilton wrote that declining to run for a second term would be "the greatest evil, that could befall the country at the present juncture, and as critically hazardous to your own reputation." When electoral votes were counted on February 13, 1793, Washington once again was the unanimous choice to lead the nation.[30]

At the beginning of Washington's second term, the unlikely issue of piracy provided an opportunity for the president to demonstrate one way to maintain the secrecy of sensitive negotiations while supporting the openness needed for congressional oversight—selective confidentiality. It also provided a forum for the Republican-controlled House to retract its earlier unconditional promise of confidentiality. From this point forward, Congress would decide one request at a time whether to keep presidential papers out of public view.

Washington reported routinely to Congress on negotiations with Morocco, Algiers, Tunis, and Tripoli, known as the Barbary States. Those predatory nations raised revenue by commandeering ships in the Mediterranean Sea, confiscating the cargo, imprisoning or enslaving the crew, and demanding millions of dollars in tribute for the return of prisoners and a promise of future safe passage. American ships, no longer protected by the French or British navies, were easy prey.

When the president sent one of his piracy reports to Congress on December 16, 1793, he asked that two items be kept confidential: the name of an informant who had provided information about the Barbary powers and the amount the government was prepared to pay for release of kidnapped sailors and safe passage in the future.

Instead of respecting this benign request, several Republican members of the House challenged it. The public had an interest in any deliberations involving commerce. The House would inspect papers received from the president and "determine whether the matter communicated requires secrecy, or not." Federalists countered that without confidentiality the government could not get essential information from foreign agents, and the president himself might be less forthcoming with information in the future.[31]

Meanwhile, Bache's opposition newspaper printed other leaked details of the president's report and criticized his secrecy. "I was struck dumb with astonishment . . . that the executive alone shall have the right of judging what shall be kept secret, and what shall be made public. . . . The practice of shutting the doors of Congress which has obtained lately begins to create suspicion; it has been so frequent that people begin to fear that it will grow into a habit. It looks a little strange that a servant should shut the door against his master," wrote an anonymous contributor.[32]

Still taking a long view of open government, Washington accepted the idea that the House could make independent judgments about confidentiality. And, having flexed their procedural muscles, members decided to do what the president had asked after all—keep secret the Barbary informant and payment amounts—but only by one vote. The House then appropriated funds for negotiation and made public the president's report, without the confidential sections.

In a second skirmish two weeks later, the president tried out yet another variation on accommodating the need for both openness and secrecy—selective deletion. Instead of providing information to Congress with a request to keep some portions confidential, a request that the partisan Congress might now deny, he simply deleted from diplomatic correspondence sensitive passages that might endanger negotiations or risk lives.

On January 17, 1794, the Senate went on a fishing expedition. Suspecting that the nation's minister to France, Gouverneur Morris, was not abiding by Washington's professed policy of neutrality and was, instead, hostile to the new French republic that Republicans admired, the Senate directed the president to provide it all of the minister's correspondence with the French and American governments.

Trying to maintain a presumption of openness in an increasingly partisan atmosphere, Washington met with his cabinet and consulted informally with Madison. Both the cabinet and Madison, now leader of the opposition party, advised that the president had the authority to delete passages. Washington then provided the correspondence, asked that it be kept confidential, but also deleted sensitive portions. The Senate, where supporters of the administration still held a narrow majority, accepted the president's deletions and his request for confidentiality. The opposition press, however, did not. Bache's paper continued a drumbeat of criticism that "secrecy is a weapon [that] throws a splendor around the Executive" and keeps citizens from thinking for themselves.[33]

Two years later, Bache would play a leading role in a confrontation over presidential secrecy that would create the most serious crisis of Washington's presidency and suggest how difficult it was becoming for a president to keep secret any controversial proposal in an atmosphere of suspicion and distrust. The Constitution called for the Senate's advice and consent to proposed treaties. Washington's request seemed modest. He wanted to allow the Senate to debate a controversial treaty with Britain behind closed doors, free from partisan rancor, before its terms were made public.

The president believed that the treaty was needed to keep the nation from being drawn into the war between France and Britain over territory and trade. The United States would "pursue a conduct friendly and impartial toward the belligerent powers . . . forbidding our citizens to take part in any hostilities on the seas . . . and enjoining them from all acts . . . inconsistent with the duties of a friendly nation toward those at war."[34]

Washington had sent John Jay, a seasoned negotiator and the Supreme Court's chief justice, to bargain with the British. The United States would promise neutrality if Britain would cease its outrageous behavior—occupying forts on American soil, capturing American ships and forcing their crews into service, exacting prohibitive tariffs, blocking trade with the West Indies, and encouraging Indian attacks on settlers.

Republicans were suspicious of the agreement—and of Washington's secrecy. Perhaps it was a veiled attempt by the Federalists to support the British and oppose the French. Senators knew that in the proposed agreement Britain agreed to withdraw from forts in American territory, settle wartime debts, and accept American neutrality in Britain's war with France. In return, Britain received preferential trade status. Even before copies reached President Washington, Bache and other Republican editors leaked some of its pro-British terms. Articles attacked the president for considering any treaty at all.

In November 1794, Jay had sent the proposed treaty to Washington for his approval. But when the ship carrying the documents was captured by the French, the British crew threw the papers overboard. A second ship battled winter storms to bring copies to Norfolk, Virginia, where couriers finally delivered the treaty to the president five months after Jay sent it.

The problem was that by the time the Senate debated its terms in June 1795, the treaty had become a very public secret. A frustrated citizenry knew in February that a treaty had been signed, in March that the president had received a copy, and in June that the Senate was debating its terms. But no one would tell the American people exactly what it said.

A writer for Bache's *Aurora* exclaimed: "The Constitution . . . give[s] the President and Senate the power of making Treaties; but it communicates no power to hatch those things *in darkness* . . . [which] seems to imply . . . a disposition . . . to Monarchy."[35]

As the Senate was winding up its debate, Bache realized that there was money to be made in revealing this government secret. Senator Stevens T. Mason of Virginia apparently sold the entire text to the French minister, who gave it to Bache. Bache then sold the text for twenty-five to fifty cents as a pamphlet, which he personally carried up and down the East Coast, organizing anti-treaty rallies along the way. When his newspaper office in Philadelphia was besieged by eager customers in his absence, his delighted wife Margaret, selling more pamphlets, exclaimed: "It was more like a fair than anything else."[36]

When the Senate finally voted, 20 to 10, to approve the treaty, Washington despaired that public passions would interfere with his own consideration about whether to sign it. "It is not the opinions of those who were determined to support, or oppose it, that I am solicitous to obtain," he wrote Alexander Hamilton. "My desire is to learn from dispassionate men." He wanted "to ascertain, if possible, after the paroxysm of the fever is a little abated, what the real temper of the people is . . . for at present the cry against the Treaty is like that against a mad-dog; and every one . . . seems engaged in running it down."[37]

Mobs gathered outside the president's Philadelphia home day after day, cursing him. The man whom voters had twice chosen unanimously to lead the nation suddenly became an object of derision. Besieged by intemperate petitions from citizens in every state, he was called a "mock Monarch . . . blind, bald, toothless, querulous" and "a most miserable politician."[38]

Washington's home was not the only target. Protesters hurled stones at Alexander Hamilton when he spoke in the treaty's defense in New York, and stormed the British minister's house in Philadelphia, where they torched copies with "huzzahs and acclamations," as Independence Day celebrations became anti-treaty rallies. When law and order broke down and some states threatened secession, Washington despaired that the union might not survive. "Nothing comparable had been seen on so wide a scale since the founding of the Republic," historians Stanley Elkins and Eric McKitrick concluded.[39]

His Philadelphia home surrounded by angry protesters, Washington made a hot and disagreeable trip by carriage to Mount Vernon. But he found no peace there either. The petitions, vituperative attacks, and copies of Bache's scurrilous paper followed him. Less thick-skinned than his stately countenance suggested, Washington complained privately that he had been abused in "indecent terms as could scarcely be applied to a Nero, a notorious defaulter, or even a common pick-pocket." He determined to leave office at the end of his second term.[40]

Returning to Philadelphia, he consulted once more with his cabinet. When they met on August 12, most recommended signing the treaty in order to avoid war. Washington finally agreed.

But the House was not yet ready to let the issue go. Republicans, who now controlled the chamber, wanted to prove that Jay had violated the president's instructions by tilting toward Britain. They demanded that Washington disclose to the House all the confidential correspondence he had provided to the Senate. The Constitution did not give the House any formal role in approving treaties. But some of the treaty's provisions—boundary and debt commissions, for example—did require new funding.

Once again, the president had no good options. Denying the request would unleash another attack by "the scribblers." But providing the papers "will be fatal to the Negotiating Power of the government" if the president routinely had to reveal diplomatic correspondence, Hamilton advised him.[41]

He finally denied the House request but sent a conciliatory message explaining his rationale. He would not withhold "any information which the duty of my station will permit, or the public good shall require, to be disclosed." It is "my constant endeavor to harmonize with the other branches" under the oath to "preserve, protect and defend the Constitution." He pointed out that he had given the papers to the Senate. But foreign negotiations "often depend on secrecy," one reason the Constitution granted treaty-making authority to the president and the smaller Senate. Releasing correspondence, even after the negotiations were concluded, could be "extremely impolitic" and would "establish a dangerous precedent."[42]

Members of the House and even Vice President Adams were shocked by Washington's blanket refusal, an indication of how seriously leaders took the presumption of openness. Washington was staking out new ground—asserting the president's right to withhold information unless Congress could cite a specific constitutional purpose for requesting it. Adams wrote to his wife: "I cannot deny the right of the House to ask for papers." Madison wrote to Monroe that Washington "not only ran to the extreme . . . but assigned reasons worse than the refusal itself." The House should have access to any information that would assist its deliberations.[43]

At this juncture, the House could have refused funds for the treaty until the requested information was forthcoming, in effect providing the first formal check on presidential secrecy. But most members were not willing to go that far.

Federalists warned that failure to fund the treaty would result in war with Britain and economic collapse. The final vote was very close, 51 to 48, in favor of funding. The House simply recorded a formal protest against the president's secrecy.

The battle over the treaty with its accompanying volleys in the partisan press demonstrated an enduring limitation on presidents' secrets. In a representative government with a free press, a president's attempts to keep controversial policies secret were unlikely to be successful, and presidents paid a political price when such secrets were disclosed.

In his farewell address, submitted directly to the people through the *American Daily Advertiser*, a Philadelphia newspaper, Washington declined to seek a third term, warned against the dangers of political parties, and expressed the hope that the openness of his administration would provide the final judgment against those who attacked him. "The Acts of my Administration are on Record. By these . . . I expect to be judged."[44]

But in an earlier draft he had revealed his anger at the virulent abuse by the press. Newspapers had "teemed with all the Invective that disappointment, ignorance of facts, and malicious falsehoods could invent, to misrepresent my politics and affections; to wound my reputation and feelings; and to weaken, if not entirely destroy the confidence you had been pleased to repose in me." Hamilton talked the president out of including these passages.[45]

Washington attended the inauguration of John Adams as the nation's second president on March 4, 1797, at Congress Hall in Philadelphia, and departed five days later for Mount Vernon.

As the nation's first president, George Washington created the world's most open government during a time when predatory European nations and domestic turmoil threatened the nation's survival. Instead of claiming extraordinary powers to act unilaterally and secretly in these turbulent times, Washington initiated cabinet deliberations, granted nearly all congressional requests for confidential documents, established the validity of congressional investigations of executive actions, invented means of accommodating a president's need for secrecy with the Congress's need to provide accountability, rejected the tradition of government surveillance of private mail, and supported and subsidized the annoying and increasingly partisan free press. Lasting accommodations between secrecy and openness were not part of a grand plan. They were made in the heat of the moment, the product of chance circumstances, uncertain advice, and a quixotic public mood.

Washington's temperament served the nation well. He made decisions slowly and deliberately, had a high tolerance for dissent, understood his own limitations, and had a lifelong sense of public duty. He was acutely aware of citizens' fears that they would again become subjects of a secretive and autocratic monarchy. Despite the tawdry politics of the moment, foreign and domestic threats, and a crushing national debt, he maintained his vision of an orderly, secure, and prosperous nation that would protect personal freedom and provide the world with a unique example of republican government.

Within this open landscape, Washington began the construction of a limited but important space for confidential deliberations and diplomacy. He did so by emphasizing that each action represented a narrow exception and taking pains to explain his rationale. In fact, Washington withheld requested information for only one reason—to protect sensitive diplomatic negotiations, including the personal safety of those involved. He pointed the way to combining bounded secrecy with accountability, asking Congress to keep limited portions of papers confidential or deleting them. He was roundly criticized for his failure to explain the terms of Jay's treaty with Britain while the Senate debated behind closed doors. That judgment call cost him an opportunity for leadership and skewed later public reaction. He ceded to opponents and their newspapers the initiative to frame the issues on their terms.

By the end of Washington's second term, the Constitution was no longer merely a set of parchment promises. It now anchored a working government. But American politics had little in common with the vision of Washington and his fellow delegates to the Constitutional Convention. They had proposed a government based on an understanding of competing factions and divided powers. But they had not foreseen that factions would become enduring political parties that battle over issues between elections. They believed in an orderly democratic process in which voters chose representatives and then stood by as their representatives engaged in civil discourse while a free press provided accurate information to the people. Instead, politics featured vitriolic rumors, rowdy demonstrations, and a partisan press eager to publish a president's secrets.

Washington's culture of openness would endure until advancing technology erased the security provided by two great oceans and fear of communist aggression led presidents to build a ramshackle edifice of secretive agencies and practices that grew larger than any had intended.

Woodrow Wilson: A Foundation for Secret Government

*At a time of international instability and domestic unrest
in the wake of World War I, President Woodrow Wilson, his wife,
and his doctor kept secret his incapacitating stroke. Their ruse and
Wilson's earlier claims of conspiracies among workers, immigrants,
and Bolsheviks led to domestic spying, roundups of immigrants, and
loyalty investigations that became endemic. Confused and belligerent,
Wilson also refused to accept a congressional compromise to save his
cherished League of Nations. These events laid the foundation for peacetime
secrecy and demonstrated a president's power to hide his incapacity to
govern, a problem not entirely solved today.*

"MY GOD, THE PRESIDENT IS PARALYZED." Dr. Cary Grayson emerged from the Lincoln bedroom. Moments earlier, Grayson, President Woodrow Wilson's personal physician, had knocked on the bedroom's locked door. Wilson's wife unlocked the door and led him to the president, semiconscious on the bathroom floor. Grayson and Edith Wilson helped the president back to the large mahogany bed. The forty-one-year-old Grayson, who had served as personal physician to Presidents William Howard Taft and Theodore Roosevelt and had become the Wilsons' trusted friend, examined the president briefly and called for help.

Dr. Francis X. Dercum, an eminent neurologist from Philadelphia, found the president's left side paralyzed, the left side of his face drooping, and his vision impaired. The president was awake, though "somewhat somnolent," and answered questions slowly. Dercum told Mrs. Wilson and Wilson's daughter Margaret that the sixty-two-year-old president had suffered a severe stroke, probably caused by a thrombosis of a cerebral artery in the brain's right hemisphere.

Admitted to the bedroom later in the day to help rearrange furniture for the medical equipment the doctors ordered, White House usher Ike Hoover stared at the president as he lay in bed. "He looked as if he were dead. There was not a sign of life. His face had a long cut about the temple. . . . His nose also bore a long cut lengthwise."

It was Thursday, October 2, 1919. Days earlier, newspapers had reported that the president had suddenly cut short a ten-thousand-mile rail trip. He had set out a month earlier in order to persuade the American people that the United States should join a new League of Nations. He planned to make thirty-two speeches in twenty-two days. The League, now part of the proposed Versailles Treaty to end World War I, was Wilson's plan to provide a lasting peace through international cooperation. It would be his most important legacy. But the treaty required Senate approval, and Republicans, who held a narrow majority, wanted changes to clarify Congress's authority.

Confused, weakened, and paranoid, Wilson would remain in office for the remaining eighteen months of his term. With his wife and doctor, he managed to keep his stroke secret from his vice president, his cabinet, members of Congress, world leaders, and fellow Americans.[1]

The Constitution provides no guidance about when a disabled president should step down or who should make that decision. Article II, Section 1, says only: "In case of the removal of the President from office, or of his death, resignation, or inability to discharge the powers and duties of the said office, the same shall devolve on the Vice President." "What is the extent of the term 'disability' and who is to be the judge of it?" John Dickenson of Delaware had asked his fellow delegates at the Constitutional Convention, more than one hundred years earlier. The question remained unanswered.[2]

The Constitution's silence, an imperious first lady, a conflicted doctor, an intimidated vice president, a solicitous cabinet, and the power of secrecy allowed an incapacitated president to remain in office.

It was a terrible time to lose a president. The war had sped the demise of nineteenth-century empires and destabilized international relations. The Versailles Treaty redrew national boundaries, but lasting peace remained uncertain.

At home, there were strikes, protests, and bombings. Before his stroke, Wilson had endorsed actions by his attorney general and postmaster to extend harsh wartime measures to secretly investigate radicals, break up workers' meetings, censor mail, monitor international communications, and summarily deport immigrants. He imagined conspiracies among revolutionary Bolsheviks, anarchists, workers, and radicals that justified repressive measures. His accusations stirred up fears that inaugurated new and lasting dimensions of presidential secrecy.

At the start of the twentieth century, the United States was not yet a nation of secrets. It remained a nation of limited government and limited secrecy. George Washington's culture of openness endured. For the most part, presidents limited their actions behind closed doors to sensitive military and diplomatic matters.

Even during the Civil War, President Abraham Lincoln confronted crises openly, and left no postwar legacy of official secrecy. In the early days of the war, when Congress was not in session, Lincoln suspended the writ of habeas corpus, which allowed prisoners to challenge their custody. He did so to prevent Maryland officials from blocking rail lines to Washington, D.C., that transported union troops. Because he did so openly, his controversial action triggered the kind of constitutional checks the founders had intended. Exercising legitimate oversight, Supreme Court chief justice Roger Taney, sitting as a federal circuit court judge, struck down the president's action. The Constitution reserved suspension of the writ to Congress. Also exercising legitimate oversight, Congress then came back to town and affirmed Lincoln's order.

In the early days of the war, Lincoln began what became an annual disclosure of diplomatic correspondence that continues to this day, the *Foreign Relations of the United States* (FRUS) series. In 1861, he appended to his annual message to Congress 425 pages of correspondence that Congress had requested concerning the Confederate states, redacting passages on arms procurement, battlefield reversals, defectors, and other sensitive matters.[3]

Lincoln did create a new agency to initiate wartime investigations that carried over to peacetime, but only for one purpose. On the afternoon of April 14, 1865, he met with Treasury Secretary Hugh McCulloch and agreed on the creation of what became the Secret Service. The agency's sole mission was to stop counterfeiting. Between a third and half of wartime currency in circulation was counterfeit, threatening the nation with economic collapse. Congress would soon add fraud, smuggling, and tax evasion to the service's missions. That evening, after his meeting with McCulloch, Lincoln was shot by John Wilkes

Booth as he watched a play at Ford's Theatre. But protection of the president was a congressional afterthought, Philip H. Melanson explains in *Secret Service*. The first twenty-five presidents had no official guardians. Not until 1906 did Congress provide an annual appropriation for that purpose.[4]

Military intelligence remained minimal in a nation that still relied on the protection of two great oceans. A peacetime office of naval intelligence, created in 1882, by 1900 had only five clerks, one translator, an assistant draftsman, and a laborer. An army intelligence unit, created in 1885, began with one officer and a clerk.

Presidents did, of course, keep political secrets. President James Polk refused to give Congress the records of a contingency fund used in part for political purposes. President James Buchanan, who received illicit reports about the Supreme Court's deliberations leading up to the Dred Scott decision in March 1857, secretly pressed Justice Robert Grier to vote with the proslavery majority. President Grover Cleveland's surgery on a yacht for mouth cancer while on a "fishing trip" in 1893 was kept secret for more than two decades.[5]

Even before World War I, Wilson had shown little tolerance for dissent. The former college professor and Princeton University president championed a remarkable array of progressive policies—lower tariffs, a Federal Reserve banking system, a Federal Trade Commission, antitrust laws, a graduated income tax, and child labor and workers' compensation laws. With his carefully combed gray hair, rimless glasses, and piercing blue eyes, Wilson looked the part he had played so well—the nation's teacher.

But two years before the United States entered the European war, Wilson began giving fiery speeches that linked the misdeeds of a few violent anarchists and German agents to the legitimate activities of law-abiding citizens—workers trying to improve wages and hours, pacifists and other dissidents expressing principled objections to war, socialists peacefully questioning capitalism, and residents of German descent or citizenship going about their daily lives.

Wilson surely had no intention of making lasting changes in the United States' culture of openness. His limited aim was to solve two pressing problems. He wanted to convince a comfortably isolated nation to spend vast resources rearming in order to enter a European war that posed no direct threat to the American people. And he wanted to convince a public that included German business, political, and artistic leaders that that nation—and even those individuals—had become the enemy.

But Wilson's political choices had large consequences. He could have reined in zealots in his own administration, calmed public fears, and targeted only criminal activities. Instead, he chose to stir up those fears. As Senator Daniel Patrick Moynihan's commission on government secrecy concluded in 1997: "Never before, never since, has the American government been so aroused by the fear of subversion." Upon the base of Wilson's ad hoc responses to imagined conspiracies, decades of secret surveillance, mail opening, loyalty investigations, and summary deportation of immigrants would be built.[6]

While the nation was still at peace, Wilson warned Congress in 1915 that "there are citizens of the United States . . . born under other flags who have poured the poison of disloyalty into the very arteries of our national life. . . . Such creatures of passion, disloyalty, and anarchy must be crushed out." In June 1916—ten months before the United States entered the European war—the president asked for legislation to criminalize subversive activities. He insisted on adding an "Americanism" plank to the 1916 Democratic platform, condemning as subversive those who conspired to embarrass or weaken the government or tried to destroy the nation's unity of purpose. Among suspicious groups were German immigrants, socialists, radical labor organizers, pacifists, anarchists, and opponents of the war.[7]

An incident in July 1916 added to the public's fears. German agents apparently posing as guards blew up two million pounds of explosives at the Black Tom munitions depot across the Hudson River from lower Manhattan, causing tremors equivalent to a moderate earthquake. Later reports confirmed that the German government had sent agents to the still-neutral United States to spread pro-German propaganda and to search for evidence of U.S. aid to the Allies.[8]

Asking Congress for a declaration of war against Germany on April 2, 1917, Wilson escalated his warnings of conspiracy. Germans had filled communities and government offices with spies and set criminal intrigues against American industries.[9] Americans who opposed the war effort could be German sympathizers.[10] "The most learned and liberal of presidents," Senator Moynihan observed in *Secrecy,* "endorsed absurd caricatures."[11]

Wilson followed up with three secretive programs that allowed officials, assisted by private groups, to investigate Americans without their knowledge and to take summary action against suspicious immigrants. These wartime measures would provide the foundation for a new kind of peacetime secrecy.

Missing from each were standards to protect individual rights, limits to keep them from getting out of hand, and effective oversight.

The president, a student of history, suggested that intolerance was an inevitable part of war. "Once lead this people into war," Wilson told the editor of the *New York World* as he prepared to ask Congress for a declaration of war, "and they'll forget there ever was such a thing as tolerance. To fight you must be brutal and ruthless, and the spirit of ruthless brutality will enter into the very fibre of our national life, infecting Congress, the courts, the policeman on the beat, the man on the street."[12]

Two days after Congress declared war, Wilson directed cabinet members to dismiss any employee whose service they believed was "inimical to the public welfare," based on the employee's conduct, sympathies, or conversations related to the war. But he did not do so openly. Instead, he issued a secret order that dismissal would be "without formality" and reasons kept hidden. So broad that it was an open invitation to fire employees at will, this order led to more than 2,000 investigations and at least 660 rulings that individuals were not suitable for employment. Wilson's secret orders inspired decades of over-broad scrutiny of federal employees' personal lives.[13]

Weeks later, a second executive order gave the war department and the navy broad authority to monitor and censor international telephone and telegraph communication, including news reports sent abroad. The same order required the foreign-language press to apply for government permits in order to publish.[14]

In a third set of actions, Wilson and his attorney general launched a propaganda campaign against immigrants and radicals, and invited local police and private citizens to investigate and report on suspicious persons. Wilson enlisted journalist George Creel to head a government Committee on Public Information that supported the war effort with pamphlets and movies. But the committee also portrayed Germans as beasts who raped and pillaged, linked German sympathies to labor unrest and pacifist antiwar efforts, and demanded that all Americans demonstrate their support of the government. Attorney General Thomas Gregory officially deputized private organizations to investigate citizens' loyalty. They monitored suspicious persons and hunted down draft dodgers in "slacker" raids. Local police initiated surveillance of pacifists and German sympathizers while private citizens served as volunteer detectives, reporting their suspicions to the government. Investigators in the department's

Alien Enemy Bureau, led by a young, zealous attorney, J. Edgar Hoover, kept thousands of individuals under surveillance.[15]

This unprecedented combination of fear, secrecy, and officially sanctioned vigilante actions produced harassment, beatings, and lynchings. Hundreds of thousands of Americans joined the American Protective League, the Boy Spies of America, and other organizations that exposed individuals who were rumored to be disloyal. Some wiretapped, burglarized, bugged, tarred and feathered, or horsewhipped suspects. In his detailed account of the times, *World War I and the Origin of Civil Liberties in the United States,* historian Paul L. Murphy shows how the government's mandate triggered mob violence. One mob murdered a suspected German spy in Illinois. Another tarred and feathered a former minister in Oklahoma. Outraged citizens attacked a man in Michigan whom they thought should have bought more liberty bonds. German immigrants were barred from doing business in Cleveland, Ohio. Farmers in Texas who did not contribute to the Red Cross were horsewhipped.[16]

Wilson also successfully urged Congress to approve the espionage legislation that he had proposed while the nation was at peace. His bill was so broadly worded that it was used during and after the war to prosecute political opponents and antiwar protesters, and, with amendments, is still employed a hundred years later to prosecute government employees who leak classified documents to the press.

The Espionage Act of 1917 placed limits on free speech that set the stage for peacetime restrictions. It provided that individuals could be sent to jail for up to twenty years for willfully making or publishing false statements during wartime to interfere with military operations, promote disloyalty among the armed forces, or disrupt military recruiting. It also allowed the federal postmaster to censor any letters or publications that violated those provisions or advocated treason or insurrection.

The Sedition Act of 1918, an amendment proposed by the White House and strengthened by the Senate Judiciary Committee, made it a crime to willfully use disloyal language about the government, the flag, or the military when the nation was at war, and allowed the postmaster to return to senders any mail that violated the act, stamping it "Mail to this address undeliverable under the Espionage Act." Geoffrey R. Stone, in *Perilous Times,* his history of free speech in wartime, called it "the most repressive legislation in American history."[17]

Wilson proposed that the law include a censorship provision so extreme that even the wartime Congress would not accept it. He wanted the president alone to decide when speech might be useful to the enemy, and therefore was punishable as a crime.[18] He insisted that "authority to exercise censorship over the press . . . is absolutely necessary to public safety." But Speaker of the House James Beauchamp Clark, a Democrat from Missouri, declared that censorship was in flat contradiction of the Constitution. And Republican Henry Cabot Lodge said that censorship that would give the president the power "to exclude practically anything from the newspapers of the country." Congress rejected the president's proposal, with thirty-six members of his own party voting against him.[19]

These laws suggested three aspects of the growing power of secrecy. First, secrecy blocked constitutional checks. Investigations could not be monitored by Congress, the courts, the press, or the public because their targets and procedures were secret. Second, secrecy fostered fear and intimidation, making it uncertain whether its critics might themselves become targets. Third, secrecy invited abuse.

Among the more than three thousand individuals caught in the broad net created by the espionage and sedition laws was Eugene Debs, the leader of the Socialist Party, whose crime was making a droll speech opposing the war and ridiculing Wilson's limits on free speech. As the war ended in November 1918, Debs, who had received nearly a million votes in the 1912 presidential election, was sentenced to ten years in prison, ran for president from his prison cell in Atlanta in 1920, and again received nearly a million votes. Sick and bitter, Wilson refused to commute Debs's sentence as his attorney general recommended. Wilson's successor, Warren G. Harding, finally reduced Debs's sentence to time served on Christmas day, 1921, more than three years after the war ended.[20]

When Wilson acted openly, courts tried to make sense of these measures. The Supreme Court ruled after the war that Congress could constitutionally limit freedom of expression when there is a clear and present danger that words will bring about substantive evils that Congress had a right to prevent. The Court also upheld Debs's conviction under the Espionage Act.[21]

Wilson's aggressive postmaster general, Albert S. Burleson, interpreted the laws expansively. He sent a secret order to local postmasters to watch out for any publications that would "embarrass or hamper the Government in conducting the war." Burleson, a former member of Congress from Texas, is also remembered for leading the resegregation of the federal workforce. Within a month, fifteen left-leaning or socialist publications were banned from the mails. Burleson also banned ethnic publications and scholarly books, including the writings of Vladimir Lenin, the Russian communist leader. When Justice Department officials raided the New York offices of the most prominent civil liberties organization on August 30, 1918, the National Civil Liberties Bureau (later the American Civil Liberties Union), and threatened to prosecute its leaders, the postmaster barred its publications as well.[22]

Wilson's administration added one more lasting contribution to the presidential secrecy that would expand in the coming decades. A sweeping order made secrecy the rule rather than the exception for all military information, without balancing Congress's or the public's need to understand or influence what the military was doing. Again, there were no clear boundaries to keep secrecy in check. The War Department's three categories for sensitive information— Secret, Confidential, and For Official Circulation Only—were drawn from British and French classification systems. Unauthorized disclosure could be punished under the Espionage Act.[23]

World War I ended with the armistice of November 11, 1918. But secretive investigations, surveillance, unchecked detention of suspected radicals, and monitoring of private communications did not end. The president, the Justice Department, the postal service, state and local governments, and cadres of vigilantes shifted their sights from German immigrants to suspected Bolsheviks, striking workers, and those who questioned the American system of government. The period that followed World War I was not called a cold war, but it had many of the characteristics of the four decades that followed World War II: fear of communism, zealots who stoked the flames of intolerance, presidential secrecy that invited abuses, and a failure of constitutional checks.

As the war ended, three separate and disruptive events shook the nation and fueled the growth of peacetime secrecy. First, the Russian Revolution of 1917 and the spread of communist ideology in Europe refocused fears of radical threats within the United States. A splinter group of socialists formed the American Communist Party, which supported greater economic equality, workers' rights, nationalization of key industries, and eventual revolution.

Second, a postwar wave of strikes threatened manufacturing and transportation. In January 1919, workers in Seattle called a general strike over shipyard wages and hours, crippling the city for five days. In September, a Boston police strike triggered riots; 365,000 steel workers went on strike, followed by 394,000 coal miners. Railroad workers threatened to join them.

Finally, in April and again in June, more than three dozen bombs, most of them sent through the mail, probably by anarchists, targeted more than thirty prominent leaders, including Seattle's mayor, John D. Rockefeller, and Supreme Court justice Oliver Wendell Holmes, Jr. Some were discovered in post offices. They had not been delivered due to insufficient postage. But one intended for Wilson's attorney general A. Mitchell Palmer blew up prematurely, killing the perpetrator on the front steps of Palmer's Dupont Circle home. His neighbor, Franklin Roosevelt, then assistant secretary of the navy, rushed over to offer assistance.

By unlucky chance, a deadly strain of influenza spread from army camps to cities in 1918 and 1919, infecting a quarter of Americans and killing more than half a million. Public health officials distributed gauze masks, and rail passengers had to show certificates of health for travel. Between twenty and forty million people worldwide died of the flu, more than died in World War I.

The strikes, bombs, and new interest in communist ideology were largely unrelated. Workers struck because postwar inflation made food and other basic goods unaffordable as employers held down wages. Prices had more than doubled between 1914 and 1920. Steel workers were working twelve hours a day, seven days a week. A small number of violent anarchists and deranged individuals were responsible for the bombings. And the U.S. communist party, which did receive subsidies from Russia, remained small—fewer than fifteen thousand members in 1920—and aimed for more alliances with American workers than it achieved. Nonetheless, government officials, employers, and private groups stitched these events together into a Bolshevik conspiracy.[24]

Again, President Wilson led the way. Between the end of the war and his incapacitating stroke eleven months later, his words and actions encouraged peacetime surveillance and roundups of suspicious foreigners. Preoccupied with gaining approval for his proposed League of Nations, he suggested that without such international governance radicals would first destroy European governments and then spread the poison of revolt and chaos to destroy American democracy. The Boston police strike was an early sign of such destruction. Simply opposing the League could be a sign of disloyalty. Shunning the majority of anarchists who peacefully opposed government intervention in private affairs, Wilson successfully urged Congress to provide for summary deportation of any member of an anarchist organization. Wilson did nothing to stop postmaster Burleson from censoring private mail and denying second-class mail rates to left-leaning publications. Burleson maintained that revolutionary organizations were even more dangerous in peacetime than during the war.[25]

Meanwhile, Wilson's new and ambitious attorney general warned that overthrow of the government was imminent. He sent out agents who carried out raids based on secret—or nonexistent—information, resulting in massive violations of civil liberties. A. Mitchell Palmer had been in charge of managing property seized from suspected disloyal immigrants during the war. Before that, he had served as a progressive member of the House of Representatives from Pennsylvania, championing women's suffrage, child labor laws, and reduced tariffs. Among his first acts as attorney general was the release of ten thousand persons of German descent who had been held during the war, and the condemnation of the excesses of the American Protective League's vigilantes.

But Palmer now aimed to succeed Wilson as president. His home had been bombed by a suspected anarchist three months after he became attorney general, and the public had been primed by Wilson's wartime warnings to demand action against revolutionaries who were hiding in their midst. Seeking additional resources to hunt radicals, Palmer told the Senate that an attempt to overthrow the government was planned for July 4, 1919. The explosives sent through the mail and ignited on his front steps had been just a first step.

Despite markedly peaceful Fourth of July celebrations, Palmer secretly ordered agents to undertake investigations of agitators, without standards, controls, or congressional authority, and began planning a massive roundup of individuals suspected of engaging in subversive activities. Wilson was still directing the activities of his cabinet while Palmer arranged with the secretary of labor to handle deportations, and briefed immigration officials and intelligence agents about these plans. By fall, when postwar strikes spread and Wilson collapsed, Palmer was declaring that the blaze of revolution was eating its way into the homes of workers.

To gather information about subversive groups and to identify targets for his planned roundup, Palmer created a new office within the Justice Department, the General Intelligence Division, an agency that would outlast him, outlast the threats of 1919 and 1920, and grow into the Federal Bureau of Investigation (FBI). The twenty-five-year-old lawyer Palmer chose to head the agency,

J. Edgar Hoover, would preside over domestic spying as director of the FBI for forty-eight years.

Hoover had already made his reputation in the department by arresting and deporting immigrants during the war. He eventually built a government agency that would wiretap, bug, and monitor immigrants, dissenters, civil rights leaders, celebrities, journalists, members of Congress, cabinet officers, and even the presidents who encouraged or tolerated him, protected by a wall of officially sanctioned secrecy. Hoover used secrecy so masterfully to build power and avoid legal restraints that the attorneys general and presidents who were supposed to oversee his work often did not know what he was doing.

Convinced there was a communist conspiracy, Hoover started by directing his undercover agents to monitor radical meetings and gather names of suspected leaders. He encouraged local police to investigate dissidents and send him information. By the time Wilson left office, Hoover had identified 450,000 radical leaders, and created detailed files on 60,000.

State and local governments followed the national lead. A committee of New York's state legislature suggested that universities, magazines, civil liberties lawyers, and liberal members of Congress were associated with Bolsheviks, and expelled the legislature's socialist members. By 1920, thirty-six states had laws that limited free expression in one way or another. Police chiefs permitted or banned radical meetings as they saw fit.

Private groups, too, redoubled their efforts after the war. The American Protective League continued to target socialist groups and labor organizations. The Ku Klux Klan, active in the South and in some northern states, hunted radicals. In New York, four hundred war veterans stormed the office of a New York socialist newspaper and beat up the staff. In Los Angeles, the American Legion supported police action against union organizing.[26]

It was at this moment, as essential workers went on strike for better wages, bombs targeted prominent leaders, fear of communism took hold of reasonable people, the attorney general prepared to raid suspect organizations, and the fate of the League of Nations hung in the balance, that Wilson suffered a massive stroke. Overnight, the nation lost its leader—without knowing it. The most remarkable deception in presidential history became a tragic display of another dimension of executive secrecy—a president's power to keep secret his mental and physical incapacity to govern, an issue not fully resolved today.

Wilson's cabinet, members of Congress, world leaders, and fellow Americans were not told that the president could no longer lead. As Wilson remained prostrate and confused, Dr. Grayson issued statements saying that he suffered from nervous exhaustion, that he was improving every day, and that his mind remained clear.

At 11:00 a.m. on October 3, the day after the president was stricken, Grayson issued the first of what would become a daily drumbeat of uninformative statements. "The President had a fairly good night but his condition is not at all good this morning." This was followed at 10:00 p.m. by: "The President is a very sick man. His condition is less favorable today and he has remained in bed throughout the day." The president's illness was simply a worsening of the "nervous exhaustion" that had caused him to cut short his western trip.[27]

In an article written in 1994, historian Arthur S. Link, editor of the *Papers of Woodrow Wilson*, described Grayson's dilemma. Grayson held the information that the cabinet and the Congress needed in order to make a constitutional determination of presidential disability. As a physician treating a very sick patient, Grayson was obliged to respect Wilson's privacy. As physician to the president of the United States, Grayson was obliged to inform the nation when its chief executive could no longer carry out his duties. Neither the Constitution nor Congress provided guidance about how to reconcile these conflicting obligations.[28]

Born and raised in Virginia, Grayson had served as Wilson's physician since his election in 1912, and the two had become close personal friends. The son and grandson of country doctors, Grayson was known for his discretion, gentlemanly qualities, sense of humor, and talent as a storyteller.[29]

For the next seventeen months, Grayson chose to follow the wishes of the president and his wife. Wilson remained in office, partially paralyzed and mentally impaired, too weak and confused to lead during a time of national turmoil. By the time he left office he could sit up, walk a short distance with a cane, and work at his desk for an hour or two. As he gained physical strength and became more alert, his irrationality became a problem. He was not functioning as president, his biographer John Milton Cooper, Jr., wrote. In the absence of constitutional direction, an incapacitated president, a protective wife, and a solicitous doctor placed the nation at risk. Foreign and domestic policy became the byproducts of the domestic drama that unfolded in the White House.

Only the president's wife and his doctors knew the extent of Wilson's impairment. Ike Hoover wrote later that "an air of secrecy had come over things during the [first] day. Those on the outside, including family and employees, could learn nothing." Even the president may not have known his true condition. As Edith Wilson told the story in her memoir, "I would have to wear a mask—not only to the public but to the one I loved best in the world; for he must never know how ill he was, and I must carry on."[30]

At first, Grayson may have thought that the president might recover. "As these symptoms . . . are often transitory," he wrote two weeks after the president was stricken, "it was hoped that they would speedily disappear." When paralysis persisted, Grayson thought it wise to issue only general statements because the president was improving. "Further, Mrs. Wilson, the President's wife was absolutely opposed to any other course."[31]

Strong-willed, possessive, and convinced that staying in office would encourage her husband's recovery, Edith Galt Wilson controlled the flow of information. Wilson had married Edith four years earlier, after his first wife, Ellen, died of Bright's disease. Like Wilson and Dr. Grayson, Edith had grown up in Virginia. She was the seventh of eleven children of a circuit judge, had little formal education, and inherited enough wealth from her first husband to enjoy Washington's social life as well as annual European tours.

The morning after the president's stroke, Secretary of State Robert Lansing and the president's longtime secretary Joseph Tumulty met quietly in the cabinet room. Lansing, an expert on international law, veteran negotiator, and grandson of an earlier secretary of state, cared about the letter of the law. He had often annoyed Wilson by questioning the practical details of the president's sweeping international visions. Tumulty, Wilson's tough and politically savvy guide in dealing with Congress, patronage, and public opinion, came from a large Irish Catholic family of eleven children and was raised in an apartment above his father's grocery store in Jersey City. He had gone to work for Wilson as his private secretary in 1911 at age thirty-one, when Wilson was governor of New Jersey.

When Lansing asked Tumulty what was wrong with the president, Tumulty signaled with a hand gesture that the president's left side was paralyzed. Tumulty then sent for Grayson, who told them that the president was suffering only from nervous exhaustion. It would be weeks and perhaps months before he could resume work, but his mind was unaffected.

The meticulous Lansing had brought with him a copy of the Constitution. He suggested that it would be up to Tumulty or Grayson to declare that the president was unable to discharge his duties. Tumulty became emotional. He recalled in his memoir that he responded: "You may rest assured that while Woodrow Wilson is lying in the White House on the broad of his back I will not be a party to ousting him. He has been too kind, too loyal . . . to receive such treatment at my hands." Grayson agreed.

Still concerned, Lansing called a special meeting of the cabinet for Monday, October 6. When the heads of the federal departments gathered in the cabinet room, he brought up the question of whether the vice president, Thomas Riley Marshall, should assume the president's duties, and asked Grayson to explain to the cabinet members the seriousness of the president's condition. Dissembling again, Grayson reported that the president suffered from a nervous breakdown and indigestion, was improving, and should be bothered as little as possible. His mind was clear, and he had sent word that he resented the cabinet meeting in his absence.

In light of this rosy report, the members of the cabinet simply sent the president their good wishes. Lansing, stunned by Grayson's masquerade, was alone in wanting to confront the issue. Lacking a statement of disability from the president's doctor, he gave up his effort to get the cabinet to consider constitutional succession. Wilson historian August Heckscher concluded: "Thus began, with the silent assent of some, with the active maneuvering of others, such a cover-up as American history had not known before."[32]

During the weeks that followed, White House usher Ike Hoover spent some time each day with the president. "There was never a moment during all that time when he was more than a shadow of his former self," he wrote in his memoir. "He could articulate but indistinctly and think but feebly. . . . For at least a month or more not one word, I believe, was mentioned to him about the business of the office and he was so sick he did not take the initiative to inquire."[33]

Edith Wilson and Grayson organized a routine to conceal the president's condition. Wilson remained in bed. No visitors were allowed. Gilbert Close, the president's confidential secretary, was banished. Secretary of State Lansing never saw Wilson again. Eleven days after the president's stroke, Attorney General Palmer told the *New York Times* that no member of the cabinet knew any more about the president's condition than appeared in the newspapers. Even his closest aide, Tumulty, was not allowed to see Wilson for several weeks. Newspapers reported that the president suffered from "nervous exhaustion" and "might be definitely on the road to recovery."[34]

During the months after Wilson's stroke, Thomas Marshall, the vice president, remained the outsider he had been throughout Wilson's presidency. A modest and likable man and a seasoned politician, the former governor of Indiana had been chosen as Wilson's running mate as part of a secret deal that promised Indiana's delegates to Wilson at the divided 1912 convention. Once in office, Wilson gave him little to do, and Marshall had given up attending cabinet meetings long ago. When he came to the White House after Wilson's stroke, as the secretary of the navy, Josephus Daniels, wrote later, Edith turned him away just as she turned away all visitors.[35]

Marshall simply read the newspapers and waited. He wanted some time to prepare if he was going to assume the presidency. But he also wanted to avoid Edith Wilson's wrath. "I am not going to get myself entangled with Mrs. Wilson," he told Arthur Krock of the *New York Times*. "No politician ever exposes himself to the hatred of a woman, particularly if she's the wife of the President." When groups of senators approached Marshall about assuming the presidency, he demurred. The only way he would agree to even temporary authority would be if Congress passed a resolution that was then approved by Mrs. Wilson and Grayson.[36]

The role that Edith created for herself after Wilson's stroke became an unconstrained extension of her effort to be part of Wilson's work when he was well. When they were courting, she wrote to Wilson: "How I wish I could help you ... in a practical way." She wanted him to let her "take some of the responsibility."[37] She began by asking him for daily updates on confidential matters. Wilson was soon sending her official papers to read just as he sent them to his cabinet. He assured her that "whatever is mine is yours, knowledge of affairs of state not excepted."[38]

Edith's possessive temperament quickly turned her interest in affairs of state into harsh judgments of Wilson's advisers and his cabinet. In one of her early letters to Wilson, she observed that his closest adviser, Edward House, seemed "a weak vessel." His faithful secretary, Joseph Tumulty, did not have the appropriate taste and manners to represent the president.[39]

Once they were married, Edith waged full-scale campaigns to depose advisers she didn't like. When Wilson agonized over William Jennings Bryan's resignation as secretary of state, Edith wrote to Wilson, "Hurrah! Old Bryan is out!" When he proposed State Department counselor Robert Lansing as Bryan's successor, she complained, "He is only a clerk . . . isn't he?" In fact, Lansing was the department's second most senior official. When Wilson explained that House was the only person with whom he could talk freely, Edith tried to eliminate him.[40] When he was healthy, the president gently rebuffed these accusations. When she referred to Bryan as a traitor, Wilson responded, "My how I like you . . . And how you can hate too."[41]

Early in their marriage, Edith established a routine. Each morning she brought the president papers he needed to sign from a drawer where his advisers left them. She sometimes accompanied him to meetings with advisers, cabinet members, and foreign dignitaries, and worked hard to school herself in the issues they would discuss. Press reports at the time observed that she was much more active in her husband's duties than were earlier first ladies.[42]

After his stroke, Edith became a self-appointed gatekeeper. She explained in her memoir, "I began my stewardship. I studied every paper . . . and tried to digest . . . the things that, despite my vigilance, had to go to the President."[43] Asked by reporters how she decided what issues to raise with the president, she said, "I just decided . . . I talked with him so much that I knew pretty well what he thought of things."[44]

Without knowing it, the American people had elected and reelected a president who was a very sick man. But then, as now, no law required candidates to tell voters about their physical or mental health. More than twenty years earlier, in May 1896, when he was forty, Wilson suffered a stroke that caused weakness in his right hand. Ten years later, when he was president of Princeton University, he awoke one day blind in his left eye because of a burst blood vessel. An eminent neurologist, S. Weir Mitchell, who examined him when he was elected president in 1912, predicted he certainly would not survive his first term, a prediction that may not have been published at the time.[45]

At the Paris peace conference in 1919, Wilson probably suffered a small stroke. A neuropsychiatrist who examined him reported that it affected his personality and gave him markedly lessened mental ability. Grayson eventually acknowledged that Wilson had minor strokes while abroad. At least by 1918, Wilson showed changes in temperament and memory, according to a later expert analysis. When he was asked by Arthur S. Link to summarize the medical evidence and its impact on Wilson's behavior, the neurosurgeon Bert E. Park wrote that Wilson suffered memory loss and became increasingly irascible and suspicious a year before the massive stroke.[46]

Two weeks after the president's massive stroke, in mid-October, a leak to the *New York Times* nearly ended Edith's ruse. A Republican senator, George H. Moses of New Hampshire, suggested in a letter to a constituent that Wilson had suffered a cerebral lesion and was paralyzed. "The statement that the President has had a cerebral lesion . . . continues to be circulated by men in and out of public life," the *Times* reported.[47]

Faced with this explicit report and torn between his duty to his patient and his obligation to inform the public, Grayson decided to issue a detailed memorandum describing exactly what had occurred. Gathering notes from consulting doctors, he explained that "it was . . . desired by all the consultants in the case to make a full statement of the President's condition."[48]

However, when he gave the memorandum to Mrs. Wilson for her approval, she absolutely refused to allow him to release it. Grayson told Josephus Daniels, the navy secretary, "I am forbidden to speak. . . . The President and Mrs. Wilson have made me make a promise to that effect." Instead, Grayson continued his routine of daily bulletins to reassure the public. A month after his stroke, "the President's improvement steadily continues. He is eating, sleeping, digesting and assimilating well."[49]

Grayson's close friendship with the Wilsons made the situation more complicated. It was Grayson who had introduced Edith to the grieving president months after Wilson's first wife had died. Grayson accompanied the Wilsons to the Paris peace conference, where the president trusted him to carry messages to other heads of state and to brief the press on developments.

Secrecy bred rumors. The president had died and Edith was acting in his place. The president was insane and Grayson had locked him up. The president's advisers were urging him to step down but he wouldn't. Grayson complained that people were saying the president would never be well enough to work and that Grayson was conspiring to keep secret the true state of Wilson's health.[50]

That was true, of course. The nation no longer had a working president.

To reassure the public, Edith Wilson and Grayson staged burlesque audiences with ceremonial visitors. On October 30, the bedridden president, covered from neck to foot in a darkened room, received the king and queen of the

Belgians for a ten-minute visit. Front-page stories said the president had had a cordial talk with the king and was cheered by the visit. In a similar scene two weeks later, the Prince of Wales visited the president for twenty minutes. Grayson told the press that the prince and the president had a "fine old time."[51]

Meanwhile, pressing international and domestic issues remained unaddressed. Secretary of State Lansing, who had the most urgent matters for the president's attention, could not get responses to most of his messages. Should the United States recognize the provisional government of Costa Rica? Should the United States return Britain's ships? What role should the United States take in the allies' negotiations concerning future relations with Turkey, Syria, and other nations? Inquiries large and small were returned with Edith's notes: "the president says" that he will not act on these matters until he is well.[52]

Tumulty drafted the president's warning to mine workers not to go on strike. "There is no evidence that Wilson ever saw that statement," according to Link. Tumulty also issued a presidential veto of Congress's bill to ban the sale of alcoholic beverages, the Volstead Act. The veto message protested the perpetuation of wartime prohibition rules that had been put in place so grain would be used to make bread for soldiers rather than alcoholic beverages for civilians. Without the president's leadership, however, the House and the Senate overrode the veto, and Prohibition became the law of the land for the next thirteen years. "Insofar as we know, Wilson never knew about the veto message," Link notes.[53]

Two months after the president was stricken, the Senate Foreign Relations Committee sent two members to ascertain the president's true condition. Albert B. Fall of New Mexico, a Republican opponent of Wilson's, and Gilbert Hitchcock, the committee's senior Democrat, spent forty-five minutes with the president in his bedroom. Ike Hoover recalled that Mrs. Wilson and Grayson again engaged in a "great camouflage" of darkening the room and covering the president to disguise his weakened condition. The senators did not question the president about his illness. News reports said that the president listened attentively to Senator Fall's report on the situation in Mexico and asked him to send the facts in a memorandum.[54]

White House usher Ike Hoover, who saw Wilson every day, found him "a shadow of his former self. . . . [He] could articulate but indistinctly and think but feebly."[55] Park, the neurosurgeon who examined the medical evidence for the editors of the Wilson papers, concluded that "neither Wilson's thought processes nor his conduct in office would ever be the same again."[56]

As he regained a measure of physical strength and became somewhat more alert, Wilson's impaired judgment and emotional volatility—typical aftereffects of stroke—created a new set of problems. Wilson scholars have struggled to describe the president's mental impairment. Link noted that the stroke had "devastating effects on his personality; among other things, it made him incapable of abstract thinking, intransigent, oblivious to political reality."[57] Park wrote that Wilson suffered from nervous anxiety, delivered uncharacteristic diatribes against those whose opinions differed from his, and remained unwilling or unable to act on critical matters of state.[58] Wilson biographer August Heckscher concluded: "He was afflicted by symptoms typical of such cases—depression, paranoia, rigidity of mind, brief attention span, and loss of control over the emotions."[59]

In December, Wilson came up with a bizarre idea. He told Tumulty to draft a letter to the American people calling on all senators who opposed the League of Nations to resign and run again for reelection to test their popular support. If most were reelected, the president himself would resign.[60]

Then, in February 1920, Wilson shocked members of Congress and the public by summarily firing his secretary of state. Robert Lansing had not been allowed to see the president since his stroke on October 2. A letter signed by Wilson asked whether "during my illness you have frequently called the heads of the executive departments into conference?" The cabinet usually met twice a week before Wilson's stroke and had met twenty-five times since Wilson was stricken, a fact that the president and his wife knew. When Lansing responded by letter that he had participated in calling cabinet meetings, Wilson asked for his resignation. The *Los Angeles Times* called it "Wilson's Last Mad Act."[61]

Wilson's action prompted the House Judiciary Committee to hold two days of hearings on the president's disability. Members debated the questions the Constitution did not answer. Did Congress have the authority to determine the process of presidential succession? Did appointed officials—cabinet officers or the president's physician, for example—have the power to oust an elected president? Members introduced bills to empower the cabinet or the Supreme Court to determine presidential disability or to provide for the vice president to serve as acting president. Some members believed that a constitutional amendment rather than an act of Congress would be appropriate. But no consensus emerged and Congress took no action.[62]

It was during this time that the attorney general, Mitchell Palmer, used the power vacuum to stage roundups of alleged Bolsheviks and other radicals, based on secret—or nonexistent—information about their activities. Unconstrained by the stricken president, Palmer ordered agents to infiltrate radical groups, interrogate and arrest suspicious persons, and summarily deport immigrant workers as communist agents.

In early November, a month after the president's stroke, Palmer's agents stormed meetings of the Union of Russian Workers in twelve cities, arrested several hundred suspects, and summarily deported 249 to Russia. Two months later they rounded up four thousand suspected communists in thirty-three cities and held them without access to lawyers. They arrested suspects based on secret information, denied them lawyers, and jailed them. Historians would later observe that the government indulged in greater excesses during this period than at any earlier time.[63]

Palmer's actions were so extreme that they helped provoke a lasting counterweight to growing peacetime secrecy, a durable movement to protect civil liberties. In May 1920, Felix Frankfurter, Roscoe Pound, and other prominent lawyers documented the illegal arrests and detention of dissenters during Palmer's raids. Their report confirmed that federal agents had infiltrated radical organizations and that those arrested were not allowed to consult with lawyers or talk to friends. The same year, civil liberties advocates formed the American Civil Liberties Union (ACLU).[64]

As the Senate considered whether to approve the League of Nations in the fall of 1919 and the spring of 1920, the president remained an isolated, powerful, unpredictable actor in a political drama with grave consequences. When he was well, no policy issue mattered more to him than the creation of this new world order of international cooperation. Wilson had insisted that the League be the first article of the Versailles Treaty that would officially end World War I. Senate consent to the treaty would make Wilson's vision of international peace a reality. The Senate was scheduled to vote on November 19, six weeks after Wilson's stroke.

However, Republicans had gained a one-vote majority in the 1918 midterm elections, and now sought changes. The treaty stated that all members of the League would come to the aid of any member state whose independence was threatened. Republican senator Henry Cabot Lodge of Massachusetts, chairman of the Foreign Relations Committee, believed that the treaty should say explicitly that such economic or military aid required congressional approval. Before his stroke, Wilson had argued that the constitutional requirements that Congress declare war and appropriate funds need not be repeated in the treaty.[65]

These issues were solvable. When he was well, Wilson told Lodge's committee confidentially that he did not dispute that congressional action would be required to authorize intervention against aggressors that attacked an ally nation. The treaty was "a moral, not a legal, obligation, and leaves our Congress absolutely free to put its own interpretation upon it."[66] On September 3, he had written a memorandum acknowledging that the treaty's commitment "is to be regarded only as advice and leaves each Member State free to exercise its own judgment." That principle should be stated in interpretive documents rather than the treaty itself so other nations would not be tempted to add treaty modifications.[67]

But after his stroke, the bedridden president became belligerent. There would be no compromise. On October 28, Lodge once again proposed several minor changes that would make the treaty obligations acceptable to him. The White House never responded.

When Senator Hitchcock went to see the president on November 17, just two days before the crucial vote, he found the president much changed. Wilson explained to him: "I have been lying on my back and have been very weak, and it has fatigued me to read and to discuss matters in my mind, so to speak. I have been kept in the dark to a certain extent except what Mrs. Wilson and Doctor Grayson have told me, and they have purposely kept a good deal from me." Hitchcock told Wilson that the treaty could not be approved without accepting modest changes in language. Wilson groaned, "Is it possible? Is it possible?" When Hitchcock suggested it might be wise to compromise, Wilson responded: "Let Lodge compromise."[68]

On November 19, the Senate rejected the proposed treaty with and without the Lodge reservations. Both votes were 38 in favor and 53 opposed. The Senate would take one more vote in the spring. The White House issued a statement on December 14 stating that the president had "no compromise or concession of any kind in mind."[69]

A final Senate vote was scheduled for March 19, 1920. As the date approached, Wilson became increasingly strident. Ignoring the pleas of his advisers and of Democratic senators, he simply refused to discuss any changes. On January 15, he issued a statement to the press that he would make no compromise on the treaty. Wilson instructed Senator Hitchcock, who was leading the Senate fight for the Democrats, not to entertain any proposals.[70]

Noting the president's intransigence, Grayson again suggested to Wilson that he resign, now telling him it would speed his recovery. Professor Link described Grayson's action as "his final plan to save the treaty." For a brief time, Wilson talked about appearing before the Senate in a wheelchair to deliver his resignation speech. But he dropped the plan to resign when he was angered by a letter from a recent British envoy that seemed to accept Lodge's compromise.[71]

On March 8, as the final vote approached, Wilson warned Congress that failure to approve the treaty as submitted would be acting "in bad faith to the opinion of the world" and mean "repudiating our own principles." The *New York Tribune* noted that "leaders of all factions . . . were absolutely hopeless of ratification. . . . The president has again said 'Take it or leave it.' "

On the day of the final vote, the galleries were full. Many curious members of the House attended as well. Senators made their last speeches, many encouraging ratification. Six hours later it was over.

The Senate rejected both the treaty Wilson had worked so hard to negotiate and membership in the League of Nations that he had conceived, despite the fact that more than two-thirds of senators certainly favored both. Forty-nine senators voted to accept the treaty and the League with the modifications favored by Senator Lodge; thirty-five opposed it. The vote fell seven short of the two-thirds majority required by the Constitution for approval. Twenty-one Democrats broke with the president to support Lodge's modifications. Ironically, Democrats who remained loyal to Wilson's rigid view joined the extreme isolationists Wilson deplored to vote for his doomed version. The ailing president defeated his most important legacy.

In a poignant conclusion to a long day, Republican leaders handed back to George Sanderson, the secretary of state who had replaced the ousted Robert Lansing, the bound volume of the treaty that Wilson had presented to the Senate for ratification in August 1919. The next morning, Sanderson returned the rejected treaty to the White House.[72]

Wilson was derided in the press. It was a "colossal crime" for the president to block ratification, declared Wilson's first secretary of state, William Jennings Bryan. Republican senator Frank Brandegee of Connecticut said, "[The president] has strangled his own child."[73] The *Chicago Daily Tribune* editorialized that "in the final hour, completing his disservice, he [Wilson] was able to command enough senators to drive a knife into the heart of his own work."[74]

When Edith told the president the result of the vote the next morning, March 20, a cold and cloudy Saturday, the president became depressed, Grayson wrote later. He said he felt like going to bed and staying there.[75]

The treaty's rejection meant that the United States remained officially at war with Germany. Diplomatic relations and normal trade could not resume. In April, when both houses of Congress approved a resolution making peace with Germany, Wilson vetoed it because it did not include approval of the full treaty. Wilson also failed to respond to the secretary of war's request that he release those jailed for opposing the war under the Espionage and Sedition Acts. The attorney general's campaign against radicals continued, perhaps without the president's knowledge. The United States remained technically at war with Germany until Wilson left office in 1921.[76]

Woodrow Wilson remained in office for another year after the Senate vote, a bitter, deluded, and very sick man who alternated between dreams of running for reelection and thoughts of resigning. A few days after the Senate's vote, he told Grayson that he was considering running for a third term in November to save the League of Nations. If the convention needed someone "to lead them out of the wilderness . . . I would feel obliged to accept the nomination. . . . I have given my vitality, and almost my life, for the League of Nations, and I would rather lead a fight for the League . . . and lose both my reputation and my life than shirk a duty of this kind." The next day, he spoke more philosophically. "It is evidently too soon for the country to accept the League. . . . May have to break the heart of the world . . . before the League will be accepted and appreciated."[77]

Three weeks later, on April 13, in one of many middle-of-the-night conversations with Grayson, Wilson again pondered resigning. "I am seriously thinking what is my duty to the country on account of my physical condition. . . . I do not have much desire for work. If I am only half-efficient I should turn the office over to the Vice-President. . . . The country cannot afford to wait for me." On this occasion, Grayson reports in his diary that he suggested the president call a cabinet meeting "to determine just what your leadership represents."[78]

The next day, the president met with his cabinet for the first time since his stroke more than six months earlier. Ike Hoover wheeled Wilson into the White

House library and announced each member's name very plainly so that Wilson, whose vision had been further impaired by the stroke, could identify them. Those who attended reported that he looked old, worn, and haggard, and said little. When he tried to speak, his jaw tended to drop. He sat as if in a trance and would have agreed to anything to end the meeting, Hoover wrote later.[79]

At the end of June 1920, the Democrats held their convention in San Francisco. It was the first political convention held on the west coast and the first to use microphones.[80] Still deluded that he could run for reelection, Wilson worked behind the scenes to secure the nomination for himself. Grayson and Wilson's faithful secretary Joseph Tumulty worked to ensure that that would not happen. Edith Wilson initially humored the president but, by the time of the convention, she joined Grayson and Tumulty in discouraging his nomination.[81]

After forty-four ballots, the convention nominated James M. Cox, governor of Ohio, for president and a thirty-eight-year-old delegate from New York, the assistant secretary of the navy, Franklin D. Roosevelt, for vice president. The party's platform still favored a League of Nations.[82]

Republican Warren G. Harding, who won the election, declared that "in the existing League of Nations . . . this Republic will have no part." Harding reversed many of Wilson's progressive policies, increasing tariffs and opposing regulation of business.[83]

On March 1, 1921, Wilson met with his cabinet for the last time. He walked slowly into the room, leaning on a cane. As cabinet members took turns speaking in tribute to the president, Wilson began to cry. Apologetically, he explained, "It is one of the handicaps of my physical condition that I cannot control myself as I have been accustomed to do. God bless you all."

Leaving office three days later, Wilson moved with his wife to a house he had purchased at 2340 S Street NW, where he continued to fantasize about running for president in 1924. In June, he engaged Louis Brandeis, one of his appointees to the Supreme Court, to help draw up the principles upon which he would run. Wilson wanted to include a statement about the senators who had opposed the League of Nations or worked for a compromise. "We condemn the group of men [responsible for the treaty's defeat] as the most partisan, prejudiced and unpatriotic coterie that has ever misled the Senate of the United States."[84]

In late January 1924, Wilson's health deteriorated. Doctors administered oxygen and morphine. On February 3, Wilson's heart failed. Outside his house on S Street hundreds of people had gathered. Grayson emerged in tears to read a brief statement. "Mr. Wilson died at 11:15 o'clock this morning. His heart action became feebler and feebler, and the heart muscle was so fatigued that it refused to act any longer. The end came peacefully."[85]

Without the membership of the United States, the League of Nations was officially disbanded in 1935.

Wilson's repressive measures continued to cast a long shadow. Congress did not repeal the Sedition Act until December 1920, more than two years after the war ended, and loyalty investigations to exclude applicants from government employment, based on secret evidence, continued on through much of the twentieth century. Only in 1931 did President Franklin D. Roosevelt restore the civil rights of surviving political prisoners convicted under Wilson's 1917 Espionage Act and 1918 Sedition Act.

Once initiated, secret surveillance was hard to stop. In 1924, when President Calvin Coolidge's attorney general Harlan Fiske Stone ordered J. Edgar Hoover to stop initiating new investigations, Hoover simply expanded his existing investigations of radicals, labor groups, civil liberties organizations, and dissidents. He assisted local police in raids, shared lists of suspected dissidents with employers, and kept up his files on the ACLU and other groups that protested government interference with individual rights. Hoover's mastery of secrecy as an instrument of power continued to frustrate the attempts of attorneys general to set limits on his surveillance activities until his death in 1972.[86]

In 1975, the Senate Select Committee to Study Governmental Operations with Respect to Intelligence Activities, known as the Church Committee, noted "a consistent pattern in which programs initiated with limited goals, such as preventing criminal violence or identifying foreign spies, were expanded to what witnesses characterized as 'vacuum cleaners,' sweeping in information about lawful activities of American citizens."[87]

The stock market crash of 1929 and the Depression that followed created new domestic unrest and broadened government surveillance, again without setting clear limits. By 1930, Hamilton Fish, a Republican House member from New York, headed a congressional committee to investigate alleged communists, based on the idea that they had helped cause the economic collapse. By 1934, after Adolf Hitler seized power in Germany, President Roosevelt was directing Hoover's agency to secretly investigate the Nazi movement in the

United States. Two years later, the president may have asked Hoover to conduct a broader investigation of communists and fascists, a direction that Hoover broadened into a call to his agents to investigate any organization that advocated the overthrow of the U.S. government, with or without foreign influence. By 1938, the House Un-American Activities Committee was investigating not only Nazis and communists but also liberal organizations, left-leaning newspapers, and labor groups. By 1940 Roosevelt was asking Hoover to investigate political opponents and keep files on individuals who wrote the president opposing a U.S. role in the European war.[88]

Members of Congress who compromised on the vague wording of the Espionage Act could not have foreseen that the act would become the government's lasting instrument for punishing government officials who revealed classified information they thought the public should know. President Richard Nixon's Justice Department would use it to charge Defense Department contractor Daniel Ellsberg in 1971 when he provided to the press a classified history of the Vietnam War, and President Barack Obama would use it to charge Edward Snowden in 2013 when he provided secret National Security Agency documents to the *Guardian,* the *New York Times,* and the *Washington Post.*

Presidents' secrets about their physical and mental capacity remain a recurring issue. There had been earlier instances of disability that were not shared with the American people. George Washington suffered life-threatening pneumonia and was unable to work for several weeks in 1790. His doctors and advisers hid his illness because they did not want to worry the public. James Garfield, shot in a Washington train station by a disgruntled office-seeker, lay disabled for two and a half months in 1881 before he died. No one broached the question of removing him from office. Grover Cleveland had a secret cancer surgery on a yacht anchored off Long Island.

Nor would Wilson's incapacity in office be the last. Franklin Roosevelt may have suffered small strokes beginning in 1938, and scholars agree that his mental and physical health declined during his last years in office due to heart disease. John F. Kennedy did not disclose that he suffered from Addison's disease, and took pain-killing drugs with physical and psychological side effects.[89]

The Twenty-Fifth Amendment to the Constitution, approved by the states in 1967, did not entirely solve the problem. Congress proposed the amendment after the assassination of President Kennedy raised concerns about the health of his successor, Lyndon B. Johnson, who had suffered a heart attack eight years earlier. The amendment provided that a president could be removed from office by himself declaring his temporary or permanent disability or by his vice president and a majority of his cabinet (or another group designated by Congress) declaring a disability. The amendment also provided for congressional review and approval of presidents' appointments to fill vice presidential vacancies.[90]

However, the amendment did not resolve the two most difficult issues concerning presidents' physical or mental incapacity. It relied on the president, vice president, or cabinet to declare the president disabled. And it did not require that the president's doctor provide information about the president's health to the vice president, the cabinet, or the public, information on which a judgment of disability might be based.[91]

Writing in 1995, Professor Link noted, "It is hardly conceivable that Wilson would have acted to bring in the Vice President. . . . Wilson was emotionally and psychologically incapable of taking any such action." And "it is inconceivable that [Vice President Marshall] would have declared President Wilson unable to fulfill his constitutional duties," and all the cabinet officers except Lansing would have agreed with the vice president.[92]

Congress has never acted on proposals to supplement the judgment of the president's personal physician with a medical committee, to require that evidence of incapacity be quickly disclosed, or to require physical exams and health histories for candidates for the presidency and vice presidency with results disclosed to the public.

Presidents remain at risk of incapacity not only from illness but also from assassination attempts. Gerald Ford survived two assassination attempts within eighteen days. While he was shaking hands with citizens in Sacramento, California, on September 5, 1975, Lynette Alice Fromme, a follower of the mass murderer Charles Manson, raised a gun to shoot him from two feet away, and was wrestled to the ground by Secret Service agents. Then an angry forty-five-year-old bookkeeper, Sara Jane Moore, fired at the president across the street from the St. Francis Hotel in San Francisco. Oliver Sipple, a marine and Vietnam veteran who happened to be standing next to Moore in the crowd, knocked her arm down before she could fire a second shot.

Ronald Reagan was shot by John Hinckley, Jr., as Reagan left Washington's Hilton Hotel on March 21, 1981, only two months after he took office. Neither

Reagan nor Vice President George H. W. Bush transferred power as provided by the Twenty-Fifth Amendment while Reagan was incapacitated for several weeks. Unsuccessful assassination plots were also aimed at George H. W. Bush, Bill Clinton, and Barack Obama.[93]

In matters of presidential health, then, secrecy still rules. Presidents now write contingency plans. But those plans are kept secret. Dwight D. Eisenhower and his vice president, Richard Nixon, exchanged letters agreeing that Eisenhower would transfer his duties (but not the office) to Nixon if Eisenhower deemed himself incapacitated. If Eisenhower could not make that judgment, Nixon would decide what to do. Kennedy and Johnson also exchanged letters, as did Johnson and his vice president, Hubert Humphrey. George H. W. Bush and Bill Clinton framed contingency plans for presidential succession but did not disclose them. Barack Obama apparently approved a detailed contingency plan, but that plan too has remained secret. Since presidents do not discuss these plans, there has as yet been no opportunity for debate about an issue of intense public interest.[94]

Voters often know little about the health of presidential candidates when they go to the polls. Revealing medical records remains a matter of choice. Candidates usually provide some information about their health voluntarily, but the completeness and amount of detail vary widely. In 2015, the Republican presidential candidate Donald Trump released letters from his doctor that provided few specifics. The Democratic candidate Hillary Clinton also released a letter from her doctors summarizing her good health. In 2008, Democratic candidate Barack Obama released six paragraphs summarizing his previous twenty-one years of physical exams along with a statement from his physician attesting that he was in excellent health. Republican candidate John McCain allowed reporters a laughable three hours to review more than 1,100 pages of medical records. George H. W. Bush and Michael Dukakis set a better example in 1988, when each candidate allowed his physician to discuss his medical histories with at least one reporter, Lawrence K. Altman of the *New York Times,* himself a physician. Bill Clinton revealed less about his health during his presidential campaign than any nominee in the previous twenty years, according to Altman.[95]

Woodrow Wilson's need to solve immediate political problems, his low tolerance for dissent, and his failure to restrain zealous department heads led to new fears of hidden conspiracies that justified new kinds of government secrecy. Walled off from constitutional checks, secret programs and practices continued to expand without clear limits after he left office.

A president's lifelong denial of ill health, a headstrong wife's determination to protect him, and a doctor's divided loyalty became a nation's tragedy—a tragedy that could recur. Nearly a hundred years after Wilson's stroke, Professor Link's warning remains prescient. "The story of President Wilson's disability clearly foretells what might well happen under the Twenty-fifth Amendment today."[96]

4

Harry Truman: Institutional Secrecy

Responding to the immediate crises of the early Cold War, Harry S Truman built on President Wilson's foundation a lasting framework of secret loyalty investigations, domestic surveillance, and covert actions that purposefully skirted congressional oversight. Secrecy about atomic weapons limited the president's information and his opportunities for leadership, and skewed later public debate.

"I KNIGHT YOU THE CLOAK AND DAGGER group of snoopers and director of centralized snooping." Harry Truman presented his military aide Admiral William Leahy and navy intelligence officer Sidney Souers with black cloaks, black hats, and wooden daggers. Souers got a black mustache as well.[1]

The president was in a celebratory mood. He had invited Leahy, Souers, and his press assistant, Eben Ayers, to a private lunch in the executive dining room of the White House. It was January 24, 1946. After wrangling for nine months with army and navy brass and with William J. (Wild Bill) Donovan, who had headed President Roosevelt's Office of Strategic Services during the war that had just ended, Truman had finally gotten what he asked for. It had seemed a small request.

All the new president wanted was a small staff in the White House to prepare a daily intelligence summary that would make sense of the piles of cables he received from the military intelligence services and the State Department. It was part of his effort to create order and efficiency in the executive branch. The cables were too voluminous to read, and they annoyed him with their conflicting views.[2]

Truman badly needed reliable information. When the reluctant vice president had suddenly become president less than a year earlier, after Franklin Roosevelt suffered a fatal cerebral hemorrhage on April 12, 1945, the United States was still engaged in the deadliest war in history. More than 400,000 American soldiers had died. The war had destroyed the old world order and killed more than 50 million people worldwide, most of them civilians. European countries emerged economically and politically destitute. America's stalwart ally Great Britain had lost nearly half a million people. Its economy was in shambles. The Soviet Union, also a wartime ally, had lost 20 million people.

It fell to Truman to end the war and secure the peace. But the senator from Missouri, who had served only eighty-two days as vice president, had no experience with foreign policy or diplomatic negotiations, and Roosevelt had not kept him informed. He had seen the president only twice outside of cabinet meetings.

Truman was skeptical that the wartime intelligence operations that Roosevelt had left him could provide the information he needed. Agents had failed to warn the nation of Japan's devastating attack on the Pacific fleet in Hawaii's Pearl Harbor—the event that had killed nearly three thousand Americans and brought the United States into the war. A congressional investigation in 1946 kept fresh in the minds of the president and the public the missteps that had allowed that surprise attack to succeed.

On Truman's desk the day he took office was a scathing report on the most secretive of Roosevelt's wartime intelligence agencies, the Office of Strategic Services (OSS). Roosevelt had created it to conduct covert activities. Ten thousand strong by the end of the war, its brave agents had slowed Hitler's advance by arming resistance movements and infiltrating the German leadership. They had conducted military operations against the Japanese, bought Soviet codes from a Finnish intelligence officer, and freed allied prisoners of war in enemy territory.

But its charismatic leader, Wild Bill Donovan (nicknamed for a player for the New York Yankees who threw wild pitches), operating with entrepreneurial enthusiasm and little oversight, was also accused of mistakenly blowing up guards he had sent to protect an ammunition dump in France, forgetting agents he dropped into enemy territory, sponsoring wild parties, and failing to see that Nazis had infiltrated his operations. His foiled plans included dosing Hitler's food with female sex hormones and strapping explosives to bats dropped from airplanes.[3]

Now Donovan wanted to coordinate peacetime intelligence for the president. The military intelligence services and J. Edgar Hoover of the FBI didn't want Donovan encroaching on their turf. Secretary of War Henry L. Stimson explained that taking intelligence decisions away from the military departments would be "dangerous and impractical."[4]

The report on Truman's desk reflected their opposition. The OSS had done "serious national harm to the citizens, business interests, and national interests of the United States." A leak to the *Chicago Tribune* about Donovan's plans for a peacetime intelligence agency—including the text of his proposal to Roosevelt—produced charges that his "super spy system" would create an American Gestapo.[5]

Truman concurred. Roosevelt had given Donovan a free hand during the war, but Truman feared the creation of a peacetime secret police. When Donovan arrived for an appointment to persuade the new president of the need to convert the OSS into a peacetime intelligence agency with him as its leader, Truman dismissed him in less than fifteen minutes.

A persistent Donovan kept up his arguments by letter. "All major powers except the United States have had for a long time past permanent worldwide intelligence services. . . . The United States . . . never has had and does not now have a coordinated intelligence system."[6]

To no avail. On September 20, 1945, Truman abolished the OSS and sent his trusted aide Harold Smith, director of the budget bureau, to fire Donovan.[7]

Instead, Truman would rely on his friend Admiral Souers to produce a daily digest for him and to run interference among the military intelligence agencies. His small White House office would be called the Central Intelligence Group. Truman explained to the press that his presidential directive of January 24, 1946, would make "all the information available for all the people who need it in implementing foreign policy."[8]

When Truman signed the order creating the Central Intelligence Group, he could not have foreseen that his worthy effort to coordinate intelligence gathering and to provide a daily summary would soon grow into the powerful Central Intelligence Agency (CIA), which conducted covert paramilitary operations around the world. Step by step, as fears of communist aggression increased, the CIA began operating outside domestic restraints and foreign laws. For the next thirty years, secrecy shielded its activities from debate and from integration into the public's understanding of the nation's foreign policy.

By 2013, the CIA's budget for covert operations totaled at least $2.6 billion, according to an analysis by *Washington Post* reporters. Nearly twenty years after his lunch with Souers, Truman wrote wistfully, "It was not intended as a 'Cloak & Dagger Outfit'! It was intended merely as a center for keeping the President informed on what was going on in the world."[9]

More than any other peacetime president, Truman shaped the character of secrecy in American government. Future presidents would add planks to his framework of peacetime secrecy, but the architecture remained Truman's. As communist aggression heightened foreign and domestic threats, Truman, like Woodrow Wilson before him, responded with programs that examined the loyalty of federal employees, intercepted international mail and telegrams, and investigated the private lives of law-abiding citizens. Truman turned these hidden efforts to protect Americans into lasting institutions that had in common a lack of accountability, which freed agents to improvise anti-communist strategies but which also invited abuse. Eventually, excessive secrecy itself became a threat to security and democracy.

Truman built these peacetime structures one step at a time in response to immediate threats and with limited aims, on the foundation laid by the Wilson administration after World War I. There was no grand design. And he built them in good faith. They were not political ploys. They were not attempts to accrue executive power, although they had that result. Each had deep roots and legitimate purposes, and each took on difficult tasks to protect Americans. But because the activities were secret, they were rarely questioned, evaded the normal checks of congressional scrutiny, and avoided court review. Without such checks, they just kept expanding during a Cold War that lasted longer than anyone expected.

The president came to office suspicious of wartime intelligence operations, opposed to J. Edgar Hoover's stealth tactics as head of the FBI, and sensitive to the plight of ordinary Americans. He had made his reputation in Congress investigating waste and fraud in the military. But step by step, responding to unexpected threats, he acquiesced in the creation of a CIA more powerful and more secretive than the OSS, gave the FBI a free hand in domestic spying, created a loyalty program that dismissed thousands based on secret accusations, and gave officials the broadest authority they would ever have to keep closeted national security information. It was Truman and his advisers who fostered the idea that intelligence agencies could operate outside the law when fighting an enemy that used underhanded tactics, an idea that took hold in the CIA, the FBI, and the National Security Agency (NSA).

Franklin Roosevelt's silence had left Truman unprepared for the challenges he would face. Roosevelt had led the nation through the devastating Depression and World War II. But he did not share with the American people, or with his vice president, the development of atomic weapons; his views of the Soviet Union's mercurial leader, Joseph Stalin; or his own declining health. The sixty-two-year-old president was losing weight and his hands shook. In March 1944, as he prepared to run for reelection, Roosevelt was examined by cardiologist Howard G. Bruenn at the Bethesda Naval Hospital at the insistence of his daughter Anna. Bruenn confirmed that the president's heart was failing. He might have only a year to live. Bruenn prescribed medications, and urged bed rest, but there was little he could do.

Like Woodrow Wilson's doctor twenty-five years earlier, Roosevelt's personal physician issued cheerful reports to the press. In April, Vice Admiral Ross T. McIntire, an ear, nose, and throat specialist whom FDR had chosen on the recommendation of Wilson's doctor, Cary Grayson, told the press that the president's seeming ill health was due to a head cold and bronchitis, influenza or respiratory infection, and a sinus disturbance, the *New York Times* reported. In October, McIntire described the president as "a few pounds under weight, but otherwise in perfect health." A month later, Roosevelt won reelection with 53.4 percent of the vote to New York governor Thomas Dewey's 45.9 percent. Five months later he was dead.[10]

Truman wrote later that he had only one clue about Roosevelt's declining health. Under a big old magnolia tree on the White House lawn on a muggy August day three months before the 1944 election, Roosevelt and his designated vice president had lunched in shirt sleeves and planned campaign strategy. It was the first time during the campaign that Truman had met with the president. When Truman said he planned to campaign by plane, Roosevelt responded: "Don't do that, please. Go by train. It is necessary that you take care of yourself."[11]

On a rainy April 12, nine months before his comical lunch with the new head of his Central Intelligence Group, Truman had just poured himself some bourbon and water, ready to relax with other Democratic leaders in Speaker Sam Rayburn's Capitol hideaway when Steve Early, one of the president's assistants, summoned him to the White House. In the second-floor study, Mrs. Roosevelt rose to greet Truman and put her arm around his shoulders. "Harry, the president is dead." Struggling to control his emotions, his face ashen, Truman asked, "Is there anything I can do for you?" Mrs. Roosevelt replied: "Is there anything we can do for you? For you are the one in trouble now," Truman recalled in his memoirs.[12]

Roosevelt had suffered a cerebral hemorrhage at 4:35 p.m., sitting in a chair in his cottage at Warm Springs, Georgia, where he had created a polio treatment center. He complained of a headache, then collapsed. He was spending the weekend with Lucy Mercer Rutherfurd. Rutherfurd was a widow with whom Roosevelt had had an affair many years earlier. After his wife learned of their affair, he had promised her he would never see Rutherfurd. His continuing relationship with her was another secret.[13]

Hastily sworn in by Chief Justice Harlan Fiske Stone in the cabinet room at 7:09 p.m., Truman stood under a portrait of Woodrow Wilson, his wife Bess and daughter Margaret at his side. He held a bible borrowed from the White House usher's desk drawer. Justice Stone wore a blue suit. He hadn't had time to stop at the courthouse to get his robe.[14]

Truman had served for less than three months as a reluctant vice president. He had wanted to stay in the Senate, where there was real work to be done, but Robert Hannegan, chairman of the Democratic National Committee, had put Truman's name at the top of the list. He put in a call to Roosevelt from the convention and arranged for Truman to listen in. " 'Bob,' Roosevelt said, 'have you got that fellow lined up yet?' 'No,' Bob replied. 'He is the contrariest Missouri mule I've ever dealt with.' 'Well, you tell him if he wants to break up the Democratic party in the middle of a war, that's his responsibility.' " "With that," Truman recalled in his memoir, "Roosevelt banged down the phone."[15]

In their two meetings, Roosevelt had not communicated his views about postwar stability or about Stalin. Would Stalin serve as a partner in rebuilding a free Europe? Or would he instead use his giant army to take over one shattered nation after another with communist dictatorships? Stalin had ruled the Soviet Union for twenty years by consolidating power, centralizing the economy, and ruthlessly exiling or murdering those who opposed him. Two months before he died, Roosevelt had delivered an optimistic report on the success of his negotiations with Stalin about postwar plans. But the Soviet Union remained "a riddle wrapped in a mystery inside an enigma," in the words of Britain's wartime prime minister Winston Churchill.[16]

Truman badly needed the benefit of Roosevelt's advice. He came to the presidency a seasoned politician, but with no foreign policy experience. He had grown up in Independence, Missouri, the son of a college-educated mother who prized learning and a charismatic and hot-tempered father who speculated unsuccessfully in stock and grain. Truman became the first president since Grover Cleveland without a college degree. But he loved learning and spent free hours reading history and biography, wearing thick glasses to improve the vision in his nearly blind left eye. His service in the army during World War I had left him imprinted with memories of the horrors of battle that would remain with him as he struggled to find ways to counter Soviet threats without starting another deadly war.[17]

Elected to the Senate in 1934 with the backing of Tom Pendergast's Kansas City machine, Truman made his reputation by fighting secrecy in the military. He uncovered waste and corruption in the construction of army training facilities, driving three thousand miles around the country from camp to camp in his old Dodge to see how federal dollars were being spent.[18]

Everyone liked Truman. He was warm-hearted and gregarious, with an easy laugh. His memory for names and faces, and his ability to get along with almost everyone, made him well suited for Senate politics. Truman liked plain food and plain speaking. He relaxed with bourbon and water, and a hand of poker. He was uncomfortable reading formal speeches, but his eyes lit up when he greeted voters on the campaign trail. He always felt a special affinity for ordinary Americans. He liked doers and deplored "posers." He was suspicious of the military's big brass, elite diplomats, corporate titans, lobbyists, and politicians with "Potomac fever"—an exaggerated view of their own importance.

It was Truman's discipline and hard work, not his appearance, that were imposing. At five feet nine, with thinning gray hair and thick, round metal-rimmed glasses, he looked like the bank clerk he had been at age twenty-one. But the sixty-year-old president kept his long habit of rising at 5:00 each morning, surprising passersby on his early vigorous walks around Dupont Circle. He bounded into the office around 7:00 a.m. He extolled orderly habits and orderly government. He did his homework, didn't dwell on details, made forceful decisions, and almost never looked back.[19]

Still, it was a terrible time for an inexperienced leader. The nation's most destructive war had killed more than 400,000 Americans and wounded more than 700,000. Twelve million Americans remained in the armed forces when Truman took office—about two-thirds of the nation's young men. On April 25, two weeks after Truman became president, Italian partisans captured and executed Benito Mussolini. Two days later, Adolf Hitler committed suicide in his bunker along with Eva Braun, his mistress, whom he had married the day before. On May 8, the Germans surrendered. But the Japanese fought on.[20]

The destruction of Eastern European nations left a political vacuum ready to be exploited by opportunists. Two months before he died, Roosevelt had joined Churchill and Stalin at Yalta, a resort on the Black Sea, to negotiate the peace. They divided Germany into four occupied zones. Stalin promised a free and independent Poland and free elections in all the territories that had been liberated from Nazi Germany. But so far these were paper promises.

As veterans began to return home, labor unrest threatened to cripple the economy. Manufacturing unions had agreed not to strike during the war, but inflation had taken its toll on flat salaries. A few months after Truman took office, 800,000 steel workers went on strike. Soon after, mine workers and rail workers walked out. Truman canceled wartime rationing of gasoline, tires, sugar, shoes, and other staples. He ended a fuel-saving thirty-five-mile-an-hour speed limit. Washing machines, stockings, cars, and toys became available once again as factories returned to domestic production. But remaining price controls designed to prevent runaway inflation continued to cause shortages of meat and other goods that angered voters.[21]

Truman, who relished order and calm, at first felt overwhelmed. He wasn't big enough for the job. "Within the first few months I discovered that being a President is like riding a tiger. A man has to keep on riding or be swallowed," he wrote in his memoirs. A year after he took office, he showed his inexperience in an outlandish speech to Congress in which he announced that he would draft railroad workers into the army if they went on strike. He complained in a letter to his mother and sister, "The Congress are balking, labor has gone crazy and management isn't far from insane in selfishness."[22]

Excessive secrecy left Truman with incomplete and inaccurate information when he made his most momentous decision. Only four months after taking office, he would execute a plan to drop atomic bombs on two Japanese cities. It was an effort to end the war without further loss of American lives. But Truman was ill-served by Roosevelt's silence about the project, a lack of intelligence about Japan's willingness to surrender, and inaccurate information about anticipated civilian casualties.

Roosevelt never told Truman the nation's biggest secret: a project nearing completion in the New Mexico desert. For two years, many of the nation's leading physicists had worked feverishly to harness the power of nuclear fission to create a bomb more powerful than any known to mankind. No one knew yet if they had succeeded. The effort had cost $2 billion and involved more than 125,000 people. But the secret had held. It was not until two weeks after Truman became president that Secretary of War Henry Stimson briefed him. There was little time for learning. The bomb was nearly ready for testing.[23]

On April 25, the same day Mussolini was captured, Stimson came alone to the White House. The seventy-seven-year-old respected elder statesman had served as an artillery officer in World War I, secretary of state under President Hoover, and secretary of war under Franklin Roosevelt. For the previous two years, Stimson had overseen the secret development of the atomic bomb. At this noon meeting, he wanted to prepare the new president for the decision he would soon have to make. If a test was successful, Truman would have to decide whether to deploy the bomb against the Japanese.

Stimson brought with him a short memorandum that he had finished writing that morning. It was marked "Top Secret." "Within four months," it began, "we shall in all probability have completed the most terrible weapon ever known in human history."[24]

These first atomic weapons would have two thousand times the force of conventional explosives that had already killed 300,000 Japanese civilians in Tokyo and other cities. They would also release radiation that contaminated water and food, and cause civilian illnesses and deaths over a much larger area long after the event.[25]

Truman recalled later that he listened with absorbed interest, for Stimson was a man of great wisdom and foresight. Stimson seemed at least as much concerned with the role of the atomic bomb in the shaping of history as in its capacity to shorten this war.[26]

Truman approved plans for the bomb's test. On July 16, 1945, the project's leaders detonated the first atomic bomb in the desert near Alamogordo, New Mexico. "The whole country was lighted by a searing light with the intensity many times that of the midday sun. It was golden, purple, violet, gray and blue. It lighted every peak, crevasse and ridge of the nearby mountain range. . . . Thirty seconds after the explosion came first, the air blast pressing hard against people and things, to be followed almost immediately by the strong, sustained, awesome roar which warned of doomsday," a senior military official wrote at the time. The bomb's flash was visible two hundred and fifty miles away, and the blast could be heard for fifty miles.[27]

The future of warfare now rested with the new president. Truman had choices. He could direct that a nuclear device be detonated on a remote island to demonstrate its power to the Japanese. He could target a military facility. He could forgo the bomb's use entirely and approve instead a planned invasion by allied troops. Or he could drop the bomb on Japanese cities in a surprise attack. Roosevelt had anticipated that the bomb would be used against Germany, if necessary. But with Germany's surrender, its deployment against the Japanese became the issue.

Truman did not know if and when the Soviet Union might develop atomic weapons, and he did not know if Japan would surrender without the bomb's use. Historians still debate that question. Japan's leaders had approached Soviet officials to ask for talks about ending the war. An independent U.S. government assessment in 1946, based on interviews with hundreds of Japanese officials and civilians, concluded that Japan would have surrendered by November or December without the atomic bomb or an invasion.

He also thought that he had warned the Japanese. At their conference in Potsdam, Germany, in July, the Allies had informed the Japanese that they faced "prompt and utter destruction" if they continued fighting. But after four years of war propaganda, those words were not specific enough to be understood by Japanese leaders as a warning about a new kind of weapon.

Truman also made his decision based on an apparent misunderstanding about civilian casualties. He told the American people that the bombs were directed at military targets. After approving a list of cities, Truman noted in his journal that military objectives would be the target, not women and children. In fact, the targets were major cities. Both cities were commercial centers that housed limited military and industrial facilities on the periphery. Either Truman was misinformed or he did not understand the power of the explosives.

Finally, the president left to the vagaries of weather and last-minute pilot preferences the decisions about which cities to hit and when—factors that determined not only how many civilians were killed but also whether the Japanese would have time to consider surrender before a second bomb was deployed. On July 24, while still at the Potsdam conference in Germany, the president made a final decision. He signed an order that gave the air force broad discretion to deliver its first bomb as soon as weather permitted on Hiroshima, Kokura, Niigata, or Nagasaki, and additional bombs as soon as they were ready.

Based on weather forecasts and working from the president's open-ended order, the air force dropped the first bomb on Hiroshima and dropped the second bomb only eighty-two hours later—too soon for the Japanese to have understood what happened at Hiroshima and to respond. Nagasaki was a last-minute choice. Haze prevented the pilot from targeting the Kokura arsenal, the military's first choice. Running low on fuel, the pilot saw Nagasaki through a momentary hole in the cloud cover and dropped the bomb there.

On August 6, 1945, at 8:15 in the morning, most factory workers were already at work in Hiroshima. Schoolchildren were building firebreaks, anticipating future allied air strikes. No air-raid siren announced the approach of American planes. The *Enola Gay* dropped the atomic bomb from 30,000 feet. Some 80,000 people were killed instantly. Another 80,000 were injured. Nearly two-thirds of the city's buildings were destroyed. Of two hundred doctors in the city, only thirty were left to offer help; 1,654 of 1,780 nurses were killed or injured. Radiation poisoning added more casualties in the weeks that followed. The immediate death toll from both bombs was approximately 135,000 people, although the exact numbers remain uncertain. The final death toll from both bombs would be about 200,000, which included those who died later of burns or radiation poisoning. Most were civilians.[28]

Truman continued to say that the Japanese had been warned and that Hiroshima was a military target. In a terse 1,100-word statement to the American people announcing the bombing, he said: "It was to spare the Japanese people from utter destruction that the ultimatum of July 26 was issued at Potsdam. Their leaders promptly rejected that ultimatum." He followed with a brief radio address on August 9: "The world will note that the first atomic bomb was dropped on Hiroshima, a military base. That was because we wished . . . to avoid, insofar as possible, the killing of civilians."[29]

It would have been difficult for any new president to counter the momentum that had been building since the Manhattan Project began two and a half years earlier. John Lewis Gaddis, a leading scholar of the Cold War, wrote that "the possibility of employing the bomb to shorten the war had long been taken for granted by American and British political leaders." Lieutenant General Leslie Groves, who led the development of the bomb, concluded: "His decision was one of noninterference—basically a decision not to upset the existing plan."[30]

On August 14, in a 7:00 p.m. press conference, Truman announced Japan's unconditional surrender and proclaimed a two-day holiday. Three hours later, two million people had crowded into Times Square in New York amid paper, confetti, and streamers tossed from windows above.[31]

After the bombings, American officials tried to keep the devastation secret by controlling access to the two Japanese cities and denying that there were radiation effects. When one reporter found his way to Hiroshima independently and wrote that people were still dying mysteriously thirty days after the bomb was detonated, the military called it Japanese propaganda.[32]

The ideas that the Japanese were given fair warning and that the bombs were dropped on military targets, inaccurate though they were, also became the dominant media narratives. In December, *Time* magazine named Truman "Man of the Year," his cover picture flanked by a mushroom cloud and a lightning bolt. "It was no scientist who, by historical accident, somewhat unwittingly, somewhat against his own will, became more than any other man responsible for the bomb, its use in 1945 and its future," *Time*'s article read. "It was an ordinary, uncurious man without any pretensions to scientific knowledge, without many pretensions of any kind, a man of average size and weight, wearing bifocal glasses, fond of plain food, whiskey & water and lodge meetings. It was Harry Truman, 32nd President of the U.S."[33]

Later assessments criticized Truman for letting the military decide when and where the bombs would be dropped. "The president was much too detached from the decision on Nagasaki," wrote Truman's generally sympathetic biographer Robert J. Donovan, "which resulted in the death of an additional forty thousand persons and the wounding of sixty thousand more. It was a decision that should have been reviewed by him and his senior advisers."[34]

Targeting major civilian populations with atomic bombs created immediate fear about what would happen if these new weapons were deployed against American cities. In November, *Life* magazine imagined for its four million subscribers a thirty-six-hour war in which American cities were destroyed by atomic bombs. Drawings and doctored photos showed "a great shower of enemy rockets falling on 13 key U.S. centers," including New York, Chicago,

San Francisco, Los Angeles, Philadelphia, Boulder Dam, New Orleans, Denver, Washington, Salt Lake City, Seattle, Kansas City, and Knoxville. Two drawings of people in gas masks and protective gear illustrated the aftermath of an attack. *Life* quoted an army general's account: "Hostilities would begin with the explosion of atomic bombs in cities like London, Paris, Moscow or Washington. Radar would give about 30 minutes' warning. The destruction would be so swift and terrible that the war might well be decided in 36 hours."[35]

As the war ended, the new president foresaw a time of peace and new government openness. He was optimistic that Stalin would become a partner in rebuilding Europe. Three months after Roosevelt's death, Truman came home from the Potsdam conference, his only meeting with the Soviet leader, believing that he could deal with Stalin. Without experience in international negotiations, Truman drew on his Missouri roots. Stalin reminded him of Tom Pendergast, the Kansas City political boss who had launched Truman's political career. Pendergast was tough, but he always kept his word, a value of utmost importance to Truman. Stalin, of course, did not keep his word. Truman's view was "naïve and ill-informed," Truman historian Alonzo Hamby notes.[36]

Anticipating postwar peace, Truman drastically cut military and intelligence budgets. He reduced the number of people serving in the military from 12 million to 1.5 million and the defense budget from $91 billion to $10 billion during his first two years in office.

In a remarkable feat of leadership, he persuaded the Republican Congress to approve George Marshall's $13 billion plan to support the reconstruction of the devastated nations of Eastern Europe. The Truman Doctrine promised U.S. support for all free peoples threatened with takeover. He hoped that the United Nations would control nuclear materials and police a ban on bomb building.[37]

This imagined fabric of postwar peace began to fray almost immediately. When the Soviets insisted on keeping control of Bulgaria, Romania, and Poland instead of holding free elections, an exasperated Truman told his secretary of state, James Byrnes, to get tougher with Stalin. The president was determined not to recognize these police-state governments.[38]

Then in early 1946 came clues that Stalin had sent agents to the United States to learn atomic secrets even while the two nations were wartime allies. A cipher clerk working in Canada revealed that a Soviet spy ring operating out of the embassy in Ottawa was trying to steal information about the atomic bomb, radar technology, and other military secrets. It turned out that the Soviets knew a great deal about the intentions of the United States and its allies. The U.S. government knew almost nothing about the Soviets.[39]

In February, Stalin told the Russian people in a radio address that eventual war was inevitable between capitalist and communist nations. Capitalist nations would grow weaker as they competed with one another, while communist regimes would spread throughout the world.

Truman told his staff that he was getting tired of being pushed around by the Russians. Two weeks after Stalin's speech, he traveled with Winston Churchill to Missouri, where Churchill gave a speech declaring that "an Iron Curtain" had descended across Europe. By November, Truman began to express privately his view that there wasn't much difference between the totalitarian regimes of Hitler and Stalin. He was beginning to see the Soviet Union as an adversary.[40]

In response to Stalin's speech, George Kennan, a young foreign service officer assigned to the U.S. embassy in Moscow, dictated an eight-thousand-word telegram that would provide a rationale for covert activities.

Kennan proposed what would become a Cold War strategy of containment. Soviet aggression could not be stopped by negotiation. It could be limited, but only by forceful countermeasures. The Soviets operated on two levels—by means of formal diplomatic channels but also by stealth, providing financial support and weapons to communist parties around the world, engaging in propaganda campaigns and sabotage, and deploying spies in Western nations. The United States would have to operate on two levels as well. Later, as head of the State Department's planning office, Kennan would be assigned to oversee the CIA's covert operations.[41]

Growing uncertainty about Soviet capabilities and intentions created a politics of fear. Arguing for a buildup of forces, James V. Forrestal, secretary of the navy, warned that "half or maybe all of Europe might be communistic by the end of next winter."[42] Robert Patterson, the secretary of war who replaced the ailing Stimson in September 1945, warned that "we must envisage the possibility of the U.S.S.R. adopting open use of armed forces on a global scale."[43]

By late 1946, Republicans were using fear for partisan purposes, painting Truman as soft on communism. Economic distress, real and imagined threats, and the new president's inexperience helped Republicans gain control of both houses of Congress in November for the first time since 1928, with eleven new seats in the Senate and fifty-five in the House. Richard Nixon, a young navy veteran, won a seat representing Los Angeles while suggesting that the Democratic incumbent Jerry Voorhis had ties to communist organizations. When he ran in 1950 against the Democrat Helen Gahagan Douglas, he accused her of being "pink right down to her underwear." Marine veteran Joseph McCarthy won a Wisconsin Senate seat. He went on to claim that the government was infested with communists. The absence of reliable information about Stalin's intentions left a void that was filled by demagogues like McCarthy who waged their own politically motivated information wars.[44]

As Soviet aggression persisted, a president with sturdy values and an instinctive suspicion of skulduggery became convinced that the United States needed to employ underhanded tactics to counter a Soviet adversary that used them masterfully. This judgment supported a new generation of surreptitious national security activities. Truman and his advisers explicitly acknowledged that the CIA, the FBI, and later the NSA would operate outside the law when necessary, without telling the American people what they were doing. There would be a double standard, sustained by secrecy. Patriotic agents undertook illicit activities with orders or acquiescence from superiors and sometimes from presidents. When agents' activities were revealed in the 1970s and the double standard was disavowed, what they had done was scorned.[45]

The Central Intelligence Agency was not created in any orderly way. It just grew. Truman's small request for a daily summary and some help coordinating military intelligence became a constellation of undercover operations around the world, carried out with much zeal and little oversight. Budget and policy reviews were cast aside to give the agency a free hand to do an urgent and difficult job.

During its first year, Truman's Central Intelligence Group had three leaders, no budget, no authorization from Congress, and no cooperation from jealous army, navy, and State Department intelligence agencies. Legally, it did not exist.

Truman did get his intelligence summary. Every afternoon after lunch, Admiral Souers, the recipient of the wooden dagger and the first head of the small group, brought to the president a three-page single-spaced account of the day's national security concerns, drafted by the fifteen staffers he had borrowed from military and State Department intelligence agencies.[46]

But Souers soon quit. He had not wanted the job. In his place Truman appointed a dashing air force officer and War Department intelligence director, General Hoyt Vandenberg. Vandenberg's good looks and military record had already landed him on the covers of *Time* and *Life* magazines, and he had alleg-edly gained additional renown as one of Marilyn Monroe's three choices of men she would like to be stranded with on a desert island. (The other two were Joe DiMaggio and Albert Einstein.)[47]

Secretary of the Navy Forrestal and Secretary of War Patterson didn't want to be responsible for sabotage, election fixing, and assassination plots. They began pressing CIA director Vandenberg to take the lead. Uncertain whether his group was authorized to conduct such operations, Vandenberg sent two staff members to see Clark Clifford, Truman's trusted White House counsel. Clifford told them he would go to the president to ask for legislation authorizing such activities if the agency would exclude domestic intelligence from its mission. Without waiting for Congress, Vandenberg rounded up stealth funding. Struggling to patch together resources for an agency that did not officially exist, he appealed to Patterson and Secretary of State Byrnes to transfer more than $10 million from their own budgets.

A year later, Congress finally gave the Central Intelligence Agency legal status, but without intending to authorize covert activities. To avoid attracting attention, the White House appended authorization for the CIA to a broad and important National Security Act. Truman's proposal to unite the army, navy, and a new air force under a civilian secretary of defense drew most of Congress's attention. Buried in the law was language that authorized a central intelligence agency, without spelling out its duties.

House members did question whether the agency might become a Gestapo-like secret police force. Vandenberg assured them that the agency would never interfere with American liberties. It would operate only outside the United States. It would have no police, subpoena, or law-enforcement powers. Asked in a secret hearing if it would be a good idea to spell out its responsibilities, Vandenberg said he "would prefer to let this thing grow in the hands of the people who are primarily interested in getting this intelligence, and with the safeguard that you cannot build a Gestapo, because after all, all they are trying to do is get intelli-gence." Vandenberg explained that Congress would need to give the CIA "almost a blank check in trust . . . without a public accounting." White House testimony at the hearings emphasized that the CIA would remain a small, elite cadre of intelligence analysts. There was no mention of covert activities.[48]

Congressional committees added Vandenberg's promises to the wording of the bill. The CIA would have "no police, subpoena, law-enforcement powers, or internal security functions." The agency was charged with "protecting intelligence sources and methods from unauthorized disclosure."

The committees also insisted on adding some kind of statement about the CIA's duties. They could not have known that the two simple phrases they borrowed from Truman's original executive order creating the Central Intelligence Group would alter the peacetime relationship between government and the American people. In addition to coordinating intelligence, the new agency was authorized to carry out "such other functions and duties . . . affecting national security" as the president's National Security Council (NSC) approved. Over the next four years, CIA directors would use that phrase to justify creation of a vast network of covert operations around the world with little oversight. Nearly thirty years later, the Senate committee assigned to investigate the CIA's violations of its charter would find "no substantial evidence that Congress intended . . . to authorize covert action by the CIA" in 1947.[49]

Pleased to have assured civilian control of the military by creating a new secretary of defense, Truman signed the National Security Act on July 26, 1947, aboard the *Sacred Cow,* the first presidential plane. The president was flying to Missouri to visit his critically ill mother. As he flew over Ohio, the pilot relayed a message that his mother had died.[50]

George Kennan, the foreign service officer who had urged the president to counter the Soviets with stealth tactics, soon became the central figure in encouraging the CIA's covert activities. As director of planning for the new secretary of state appointed in 1947, George Marshall, Kennan represented the State Department staff on the newly created White House National Security Council, which was supposed to monitor the CIA. Truman and the NSC would rely on Kennan. Kennan, in turn, would later regret that he neglected to keep tabs on zealous officials who led the CIA's covert operations.

Kennan believed that U.S. and British withdrawal of troops from Europe would continue to produce power vacuums that the Soviets would fill. The economic aid provided by the generous European Recovery Program, which became known as the Marshall Plan, would help stabilize European economies but would not stop the Soviets from using bribery, intimidation, and murder to install communist governments controlled from Moscow. Stalin was financing and training communists in Poland, Romania, and Hungary. He sought bases in Turkey and a role in running the former Italian colonies in North Africa.[51]

The United States could prevail only by changing what Kennan called the Soviet psychology—their leaders' perception that they could easily dominate Europe. To do that, the United States government would have to engage in the same kind of secret operations. For Kennan, who had worked with the OSS during the war while in Moscow, creating a secret organization to carry out covert activities was more a continuation of past practices than a dramatic innovation, his biographer John Lewis Gaddis concludes.[52]

Kennan noted to Forrestal, who had become the nation's first secretary of defense in 1947, that the American public probably would not approve of the kind of stealth activities the CIA might undertake, but "there are cases where it might be essential to our security that we fight fire with fire." He did not want to see the United States "handicapped by the lack of ability to use the techniques of undercover political operation which are being used against us."

Kennan's call to action was echoed by former OSS officers, by Forrestal, by the joint chiefs of staff, and by the president. Looking back, Dean Rusk, then assistant secretary of state for East Asian and Pacific affairs, and later John F. Kennedy's and Lyndon Johnson's secretary of state, explained: "The Soviet Union was already operating with such methods. It was a mean, dirty, back-alley struggle and if the U.S. had stayed out it would have found out what Leo Durocher meant when he said 'nice guys finish last.' "[53]

Hindsight produced more skepticism. Dean Acheson, who was secretary of state from 1949 to 1953, noted in his memoirs, "I had the gravest forebodings about this organization and warned the President that as set up neither he, the National Security Council, nor anyone else would be in a position to know what it was doing or to control it."[54]

Fighting fire with fire meant that an open society with democratic values and constitutional requirements would frequently leave intelligence agencies unconstrained and unsupervised. Agencies' secret activities were not reconciled with the public's understanding of the nation's foreign policy. Exposure of abuses would create new restraints and accountability in the 1970s. President George W. Bush's counterterrorism tactics later reopened issues of secrecy and accountability after the terrorist attacks of 2001.

The CIA's covert operations grew in step with Soviet aggression as fear of communist expansion replaced hope of a peacetime partnership. Gradually, the president's suspicion of intelligence agents and military brass gave way to his commitment to protecting fragile democracies by any means necessary.

Truman himself rarely attended National Security Council meetings in which CIA operations were discussed. He didn't like gatherings of four-star generals and their staffs. They had an insatiable appetite for larger appropriations. He preferred to meet informally with a few trusted advisers. But he received summaries, and when asked about proposals for covert actions, he approved them.[55]

The National Security Council approved the CIA's first official covert operation in 1947, two years before Congress authorized such actions. Truman's military leaders feared that Italy's Communist Party would win the Italian elections scheduled for April 1948 and assigned the CIA to strengthen anti-communist groups. The agency laundered money through wealthy Italian Americans to finance Italy's Christian Democrats and other organizations in ways that could not be traced back to the United States' government. When the Communist Party was roundly defeated in the April elections, the CIA considered the operation a great success.[56]

The president officially approved Kennan's plan for covert psychological operations designed to counter Soviet-inspired activities. Given his usual way of making decisions, it seems likely that he approved the general directive and didn't ask about the details.[57]

After Czechoslovakia's Communist Party took over that government and established a dictatorship in February 1948, the National Security Council hid covert activities deeper within the intelligence framework and gave agents freer rein. An NSC document reflected growing alarm. "Stalin has come close to achieving what Hitler attempted in vain. The Soviet world . . . embraces one fifth of the land surface of the earth."[58] The mission of the new Office of Policy Coordination was to counter "the vicious covert activities of the USSR," using propaganda, economic warfare, sabotage, and subversion. Its existence was to remain secret.[59]

Kennan proposed that a broader guerrilla warfare might include supporting nascent liberation movements, fortifying anti-communists, and "in cases of critical necessity," using force to protect property and human life. "We cannot afford to leave un-mobilized our resources for covert political warfare," he wrote.[60]

The Office of Policy Coordination, or OPC, represented the antithesis of Truman's view of orderly administration. Secretary of State Marshall wanted to keep control of its activities but didn't want the State Department to be held responsible for its deeds. As a result, the office was initially independent but its head was chosen by the secretary of state. An advisory committee representing the secretaries of state and defense was supposed to coordinate its activities. George Kennan, still representing the secretary of state, remained the key person directing and reviewing covert activities. He recommended the office's first head, his friend and OSS veteran Frank Wisner. Since he viewed political warfare as an instrument of foreign policy, he insisted that the State Department, not the CIA director, control covert operations. Secrecy, confused oversight, and perhaps senior officials' preference for deniability would leave agents free to plan and execute their own adventures.

Like Kennan, Wisner was steeped in the culture of wartime covert action. He had headed OSS operations in portions of Eastern Europe near the end of the war and watched the Soviets' ruthless treatment of German prisoners. After the war, he felt miscast when he returned to his job as a Wall Street lawyer. Ambitious, energetic, and still in his thirties, Wisner expanded the OPC, opening forty-seven posts in three years. Soon his covert operations had more people and more money than the entire rest of the agency.[61]

Those operations continued to be funded through stealth channels that circled around the usual oversight rules. The CIA found a steady stream of unaccountable funding when Forrestal persuaded the treasury secretary, John W. Snyder, to channel a portion of the funds that were earmarked for the rebuilding of Europe to the agency, providing a flow of cash that bypassed congressional appropriations. Avoiding normal budgeting became another way of preserving secrecy.[62]

Most of the CIA's enterprises remained secret until the 1970s, when revelations by an investigative journalist and a concerned CIA director triggered congressional investigations. Declassified CIA memos and a Senate investigation in 1977 revealed that secret interrogations of suspected double agents, part of a project code-named Artichoke, employed harsh interrogation techniques and mind-control experiments to gain information. Most of the records of that project were later destroyed.[63]

In the closed circle of officials who knew about the CIA's activities, the agency's effectiveness remained in doubt. In early 1948, Forrestal asked Allen Dulles, then president of the Council on Foreign Relations and later CIA director, to provide an independent report on the new agency. The report, declassified fifty years later, found that the CIA had not yet penetrated the

Soviet hierarchy, its intelligence work was "not impressive," it usually did not coordinate intelligence as Truman had hoped, and it would take years to fulfill its mission.[64]

Secrecy placed extraordinary responsibility on one man: George Kennan. Then as now, the CIA's covert operations were planned so that most members of Congress and the American people knew nothing about them. They were among the government's essential secrets, characterized by "plausible deniability."

Kennan told CIA officials that he would require "specific knowledge of the objectives of every operation and also of the procedures and methods employed." He needed to know the details in order to maintain "a firm guiding hand." But oversight that depended on one individual soon lapsed. Kennan had other assignments. As he remembered later, "I scarcely paid any attention to it," referring to the CIA office that carried out covert activities. That was "probably the worst mistake I ever made in government." Kennan assumed that covert actions would be rare, restrained, and supervised by a small staff. After Wisner built networks of activities around the world with more than two thousand agents, Kennan regretted "the part that I or the staff took in any of this." During the Church Committee hearings in 1975, he testified that covert action "did not work out at all the way I had conceived it."[65]

By 1949, neither Kennan, Forrestal, nor the members of the National Security Council were providing oversight. Kennan lost much of his influence when Marshall left the government in January due to ill health. Kennan himself left soon after. Forrestal suffered a breakdown and resigned in March. He was admitted to the Bethesda Naval Hospital, where he jumped or fell to his death from a sixteenth-floor window two months later.

When the president finally asked Congress for legislation giving the CIA authority for the covert operations, the agency had been conducting such operations for three years. Carl Vinson, chairman of the House Armed Services Committee, agreed in 1949 to a closed hearing to consider a bill to authorize covert operations. Vinson explained, "We cannot have a Central Intelligence Agency if you are going to advertise it and all of its operations from . . . the Empire State Building. So the Congress just has to go along or else not have any confidence in us." The House approved the bill with no debate, 348 to 4.[66]

There had never been anything like it before. The new law exempted the agency from usual government disclosure rules, required protection of "sources and methods from unauthorized disclosure," and cloaked its financing in secrecy. The agency could use unbudgeted funds and spend money "without regard to the provisions of law . . . relating to the expenditure of government funds." Congress also gave the agency its own immigration program to admit up to one hundred immigrants and their families each year in order to provide a safe refuge for foreign undercover agents.[67]

By 1950, the CIA had 15,000 employees and an annual budget of $500 million.[68]

On October 24, 1952, three months before Truman left office, CIA director Walter Bedell Smith and the executive director of the National Security Council carried to the Oval Office a file folder with an eight-page top-secret memorandum for Truman to sign. Truman penned his signature. The two men left. It had been a ten-minute meeting. The president had just ordered the creation of the National Security Agency to carry out "communications intelligence activities of the United States conducted against foreign governments." The agency's monitoring of dissidents within the United States, and of international radio transmissions, cables, and phone calls, would remain invisible until congressional investigators and journalists forced their exposure more than twenty years later. The very existence of the agency remained hidden. There would be no mention of it in the government's organization manual or in the *Federal Register*.[69]

Perhaps no story better illustrates the small decisions with large consequences that characterize the growth of peacetime presidential secrecy than the creation of the NSA. Truman created the agency to solve a limited but urgent problem. Twice in recent years, communications intelligence had failed to warn of surprise attacks. The congressional investigation of Japan's attack on the American fleet at Pearl Harbor in 1941 found that intelligence officers had deciphered from Japanese cables' oblique references to a possible attack but had not shared the information quickly enough among agencies and leaders. Nor had intelligence agencies predicted North Korea's invasion of South Korea in 1950. A review group appointed by Truman recommended the creation of a stronger coordinating agency for military and civilian communications intelligence. His secret memorandum was the result.[70]

The memorandum removed the NSA from usual military oversight requirements. The agency's director would report to the secretaries of state and defense through the National Security Council. But it would operate "outside the framework of . . . general intelligence activities," not subject to its rules or policies. The pressing problem was how to get accurate intelligence as quickly as possible. Limits would get in the way. Truman simply asked the secretary of state and the secretary of defense to create policies to "exploit to the maximum all available resources."[71]

The NSA inherited a confusing legacy of secret surveillance. After World War I, the government's so-called black chamber monitored international cable traffic involving American citizens by making private arrangements with two cable companies, Western Union and Postal Telegraph. When Henry Stimson, Herbert Hoover's secretary of state who later served as Roosevelt's and Truman's secretary of war, learned about the arrangement in 1929, he ordered the interceptions stopped, with an often quoted remark: "Gentlemen do not read each other's mail."

After a brief interlude, however, the monitoring began again. Then when Congress banned warrantless electronic surveillance in the Communications Act of 1934, President Roosevelt countered by secretly instructing the attorney general that such surveillance should continue in "grave matters involving defense of the nation, providing that investigations were limited insofar as possible to aliens." During World War II, army intelligence officials intercepted international telegrams of foreign officials and individuals of interest, including American citizens.[72]

In 1947, Secretary of Defense Forrestal met with executives of three international cable companies, RCA, Western Union, and ITT, and told them that Truman wanted them to continue the monitoring of international communications, a project code-named Shamrock. He assured them in Truman's name that they would not be prosecuted under a federal law that prohibited companies from sharing the content of telegrams. The companies resisted, citing the Communications Act prohibition, but finally agreed. The chairmen of the House and Senate Judiciary Committees were informed of the program at least by 1948.

In 1949, Forrestal's successor, Louis Johnson, renewed the request, again invoking Truman's name. Agents manually sorted copies of telegrams they received on microfilm or paper tapes, and examined them for communications of Americans on "watch lists." Versions of the program involving the interception of international telegrams to and from the United States continued until 1975. Even then, the NSA revealed the practice only when questioned under oath by Senate investigators, who concluded that it was probably the largest surveillance program ever affecting Americans.[73]

Barred from monitoring communications inside the United States, the NSA nonetheless shared surveillance information with the FBI in the 1960s on Americans traveling to Cuba, and accepted surveillance assignments from the Drug Enforcement Administration, the CIA, the Secret Service, and the Defense Department, as well as further assignments from the FBI. An estimated 1,650 Americans appeared on the NSA watch lists that were exposed in 1973. The names included prominent antiwar protesters, civil rights leaders, and government officials.[74]

The CIA and the NSA aimed to discover Soviet secrets that could threaten the nation's security and counter Soviet aggression with covert operations—the first half of Truman's security agenda. The second half of his agenda was to protect the United States' secrets from the Soviets. Over time, that created more stealth intrusions into Americans' lives.

When Truman took office, the Soviets already knew a great deal about the United States' military plans. A sophisticated network of Soviet spies had been operating in the federal government during the war.

Although a Canadian spy ring was discovered in 1945, the full extent of the Soviets' espionage network in the United States was revealed only gradually. As army code breakers began to make sense of intercepted wartime Soviet cable traffic, after the war, they gathered clues about Soviet agents who had infiltrated high levels of the U.S. government. Klaus Fuchs, a British physicist who had worked on the joint U.S.-British effort to develop the atom bomb, and David Greenglass, an army technician, revealed other alleged spies. Greenglass accused his sister, Ethel Rosenberg, and her husband, Julius, of passing atomic secrets to the Soviets. Whittaker Chambers, a senior editor at *Time* magazine, implicated Alger Hiss, a high-level State Department official. A cipher clerk working with U.S. code breakers, William W. Weisband, allegedly told the Soviets during the war that their code had been cracked, whereupon the Soviets revised their code so that U.S. agents could no longer decipher it.[75]

By the late 1940s, government cryptographers working at Arlington Hall, Virginia, knew that the Soviet spy network was far larger than anyone had imagined. The Soviets had at least two hundred spies in U.S. government agencies during the war, including several in high positions. But that too remained secret. Most spies were not prosecuted for fear of alerting the Soviets to U.S. intelligence capabilities. Not until 1995 was the full scale of the Soviet spy network revealed publicly, when Senator Daniel Patrick Moynihan's Senate secrecy commission encouraged the declassification of the Venona papers— deciphered Soviet cables.

The presence of Soviet spies was also kept secret within the government, and perhaps from the president himself. The army did not inform the CIA about the spy network until 1952, and Senator Moynihan, who had access to classified information, wrote that Truman was not informed.[76]

As suspicion mounted, the effort to protect government secrets became a search for the enemy within, a search that was conducted using stealth methods and that changed the government's relationship to its citizens, without citizens knowing it. Following Wilson's example, Truman launched an ill-conceived loyalty program based on information from secret accusers. Hoover, still the FBI director, extended his own surveillance network to spy on "subversives" without search warrants. And Truman gave government employees broad classification authority to keep virtually any national security information hidden from public view. What these measures had in common was the absence of constitutional checks by Congress and the courts, and the absence of effective oversight by the president.

Hounded by Republicans in Congress and his own FBI director for not doing enough to fight communism, Truman appointed a commission to plan a government loyalty program two weeks after Republicans gained control of Congress in 1946. It was a defensive measure. The Republicans were drafting a more intrusive program.

Uncharacteristically, Truman took the time to work on the specifics himself. He wanted to avoid a witch hunt and he wanted to limit the role of Hoover's FBI. He failed on both counts. Instead, the program he created in good faith examined the lives of applicants and employees, and Hoover controlled the investigations.

Truman's loyalty program had a legitimate purpose. The aim was to keep Soviet agents out of the government. But it did so with loose standards and secret evidence. Loyalty boards in each agency could dismiss employees if "there were reasonable grounds for belief that the person is disloyal," an undefined term, based on charges by accusers whose identity could remain hidden.

If an initial "name check" turned up negative information, the FBI could conduct a more detailed investigation. Heads of agencies appointed loyalty boards, and the attorney general made a secret list of more than two hundred "subversive" organizations, movements, and groups. Membership or "sympathetic association" with such organizations would be considered disloyalty. Truman had wanted the Civil Service Commission to run the program, but Congress, lobbied by Hoover, gave most of the funding to the FBI.[77]

More than four million employees were screened during the ten years of the loyalty program, and 27,000 were subjected to detailed investigations. It remains unknown how many careers were affected. About 1,650 civilian and military employees were dismissed while Truman was in office. Many more quit. The program did not lead to the prosecution of any spies.[78]

Truman decried the "demagogues" and "crackpots" who fed what he called the mass hysteria about communists in the United States. But Hoover, protected by a veil of secrecy, used the growing fear of communism and his political acumen to aid those demagogues and expand his own influence. Hoover invented programs that investigated ordinary Americans, members of Congress, and even administration officials. Sometimes his bosses knew what he was doing. Often they did not. He outlasted presidents and attorneys general after Woodrow Wilson gave him his start investigating aliens in 1917. Truman complained about Hoover, but he did not fire him or seek legislation to rein him in. Hoover served as FBI director from 1924 until his death in 1972.[79]

On April 23, 1945, Hoover paid a visit to the new president in order to brief him on ongoing investigations. Truman had been in office only two weeks, but he knew he wanted to keep a distance from Hoover. He asked Harry Vaughan, his military aide, to join the meeting, gave Hoover only fifteen minutes, and told Hoover that Vaughan, not the president, would be his contact for communicating with the White House.[80]

Truman disapproved of Hoover's investigation of the sex lives of members of Congress and the executive branch. "If I can prevent [it] there'll be no . . . Gestapo in this country. Edgar Hoover's organization would make a good start toward a citizen spy system," he confided to his wife Bess.[81]

But Hoover already had twenty years of experience turning presidents' political interests to his advantage, and he would not be defeated by a newcomer. After the meeting, he sent Vaughan a memorandum reporting some partisan political information. Vaughan fell into the trap. "Future communications along that line would be of considerable interest whenever, in your opinion, they are necessary," he replied.

That was all Hoover needed. Within weeks, the FBI started secret political investigations for the White House, and within two months began wiretapping of government officials and political operatives, Hoover biographer Curt Gentry wrote. He provided Truman with information from wiretaps on the prominent lobbyist Tom Corcoran as well as on Roosevelt holdovers who might not be loyal to the new president. But he also hedged his bets, providing information from his files on Truman's affiliation with the Pendergast machine to Thomas Dewey, Truman's Republican opponent in the 1948 election.

When the president rejected Hoover's proposal that he lead a worldwide intelligence operation and instead limited the FBI to domestic investigations, Hoover simply assigned "legal attaches" to American embassies around the world.[82]

But Hoover wanted broader surveillance powers. In July 1946, Truman's attorney general, Tom Clarke, ostensibly Hoover's boss, sent the president a memorandum drafted by Hoover. Because of the "present troubled period of international affairs, accompanied . . . by an increase in subversive activity here at home," the memorandum asked the president to renew Roosevelt's wartime authorization of wiretapping and other electronic surveillance of "persons suspected of subversive activities against the Government." It was a trick. Hoover's draft omitted Roosevelt's restriction—that surveillance must be limited "insofar as possible to aliens."

Assuming he was just renewing existing authority, Truman wrote, "I concur July 17, 1946." Deceived by Hoover, Truman had just authorized a peacetime program of secret wiretapping of the phones of ordinary Americans—a program that continued for thirty years. When George M. Elsey, a White House lawyer, discovered Hoover's deception and recommended the order be rescinded in 1950, Truman took no action. The Church Committee found evidence of 364 wiretaps placed in 1946 alone.[83]

By the time Truman took office, Hoover had a routine for keeping his surveillance of Americans secret from attorneys general, members of Congress, and presidents. In 1940, he established a filing system for investigations that he did not want traced. He kept a single copy of each document in his office safe. No attorney general ever knew about these untraceable memos, Hoover biographer

Curt Gentry concludes. Hoover also did not tell his superiors that he maintained a vast network of informants in government agencies, congressional offices, and the Supreme Court, and planted bugs in an undetermined number of embassies as well as in Washington homes and offices.

Hoover also kept secret from attorneys general, presidents, and Congress the fact that his agents opened mail with the aid of the U.S. Post Office. A program that Hoover initiated to examine the mail of German, Japanese, and Italian embassies before and during the war expanded to include the mail of neutral countries, and continued for twenty-six years with varied targets. Other FBI mail-opening programs targeted suspected communists within the United States, including organizations on the attorney general's list of subversive organizations.

By 1947, Hoover was also working secretly with J. Parnell Thomas, the Republican chairman of the House Un-American Activities Committee. Hoover gave Thomas unattributed memos detailing alleged communist activities in the movie industry, a source for the committee's Hollywood blacklist. Hoover also provided lists of individuals who at some point had been associated with a range of organizations Hoover considered suspect as well as lists of potentially friendly witnesses for the committee. He thoughtfully added questions for Thomas to ask those called before the committee. In principle, the FBI director was accountable to the attorney general, the president, Congress, and the courts. In practice, he was accountable to none.[84]

Truman's desire for order led to the creation of one more lasting institution that expanded government secrecy. In 1951, Truman instituted a sweeping classification system that allowed officials of forty-five government agencies—including the Smithsonian and the Fine Arts Commission—to keep secret any information related to national security. It remains the broadest secrecy order ever issued by a president. Although cut back by his successors, his system of limiting access to security information would outlast the Cold War and the Soviet Union, and finally grow so unwieldy that no one fully understood or controlled it.

Just as he created the CIA to make sense of separate military intelligence operations, Truman created the classification system with a worthy goal—to make sense of separate systems of military secrets. He extended Wilson's classification of military information to all federal agencies and to any national security matters. Roosevelt's wartime order had been narrower, allowing for secrecy of military information that could impair prosecution of the war.[85]

Truman's order provoked a bipartisan reaction. Members of both parties in Congress accused Truman of striking a blow against liberty and making the nation more like the autocratic communist regimes it was fighting. A Republican who introduced a bill to repeal the order ventured that Truman's purpose was to "cover up the crookedness and skullduggery that is going on in his administration." At least one federal office, the Office of Price Stabilization, asked to be excluded because compliance could prove embarrassing.

Editors asked why Truman was introducing censorship. Arthur Krock of the *New York Times* noted that agencies' new "right to withhold information will stimulate an instinct to deny legitimate information to the public. . . . [It] will also encourage the operations of another instinct of bureaucracy, which is to resolve any doubt in favor of suppression."

None of the criticisms of the order led to effective limitations. Truman did advise officials to limit the order's use. "To put the matter bluntly," he said in a letter to agency heads, "these regulations are designed to keep security information away from potential enemies and must not be used to withhold non-security information or to cover up mistakes made by any official or employee of the Government." But over time these exhortations came to be forgotten.[86]

The order was so broad that Truman's Republican successor, Dwight D. Eisenhower, rolled it back a few years later. Eisenhower assigned Herbert Brownell, his attorney general, to review Truman's order. A New York lawyer who came from a family of progressive leaders (his cousin was the feminist Susan B. Anthony), Brownell orchestrated unusual exercise of presidential self-restraint.

Eisenhower's revised order removed from most federal agencies and most employees the authority to keep information secret, restricted secrecy to "national defense" information—a narrower term than Truman's "national security"—and provided a process for declassification of secrets.[87]

Finally, Truman confronted the question of whether a president was obliged to provide for open debate about the peacetime development of a weapon that changed the nature of warfare, a question that George W. Bush and Barack Obama had to confront in a different time as they ordered the development and use of cyberweapons and armed drones. The hydrogen bomb was an atomic weapon so powerful that it had no military use. Truman attempted to limit debate about its development to a small circle of expert advisers. But even during the Cold War, Truman's attempt at secrecy didn't work, and his unsuccessful attempt deprived him of an opportunity for leadership and placed him at a disadvantage in the public debate that followed.

On August 29, 1949, a U.S. Air Force reconnaissance plane flying from Japan to Alaska measured levels of radioactivity twenty times higher than usual east of the Soviet Union's Kamchatka Peninsula. A week later, Robert Oppenheimer, the physicist who had led the Manhattan Project and at the time chaired the advisory committee of the Atomic Energy Commission (AEC), confirmed that the radiation came from the Soviets' test of an atomic weapon.[88]

Truman and his advisers had counted on their exclusive possession of such weapons in order to deter Soviet aggression and establish international controls. Now he had to consider whether to develop an even bigger bomb—a hydrogen bomb a thousand times more powerful than the bombs dropped on Hiroshima and Nagasaki. Triggered by uranium fission like the bombs dropped on Japan and tested by the Russians, but drawing on the more powerful force of hydrogen fusion, it could wipe out whole cities. The deployment of several such bombs might destroy civilization.[89]

Truman hesitated to share the news of the Soviet test with the American people. He told David Lilienthal, the Chicago lawyer who chaired the Atomic Energy Commission, that he was reluctant to say anything publicly just yet. An announcement might cause "great fears, troubles." By his own account, Lilienthal convinced the president that an announcement would be preferable to plugging leaks, would show that the president was in a commanding position, and would allay, not inflame, public fears.[90]

Instead of addressing the American people, though, Truman in effect whispered the news. Nearly a month after the event, the White House press office passed around to reporters a mimeographed sheet. It read in part: "I believe the American people, to the fullest extent consistent with national security, are entitled to be informed of all developments in the field of atomic energy. That is my reason for making public the following information. We have evidence that within recent weeks an atomic explosion occurred in the U.S.S.R. This recent development emphasizes once again, if indeed such emphasis were needed, the necessity for that truly effective enforceable international control of atomic energy which this Government and the large majority of the members of the United Nations support."[91]

The truth was that the United States no longer had a monopoly on atomic weapons. The press immediately grasped the significance of the test. A *New York Times* editorial began: "Thus opened Chapter 2 of the Atomic Age. The President's disclosure last week had tremendous and world-wide impact. In all the capitals of the world it was almost the sole topic of interest. It reached deeply into the lives of private citizens everywhere. Two questions stood out. The first was an immediate one: What exactly does Russia have in the way of atomic weapons? The second one was long range and far more important than the first: What does the opening of Chapter 2 of the Atomic Age mean in terms of war and peace? These questions have been put to the world with dramatic suddenness."[92]

Truman now had to decide whether to raise the stakes. Scientists had known since 1942 about the theoretical possibility of a hydrogen bomb. But its technical feasibility had yet to be proved. "I am not sure the miserable thing will work, nor that it can be gotten to a target except by ox cart," Oppenheimer groused in a letter to Harvard president James Conant, who served with him on the AEC advisory committee.[93]

Surprisingly, both the Atomic Energy Commission and its expert advisory committee recommended against developing the bomb. Meeting over two long days in late October 1949 in a second-floor conference room at the commission's offices at Nineteenth Street and Constitution Avenue NW in the nation's capital, the former wartime offices of the joint chiefs of staff, the advisory committee's distinguished members debated the bomb. Chaired by Oppenheimer, the committee included three other eminent atomic physicists who were veterans of the Manhattan Project—Enrico Fermi, I. I. Rabi, and Glenn Seaborg—and two scientists who were noted college presidents, James Conant of Harvard and Lee DuBridge of MIT. They called in George Kennan, who vigorously opposed the development of the hydrogen bomb, and General Omar Bradley, chairman of the joint chiefs of staff, who argued that it would provide a psychological advantage over the Soviets.

As Oppenheimer went around the table, the committee members agreed that the bomb, if it proved feasible, would be too big for military use, that it was hard to justify developing a weapon during a time of peace that was designed to kill mainly civilians, and that the nation should try to avoid a thermonuclear arms race. Most thought the bomb's development would not deter the Russians from building their own bomb.

In spite of pressure from the military, members agreed that the hydrogen bomb should not be developed at that time. Several stayed up late drafting the committee's secret report: "We recommend strongly against such action. We base our recommendation on our belief that the extreme dangers to mankind inherent in the proposal wholly outweigh any military advantage that could come from this development. . . . We are alarmed as to the possible global effects of the radioactivity generated by the explosion of a few super bombs. . . . Therefore, a super bomb might become a weapon of genocide. . . . The extreme dangers to mankind inherent in the proposal wholly outweigh any military advantage that could come from this development . . . [which] might be a weapon of genocide."

A minority report placed greater emphasis on the need for international controls. "A decision . . . for the development of the 'Super' cannot in our opinion be separated from consideration of broad national policy. . . . Necessarily such a weapon goes far beyond any military objective and enters the range of very great natural catastrophes. . . . We believe it important for the President of the United States to tell the American public, and the world, that we think it wrong on fundamental ethical principles to initiate a program of development of such a weapon. At the same time it would be appropriate to invite the nations of the world to join us in a solemn pledge not to proceed in the development or construction of weapons of this category."

The committee called for an open debate. "The Committee recommends that enough be declassified so that a public statement . . . can be made at this time. . . . It should explain the scale and general nature of the destruction which its use would entail." Arguing forcefully for openness, Conant declared that what mattered was how the American people viewed the moral issues.

Oppenheimer himself believed that the secrecy of the atomic bomb's development during the war had not been in the nation's best interest. If the United States explored the feasibility of a hydrogen bomb, it should be done more openly from the start.[94]

Meeting in November, the divided Atomic Energy Commission followed the advisory committee's recommendation to forgo the bomb's development. The bomb would not provide any military advantage and would hurt the cause of international peace. The commission members urged the president to be open with the public. Two of the five commissioners favored the bomb's development. They argued that it would deter Russia from initiating an atomic attack.[95]

Brien McMahon, the influential chairman of Congress's Joint Committee, and Edward Teller, a leading physicist and strong proponent of the bomb, read the advisory committee's report with dismay. Teller offered to bet a colleague that "we would be Russian prisoners of war within five years." McMahon told Lilienthal that the bomb was essential to the inevitable war with the Soviets and there wasn't much time to prepare. McMahon began his own lobbying effort. He wrote to Truman, "If we let Russia get the Super first, catastrophe becomes all but certain."[96]

The president himself had three fixed ideas about atomic weapons. First, the development of atomic energy should remain under civilian control. Second, without an international agreement, the United States would have to stay ahead of the Soviets. "I believed that anything that would assure us the lead in the field of atomic energy development for defense had to be tried out," he wrote in his memoirs. Third, information about atomic energy should be closely guarded, not only to avoid giving clues to Soviet scientists but also because public debate was not desirable—it could lead to lobbying pressure that could distort decision making. Congressional leaders would be kept informed, but the American people would be recipients of, not participants in, the decision.

When the president received the AEC reports, he decided to rely on the secret advice of three officials for his decision. He asked Secretary of Defense Louis Johnson, Secretary of State Dean Acheson, and AEC chair David Lilienthal to give him their final recommendation.

But when the three met on December 22, 1949, Lilienthal and Johnson were so far apart in their views and Johnson was so personally antagonistic to the other two that Acheson was reluctant to call another meeting. Johnson wanted the bomb so that the United States could "kick the hell out of [the Soviet aggressor] if she doesn't stay deterred," as he said in a later public speech.[97] Lilienthal remained opposed. Acheson found political reasons compelling. Congress would strongly favor the bomb's development, and he saw no prospect of negotiating with the Russians.[98]

Truman's attempt to make a controversial decision behind closed doors had two predictable results. First, secrecy opened the way for selective lobbying— just what the president abhorred. Johnson circled around the committee of three, of which he was a member, to send the joint chiefs' recommendation directly to Truman: "The United States would be in an intolerable position if a possible enemy possessed the bomb and the United States did not," the recommendation argued. Renunciation of the hydrogen bomb might be seen by the Soviets as a sign of a weakening commitment to atomic weapons. His end run worked. Truman thought the recommendation made a lot of sense. McMahon sent Truman a five-thousand-word letter calling the commission's advisory committee report "false, horror-inspired logic" and strongly endorsing the bomb's development.[99]

Second, the president paid a high political price when the secret was revealed. Truman had told his advisers to avoid mentioning the hydrogen bomb to the press. But in a televised speech on November 1, Senator Edwin Johnson of Colorado, who served on the Joint Atomic Energy Committee, declared: "Our scientists from the time that the bombs were detonated at Hiroshima and Nagasaki have been trying to make what is known as the super-bomb. . . . And that's the secret, that's the big secret that scientists in America are so anxious to divulge to the whole scientific world." Johnson described the bomb as a thousand times more powerful than the Nagasaki bomb. When Alfred Friendly, a reporter for the *Washington Post,* reported on the speech, national columnists—Stewart and Joseph Alsop, and James Reston—picked up the story. The Alsops' column noted: "Here is a pompous lawmaker, pleading with the television audience for more secrecy. . . . And in the midst of his bumbling discourse, the Senator commits the worst violation of secrecy rules that has occurred to date."[100]

So by the time Truman was holding final meetings with his advisers, the bomb had become a very public secret—known but unacknowledged. William Laurence of the *New York Times* reported in mid-January: "While a curtain of official secrecy surrounds the hydrogen super-atomic bomb, fundamental data published in scientific journals in this country, England and Germany as far back as 1935 show that such a bomb is definitely possible, and that Russia, as well as other countries, is therefore fully aware of its potentialities."[101]

Instead of providing leadership to a confused public, Truman kept up the ruse. On January 19, 1950, a reporter asked Truman at his weekly news conference: "Mr. President, do you have under consideration the production of a hydrogen bomb?" "I cannot comment on that," Truman answered. Later commentators would note that this unexpected publicity distressed the president and may have led him to rush his decision. It also led Truman to ask his attorney general to crack down on leaks.[102]

On a sunny Tuesday, January 31, the acrimonious committee of three—the secretary of defense, the secretary of state, and the head of the AEC—took their recommendation to the president for a final decision. "Possession of a thermo-nuclear weapon by the USSR without such possession by the United States would constitute a situation fraught with danger to the United States," their report concluded. "Possession of such weapons . . . may act as a deterrent to war . . . [and] will provide an offensive weapon of the greatest known power possibilities thereby providing increased flexibility and effectiveness to our operations in the event of hostilities."[103]

Acheson told the president they had reached agreement, handing him a sheet of paper with their recommendations and the text of a public statement. He asked the president to listen to Lilienthal's opposing views.

Truman glanced at their short summary. He said he had always believed that the United States should never use these weapons, but they had to go ahead and make them because of the way the Russians were behaving. When Lilienthal suggested another course was open, Truman interrupted to say that the leak to the press and the pressure in Congress meant that people were so excited he had no alternative but to go ahead. Truman signed the memorandum and approved the wording of the public announcement. The meeting had lasted seven minutes.[104]

Truman issued a short, unenlightening statement, doing everything possible to downplay the decision. While he was lunching across the street at Blair House, Charles Ross, Truman's press aide, handed out a mimeographed sheet with a brief statement by the president.

It said: "I have directed the Atomic Energy Commission to continue its work on all forms of atomic weapons, including the so-called hydrogen or super-bomb. Like all other work in the field of atomic weapons, it is being and will be carried forward on a basis consistent with the overall objectives of our program for peace and security."[105]

That was it.

The *New York Times* noted that "Mr. Truman was as undramatic in making his announcement as he was last Sept. 23 when he disclosed that Russia had achieved an atomic explosion—a development that clearly showed that our absolute dominance in atomic weapons was virtually ended."[106]

The president gave up an opportunity for leadership. Instead, he left it to the press to signal the real importance of his decision. The *Times* banner headline the next day read: TRUMAN ORDERS HYDROGEN BOMB BUILT.[107]

In the weeks that followed, the president's secrecy itself soon became the issue. The *Wall Street Journal* editorialized: "We do not have sufficient information on which to base approval or disapproval . . . because the government of the United States considers knowledge on this matter too important to be entrusted to the people. . . . Whether he acted in accordance with or in opposition to . . . advice we do not know, because all the opinions of the various advisers have not been made public. . . . It may turn out . . . that this was indeed one of the gravest decisions this country has ever had to make. But it was not made by the people of the country. . . . The decision requires nation-wide discussion. But that discussion comes only after the decision and it takes place in the darkness of secrecy."[108] Arthur Krock of the *New York Times* noted: "Except for the atomic bomb itself, the existence of which was a war time secret until it was dropped at Hiroshima, no weapon in the history of mankind became a national policy with so little understanding and discussion, though none so awful was ever projected before."[109]

Time noted that the president had treated the American people as passive recipients of information that could determine their future. "Like a patient sitting in a doctor's anteroom while the specialists discuss his case, the U.S. public . . . sat outside while the President [and his advisers] debated whether to construct the . . . most powerful explosive weapon the world has yet dreamed of."[110]

Shortly after the president's decision, *Life* magazine devoted an entire issue to the president's excessive secrecy. "For the past five years the operations and results of the U.S. atomic weapons program have been almost completely unknown to the public. The critical facts about this greatest of all publicly owned enterprises have been withheld . . . [by] the extension of secrecy far beyond the limits of true security." The accompanying article derided the president's secrecy about the atomic stockpile. "This information, so vitally necessary to the making of policy, is denied to the people who are finally responsible for determining what policy shall be: the citizens of the U.S. and their elected representatives. . . . There is no possible justification for this kind of overextended secrecy." The article also quoted General Dwight D. Eisenhower: "I can't go along with those who believe we should hide the horror of the H-bomb in ignorance."[111]

In March 1950, the American Society of Newspaper Editors and the *Bulletin of the Atomic Scientists* collaborated on an editorial charging that many "scientists believe they are being choked by secrecy requirements where no 'secrets' exist. . . . Now that the H-Bomb may be on the way many scientists would ask:

'Is the United States now strangling the geese that we may desperately need to lay hydrogen eggs?' "[112]

On November 1, 1952, at 7:15 a.m. on the Eniwetok atoll, three thousand miles west of Hawaii, the United States detonated the first thermonuclear device. A purplish fireball rose to 100,000 feet and crested at twenty-seven miles above the earth. Eighty million tons of solid material were propelled into the air, falling over a wide area. Birds were incinerated in the air. Seawater boiled. The bomb was measured at 10.4 megatons.[113]

Cold War historian John Lewis Gaddis noted: "The President himself, as if ashamed by it, would not even announce the test publicly for another two weeks." Nine months later the Soviets detonated their own thermonuclear device. By 1955, both the Soviets and the Americans had a store of hydrogen bombs as well as bombers to deliver them halfway around the world in minutes.[114]

Truman learned too late what other presidents have learned about the cost of trying to keep secret a controversial issue of national importance. If the president does not create a space for public debate, disgruntled or forgetful officials are likely to create that space for him, and the president then pays a high political price for his attempted secrecy. In this instance, when secrecy failed because of a senator's careless statement, Truman missed an opportunity to lead, rather than follow, public opinion. Without meaning to, he ceded the initiative for informing and educating a frightened public to his political opponents and to the press.

Faced with difficult decisions, dangerous times, imperfect information, and conflicting advice, a president who valued orderly administration and cared about the rights of ordinary Americans responded by adding new secretive agencies, practices, and habits that lacked limits and grew out of control. They reflected his efforts to solve immediate problems, and his conviction that Soviet aggression so threatened the free world that extraordinary steps were warranted. As he ended his second term, Truman suggested that history would remember his time in office as the years when the Cold War began to overshadow Americans' lives. He had hardly a day in office, he said, that had not been dominated by this struggle.[115]

The core idea of constitutional checks and balances among the executive, legislative, and judiciary branches of government to prevent the exercise of arbitrary power did not work when peacetime intelligence agencies lacked effective oversight, when loyalty was judged by secret accusers, and when no one looked over the shoulders of officials stamping documents as secret.

Accountability proved more problematic in practice than in principle. Truman's framework unintentionally provided enough space for single-minded zealots like J. Edgar Hoover to pursue adventures and misadventures. On occasion, government officials tried to constrain them, but they were rarely successful. Secrecy provided a shield. As a result, the boundaries between secrecy and openness remained contested, intelligence agents and investigators were hampered by uncertainty, and the institutions Truman created continued to coexist uneasily with the constitutional values of which Americans were justly proud: personal privacy, freedom of expression, protection from unreasonable searches, and open government.

A generation later, in 1966, Congress responded by trying to set limits on presidential secrecy. But that effort ended up being crippled by the political legerdemain of Lyndon Johnson, a president who had his own reasons for keeping secrets.

Lyndon Johnson: Stealth Attacks on Openness

*By the time Lyndon Johnson became president in 1963, support was
building to control the secrecy that had grown out of Truman's initiatives.
But Congress prepared to approve the Freedom of Information Act just
when Johnson needed to hide his commitment of combat troops in
Vietnam and his surveillance of antiwar protesters and civil rights
leaders. There followed a battle between a bipartisan coalition in
Congress and a president of unmatched political skills.*

"WHAT IS MOSS TRYING TO DO, SCREW ME?" the president demanded of two
surprised congressional leaders. "I thought he was one of our boys but the Justice
Department tells me his goddamn bill will screw the Johnson administration."[1]

Lyndon Johnson was meeting with the ranking members of the House of
Representatives, Speaker John W. McCormack and Majority Leader Carl
Albert, at the White House. He had just learned that the two House leaders who
were supposed to be leading his legislative juggernaut of dozens of new
domestic programs were promoting a proposal he despised.

The House was close to voting to give every American the right to obtain
information held by the government. Troubled by a generation of secrecy about
the routine workings of government, the proposed law's tireless sponsor,
Representative John Moss of California, had been working toward this moment
for a decade.

Nearly two centuries after the Constitution created a government based on an
informed public, no law gave the American people the right to know what the

president and his executive agencies were doing. Under the vague terms of legislation from 1946, officials could deny requests for information "in the public interest" or because the requester could not show a special need.[2]

Johnson's weekly session with the two House leaders focused on what he cared about most—his Great Society agenda. He hoped to equal or surpass the progressive record of his hero Franklin Roosevelt. Johnson's landslide victory over the Republican Barry Goldwater a year earlier had given him a unique opportunity. Catapulted into the presidency when John F. Kennedy was assassinated in 1963, he had won on his own against Goldwater with 61 percent of the popular vote. Democrats controlled two-thirds of the seats in the House and Senate—the largest majorities since 1936.[3]

It was April 6, 1965. Johnson had already used his mastery of legislative strategy to gain approval of the historic Civil Rights Act and the most expansive public education bill in history. Congress was close to approving his voting rights legislation that would outlaw racial discrimination in federal elections, and Medicare and Medicaid programs that would provide health care for senior citizens and the poor. Next on the president's agenda were laws to provide financial support for college students, to reform early childhood education, to rebuild American cities, and to clean up the nation's rivers. But Johnson's thirteen years in the Senate had taught him that his congressional honeymoon would soon be over. "You've got just one year when they treat you right," he told his staff. That year was 1965.[4]

That afternoon, Moss was preparing to reconvene a hearing after a lunch recess when a secretary from the subcommittee's basement office called to say that McCormack and Albert needed to see him. It was urgent. After twelve years in Congress, Moss knew that meant bad news. Passing the gavel to a committee member, he hurried to meet them.[5]

When McCormack and Albert reported to Moss the president's fury, they knew and Johnson knew that he could not openly oppose a public right to government information. The Senate had approved the bill during the previous Congress, and it had strong bipartisan support in the House. But Moss would have to negotiate with the Justice Department until the administration was satisfied that the bill was so weak it would not interfere with the president's control of information.

By 1965, information hoarding had become a habit. Years of congressional hearings had exposed its absurdities. Citizens were denied access to information about grazing permits on public lands, rent paid for government buildings, military bases where soldiers could purchase liquor, the navy's telephone books, the names and salaries of postal service employees, votes and dissenting views of regulatory commission members, past violations of labor laws, and the president's meetings with lobbyists. Dwight D. Eisenhower's secretary of state, John Foster Dulles, had refused to reveal information about a warehouse that contained six hundred gifts from foreign dignitaries: his staff said the entire building at Sixteenth and M Streets NW in the nation's capital was classified.

Leaders of both political parties acknowledged that the classification of official secrets, initiated by Woodrow Wilson and extended by Harry Truman, had spun out of control. In addition to stamping documents "top secret," "secret," or "confidential," officials routinely stamped documents "official use only," "non-public," or with dozens of other labels to limit public access. Even without secrecy stamps, agencies turned down requests by citizens and members of Congress without explanation.[6]

It was Truman's sweeping loyalty program that had inspired Moss's crusade to establish the public's right to government information. As a new member of Congress in 1953, he became suspicious that the program's secret accusations allowed officials to pad their numbers by dismissing employees for racial and ethnic reasons, because they were homosexual, or because they were unpopular with their bosses. As the son of a coal miner and the representative of the farmers of California's central valley, Moss came to Congress with a populist's zeal for protecting the rights of ordinary citizens.[7]

Assigned to the unglamorous post office and civil service committee, Moss tried to get the facts from the Civil Service Commission. When the commission refused his request, he became convinced that officials must be withholding all kinds of information from the public. "My experience in Washington quickly proved that you had a hell of a time getting any information," he told a reporter later.[8]

Fighting excessive secrecy became Moss's mission. He persuaded the House leadership to form a subcommittee to investigate what officials hid from the public and to name him chairman. He held years of hearings chronicling secrecy's many permutations. In session after session, he introduced bills to create a presumption that the public had a right to government information. In every Congress, the legislation died in committee.

But by 1965, secrecy had become a national issue. The nation had been shocked to learn that President Kennedy's CIA was behind the botched invasion of Cuba at the Bay of Pigs in April 1961.[9] Two years later, when Kennedy was assassinated, there were lingering suspicions that the government was hiding information about some kind of conspiracy, despite the Warren Commission's finding that Lee Harvey Oswald was a lone gunman. Now, the secrecy surrounding Johnson's escalation of American involvement in Vietnam was raising new questions.[10]

Johnson, a politician of legendary talents, had his own compelling reasons to oppose government openness in the spring of 1965. The previous August, he had declared to Congress and the nation that the North Vietnamese had attacked U.S. destroyers in Vietnam's Tonkin Gulf. What he did not say was that navy officers had quickly revised their first message to report that they were not certain about at least one of the attacks. A later government analysis concluded that a U.S. destroyer may have initiated the action.

The president's version of those facts misled Congress into approving his request for sweeping authority to take "all necessary measures to repel any armed attack against the forces of the United States and to prevent further aggression" not only in Vietnam but in all of Southeast Asia—an undeclared war. Five days after the reported attack, the House voted unanimously for the Tonkin Gulf resolution. The Senate approved it 88 to 2.[11]

Using that authority, Johnson ordered sustained bombing of North Vietnam. A month before he met with McCormack and Albert, he had secretly sent over 3,500 marines, the first American combat troops. By 1966 there would be nearly 275,000 American soldiers serving in South Vietnam.[12]

Publicly, Johnson expressed determination. But privately, he despaired that it was a hopeless fight—he couldn't pull out and he couldn't win.[13]

Johnson's advisers urged him to provide accurate information to Congress and the American people. Attorney General Nicholas Katzenbach told the president that the situation called for an honest public debate.[14]

But Johnson worried about taking attention away from his Great Society agenda. Instead, he cajoled journalists to report his version of America's growing involvement in Vietnam, rewarding with precious nuggets of newsworthy information those who went along with him and shutting out those who didn't. He barred reporters he viewed as hostile from White House events and recommended FBI surveillance of some to identify their sources. When the story leaked in late April that U.S. troops were going on the offensive, Secretary of State Dean Rusk tried to persuade the *New York Times*'s editors to kill it. Columnists Roland Evans and Robert Novak noted that "any White House correspondent . . . was castigated by Johnson as an ingrate and a traitor when he failed to echo the Johnson line."[15]

Johnson had another reason for protecting official secrecy. He needed to keep hidden the infiltration of civil rights and antiwar groups that his administration was carrying out under the thin rationale that such groups were national security risks because they might be involved in a communist conspiracy.[16]

Under vague orders from the president, J. Edgar Hoover's FBI investigated such groups using wiretaps, informants, and tax information. In 1965, Katzenbach authorized wiretaps on prominent antiwar and civil rights groups, including the Student Non-Violent Coordinating Committee (SNCC) and the Students for a Democratic Society (SDS).[17]

Katzenbach also authorized continued electronic surveillance of Reverend Martin Luther King, Jr., the nation's most prominent civil rights leader, who had won the Nobel Peace Prize in 1964. Hoover's FBI spread false information about King's activities and threatened him with an anonymous letter. Two of King's associates had once been members of the Communist Party, but the FBI knew their affiliation had long since lapsed. There were as many communists in the civil rights movement as there were Eskimos in Florida, King observed in a 1965 interview.[18]

Both the CIA and the FBI continued their practice of opening first-class mail, even though the CIA was barred by law from conducting surveillance within the United States.[19] CIA director Richard Helms acknowledged in a letter to Henry Kissinger that such investigation was "not within the charter of this Agency. . . . Should anyone learn of its existence, it would prove most embarrassing." The NSA, too, continued to violate its charter by monitoring international telegrams of dissident groups and individuals that "may result in civil disturbances," with the cooperation of private telegraph companies. Acting on directions from the president or attorney general, intelligence agencies frequently disregarded the law in their conduct of massive surveillance, Senate investigators concluded a decade later.[20]

By chance, Moss was pressing for revolutionary public access to government information just at the moment when Johnson most needed to protect his secret enterprises. The president's credibility gap was beginning to get him in trouble.[21] Johnson's press secretary told biographer Robert Dallek that Johnson's periods of gloom and angry outbursts were at their worst in the spring of 1965, when he was secretly sending combat troops to fight an unwinnable war while trying to shepherd his ambitious domestic agenda through Congress and, incidentally, fuming to McCormack about Moss's proposed Freedom of Information Act.[22]

Whatever the issue, Johnson was a formidable political opponent. The son of a Texas state legislator, he grew up campaigning with his father and set his sights early on the heights of national politics, even when the family's low circumstances meant that the Johnsons accepted charity to put food on the table. His mother, an educated woman from an old Texas family, expected great things of her oldest son.

It was his driving ambition, his extraordinary personal drive, and a large element of chance that took Johnson from the small farmhouse on the Pedernales River in the hill country of south central Texas to the presidency. Energy, hard work, attention to detail, persuasiveness, conciliation—and the creative manipulation of information—built an extraordinary political career: he was elected to the House of Representatives in 1936 at age twenty-eight, was elected to the Senate in 1948, and became Senate majority whip in 1951, minority leader in 1953, majority leader in 1955, and vice president in 1961. He took the presidential oath of office aboard Air Force One at Love Field in Dallas, Texas, after President Kennedy was assassinated on November 22, 1963. Johnson had been riding two cars behind the president.

Obsessed with media coverage, Johnson watched network news on three television sets on a cabinet near his desk in the Oval Office while Associated Press and United Press International news tickers clattered out current updates. In his bedroom were three more televisions. He reportedly read at least five newspapers every day.

Johnson's biographers would later struggle to describe a character with so many seeming incongruities. He had a remarkable ability to flatter, charm, and cajole his colleagues. His compassion was authentic toward those less fortunate than he. But he could also be power hungry, insecure, ruthless, mean, vulgar, and deceitful.[23]

The president's fury about a public right to government information created a quandary for the Speaker of the House, John McCormack. As a congressional leader, McCormack needed the Freedom of Information Act. Over the years, presidents—regardless of party—had used high-handed techniques to deny information to congressional committees as well as to the public. In the current Congress, McCormack had altered normal procedures to ease the bill's passage. On the other hand, he was Johnson's lieutenant, and his friend. His job was to follow his leader's priorities and maneuver the president's agenda through the legislative labyrinth.[24]

McCormack's toughness and political skills matched those of the president. Respected as a fair and impartial negotiator, the seventy-three-year-old Speaker, who liked poker and cigars, had served in the House for nearly forty years, had been chosen Speaker three times, and had brokered scores of legislative compromises. Like Moss and Johnson, he had grown up in strained circumstances. One of twelve children, he had quit school after the eighth grade to help support his family and later studied law at night.[25]

The president's outburst also created a quandary for John Moss. The simple idea that citizens had a right to know what the government was doing could finally become law. But Moss was a loyal Democrat. And even if the House and Senate decided to buck the president, he recalled in a later interview, "I knew and he knew that I didn't have two-thirds to override a veto."[26]

This historic effort by elected officials amounted to a slow-motion response to Truman's open-ended secrecy. It reflected more than ten years spent accumulating evidence, building support, and waiting for the right moment to gain approval of countervailing legislation requiring openness.

By 1950, while Truman was still in office, reporters and editors from the nation's leading newspapers had become alarmed at agencies' denials of routine requests for documents. As a first step, they enlisted Harold Cross, a prominent New York lawyer and recently retired counsel of the *New York Herald Tribune,* to document the rights of reporters and the legal grounds for secrecy, under the auspices of the American Society of Newspaper Editors. Cross's book *The People's Right to Know,* published in 1953, provided a foundation of evidence for a bipartisan effort to establish a public right of access to government information.

Cross chronicled habits of secrecy that had grown up during World War II and the beginning of the Cold War. Officials denied requests by citing executive privilege, or the president's constitutional authority to withhold information when it was in the public interest, or a "housekeeping act" from 1789 that granted agencies custody, use, and preservation of records. Or they might cite a law from 1946 that suggested citizens had to demonstrate a specific need for information. In effect, that law "enabled agencies to assert the power to withhold practically all the information they do not see fit to disclose," a Library of Congress report found in 1951, as Truman prepared to leave office.[27]

In 1956, Moss built on this foundation by convening a panel of well-known journalists to explain in a public hearing their problems in gaining access to information. Columnist Joseph Alsop described government wiretapping of investigative reporters. Russell Wiggins of the *Washington Post* disparaged the government's argument that officials needed to keep secret all the information that might aid communist governments: "The amount of rainfall, the state of the crops, the condition of the highways, the location of harbor channels . . . are . . . of even greater use to our own citizens who could not carry on their normal work without this information." Americans did not need to make a choice, Wiggins told the hearing, "between abandoning our safety and abandoning our freedom."[28]

Scientists testified that secrecy about technology and scientific theories was interfering with national security instead of protecting it. In an extreme example, the Atomic Energy Commission had ordered three thousand copies of *Scientific American* burned, and type and printing plates melted down, in 1950 because of two statements about the hydrogen bomb that the commission itself later released, editor Gerald Piel testified at Moss's hearings in 1956.

In that year, the Democratic Party platform derided Cold War secrecy. "During recent years, there has developed a practice on the part of Federal agencies to delay and withhold information which is needed by Congress and the general public to make important decisions affecting their lives and destiny. We believe that this trend toward secrecy in Government should be reversed and that the Federal Government should return to its basic tradition of exchanging and promoting the freest flow of information possible in those unclassified areas."[29]

Ironically, it was Johnson, as Senate majority leader, who had introduced the first bill to grant citizens a right to government information in 1957, and urged immediate consideration.[30] Less than five hundred words, this simple proposal provided that only national security, personal privacy, or specific legal requirements could justify secrecy. Moss introduced in the House the same bill Johnson championed in the Senate. But it was not a priority for the House Judiciary Committee, and it never got to the floor.[31]

In 1960, the Democratic Party platform again called for openness: "The massive wall of secrecy erected between the Executive branch and the Congress as well as the citizen must be torn down."[32] And in his first State of the Union address, John F. Kennedy promised not to withhold information "which is necessary for an informed judgment of our conduct."[33] Moss had campaigned for Kennedy and was rewarded with a position on the bottom rung of the House leadership ladder—deputy majority whip.[34]

Secrecy within the government left the newly elected president ill-informed when he approved the CIA-planned invasion at the Bay of Pigs in April 1961 in an attempt to wrest control of the island from communist leader Fidel Castro. The CIA failed to tell the president about the agency's doubts, Castro's military strength, and calculated risks.[35] When CIA-trained exiles landed and were quickly overwhelmed by Castro's forces, more than a hundred were killed and more than a thousand taken prisoner. A secret CIA report on the botched invasion, finally declassified in 1998, concluded that the mission failed because of the "arrogance, ignorance and incompetence within the C.I.A. itself."[36]

But the incident also made Kennedy protective of official secrecy. Ten days after the failed invasion, he called on the press to practice self-censorship while the nation was engaged in the Cold War with Russia: "Every democracy recognizes the necessary restraints of national security—and the question remains whether those restraints need to be more strictly observed. . . . Every newspaper now asks itself, . . . 'Is it news?' All I suggest is that you add the question: 'Is it in the national interest?' " To which the *New York Herald Tribune* responded: "Competent, thorough, and aggressive news reporting is the uncompromising servant of the national interest—even though it may be momentarily embarrassing to the Government."[37]

In episodes now well known, Kennedy also hid from his staff and the public his growing health problems, the strong medications he took to control pain, and his affairs with women allegedly linked to the Mafia or foreign intelligence agencies. The day after he was elected president, Kennedy denied he had Addison's disease and described his health as excellent. In fact, he took as many as seven injections a day of Novocain to control chronic back pain. He added codeine, Demerol, and methadone as needed for pain, as well as corticosteroids to control the Addison's disease. Two of the many women Kennedy allegedly had secret affairs with raised security concerns. Historian Robert Dallek noted that Ellen Rometsch was suspected of being an East German spy. Judith Campbell Exner claimed to have had affairs with both Kennedy and Mafia boss Sam Giancana.[38]

The legislative and administrative gymnastics of 1965 and 1966 showed how difficult it would be for Congress to limit excessive secrecy. Moss made the first move. In the new Congress that convened in January 1965, he persuaded the Judiciary Committee chairman Emanuel Cellar to let Moss's subcommittee handle the bill, taking the White House by surprise. Johnson's aides had assumed that the public information bill would die in the House Judiciary Committee as it had in the past.

But Johnson remained a master tactician. Instead of vetoing the bill, which would create bad publicity, he would quietly cripple it. In addition to the exceptions to openness that everyone agreed on, national defense and personal privacy, the administration quietly arranged for the committee to add an exception for trade secrets so vague that corporate executives would spend years trying to fit much of their business information under it, an open-ended provision to protect policy papers circulated within or among agencies, and a barrier to sharing personnel policies. Before he left the Senate to become Johnson's vice president, Hubert Humphrey added an exception to keep hidden investigative files and reports related to regulation of financial institutions. Senator Everett Dirksen of Illinois, the powerful minority leader, excluded from disclosure information related to oil and gas exploration.[39]

By the time the bill was approved by Moss's committee, it sparkled like a Christmas tree, its worthy purpose obscured by glittering exceptions.

Inevitably, there were leaks. Clark Mollenhoff of the *Des Moines Register* reported that "the Johnson Administration is seeking to pressure the Moss subcommittee to change proposed 'open government' legislation into a 'closed government' bill . . . a sharp departure from the original legislation."[40]

Court review of presidents' secrecy decisions was a particularly volatile issue. Moss's bill provided that citizens who were denied information could challenge the denial in court. Johnson's team declared the provision unconstitutional. Only the president could decide what documents warranted secrecy. Assistant attorney general Norbert Schlei testified that the bill "seeks to limit the Executive in its constitutional authority to determine whether . . .

documents are to be disclosed. . . . The bill would contravene the separation of powers doctrine and would be unconstitutional."[41]

"Every agency opposed the [bill], though they probably thought they could manipulate it," Attorney General Ramsey Clark told Herbert Foerstel, who wrote in detail about the law's history. "They thought it implied that they weren't trusted and feared that the [law] would force them to work in a gold fish bowl."[42]

In further meetings, Johnson's Justice Department attorneys successfully hijacked the legislative process. They told Moss that they would draft key sections of the House committee report, the statement of congressional intent that would accompany the bill and that courts and agencies would rely on to interpret the law. In other words, the report would not reflect the will of the House, as it was supposed to. Instead, it would reflect the will of the president—a means of protecting executive secrecy. The openness law would itself be the product of secret manipulation.[43]

The result became a parody of responsible government. The Justice Department lawyers did their job so aggressively that the House report accompanying the new law often contradicted the language of the law itself.[44]

As the House prepared to vote on the weakened bill in May 1966, Republicans seized the opportunity to embarrass the recalcitrant president. They made the Freedom of Information Act a Republican cause. Donald Rumsfeld, an energetic young congressman from Illinois and one of the bill's sponsors, rounded up Republican support in the House, with assistance from Minority Leader Gerald Ford. (Eight years later, as president, Ford vetoed amendments strengthening the public information law. Rumsfeld, years later, vigorously defended extraordinary presidential secrecy as George W. Bush's secretary of defense.)

Rumsfeld, Ford, and other Republicans held a press conference challenging Johnson to sign the bill into law.[45] Ford wrote to his constituents, "Republicans are in full accord with a bill . . . making it easier for any person to obtain information from public records." Nineteen Republicans spoke in support on the House floor.[46]

Rumsfeld, a member of Moss's subcommittee, expressed outrage at the administration's demand for executive secrecy. By his own later account, Rumsfeld inserted in the *Congressional Record* anything he could find to highlight the problem of government secrecy. He made an impassioned speech on the House floor noting that the bill remained stuck in committee due to "the well-known and well-publicized White House opposition." He noted that the administration continued to insist on redrafting the bill. "Asking representatives of the Justice Department to assist in the drafting of a freedom of information bill is like asking the wolf to guard the sheep."[47]

Speaking to a group of news executives in February, Rumsfeld asked, "Why should the President . . . speak frequently of his interest in people and . . . deny those people their constitutional right to information? . . . The Johnson administration has been particularly skillful and imaginative in its use of secrecy and news manipulation as a protective device. . . . Increased government secrecy has resulted in a marked loss of confidence by the people in their government."[48]

On June 20, 1966, the House approved the Freedom of Information Act by unanimous vote.[49]

In a last weekend of drama, no one knew for sure whether Johnson would sign the bill. Once Congress adjourned for a Fourth of July recess, the president could let the bill die by doing nothing—a strategy known as a pocket veto.

Johnson's staff knew that he was still angry about the proposed law. He "hated the very idea of the Freedom of Information Act," press secretary Bill Moyers recalled later in a speech to advocates of openness. "Hated the thought of journalists rummaging in government closets and opening government files; hated them challenging the official view of reality."[50]

One day before the bill would have died for lack of a presidential signature, Johnson finally ended the suspense and signed it. But across a memo from June 24 suggesting that a signing ceremony could help counter the president's credibility gap, he scrawled "No ceremony." Instead, he penned his signature without fanfare over the July Fourth weekend at his Texas ranch.[51]

In a last-minute comedy of errors, the president withdrew a positive press release that the White House had already distributed. It emphasized the importance of open government. It declared that "government officials should not be able to pull curtains of secrecy around decisions which can be revealed without injury to the public interest" and that "the decisions and policies—as well as the mistakes—of public officials are always subjected to the scrutiny and judgment of the people." But it was too positive for the president. When a revised statement was distributed, those phrases and others like them had disappeared.

The president substituted a release that stated that only "information that the security of the Nation permits" should be disclosed, that people should be able to provide information to the government without "being required to reveal . . . sources," that government "cannot operate effectively if required to disclose information prematurely," and that "this bill in no way impairs the President's power under our Constitution to provide for confidentiality when the national interest so requires." The last-minute switch put on display the president's grudging acceptance of the new law and undercut whatever credit he might have gotten for signing it.[52]

Having skewed the House report toward his restrictive view of disclosure, Johnson dealt two final blows to the new law after it was adopted. First, Attorney General Ramsey Clark issued a forty-seven-page pamphlet in June 1967, telling agencies to interpret the law's disclosure provisions narrowly. Instead of working from the language of the law, the attorney general's memorandum assumed that the House committee report was the law, wrote University of Chicago law professor and administrative law expert Kenneth Culp Davis in the first careful analysis of the act. Portions of the House committee report, of course, were secretly written by lawyers in the Justice Department.[53]

Second, each federal agency wrote restrictive rules to carry out the law. Sam Archibald, Moss's subcommittee staff director, concluded in 1979: "A weak and complicated law, weakened further by the Justice Department's emasculation of the House report, was further weakened by the Department's memorandum . . . and weakened even further by agency regulations implementing it."[54]

The crippled Freedom of Information Act combined strong ideas with weak action. In principle, all individuals and organizations would have equal and enforceable rights to government information. No longer could requests be denied on the grounds that there was no "need to know." A presumption of disclosure replaced the presumption of secrecy. The burden would be on the government to show that information should be kept locked up. Presidents would no longer have the last word on secrecy. Citizens could appeal denials of information to federal courts.

"The public as a whole has a right to know what the government is doing," the Senate report said. "A government by secrecy benefits no one. It injures the people it seeks to serve; it injures its own integrity and operation. It breeds mistrust, dampens the fervor of its citizens, and mocks their loyalty." The purpose of the bill was to "establish a general philosophy of full agency disclosure unless information is exempted."[55]

In practice, however, the law provided neither workable access to government documents nor protection of important secrets. Its nine exceptions took back much of what the disclosure requirements promised the public. Narrow exceptions became sweeping generalizations. The law set no limits on trade secrets, no time constraints on the secrecy of law enforcement investigations, no boundaries for national security secrecy. The government's financial regulators escaped accountability altogether. So did oil and gas companies and their oversight agencies.

"That the Congress of the United States, after more than ten years of hearings, questionnaires, studies, reports, drafts, and pulling and hauling, should wind up with such a shabby product seems discouraging," Davis concluded.[56]

Predictably, the new law "did not much change the practices of the bureaucracy," wrote Daniel Patrick Moynihan, who chaired the congressional commission on government secrecy thirty years later. The House subcommittee on government information concluded in 1972: "The effective operation of the Freedom of Information Act has been hindered by five years of foot dragging by the Federal bureaucracy."[57]

Speaking to the Federal Bar Association in Chicago a year after the law was enacted, Donald Rumsfeld underscored the limits of legislators' capacity to hold the president accountable. "No law can force a man to be honest, or truthful, or candid in his remarks. . . . [The Freedom of Information Act] deals with secrecy; it does not pretend to come to grips with the problems of deceit and lack of candor in government. The political system, the ballot box, may be the only real answer for the credibility problem."[58]

Johnson never paid a price for his lawyers' stealth manipulation of the legislative process. Moss and his subcommittee staff did not reveal the president's meddling. Only seven years later, in 1973, did committee counsel Benny L. Kass testify before a Senate subcommittee that Justice Department lawyers had drafted portions of the House report, substituting White House intent for legislative intent.[59]

As popular sentiment grew for measures to rein in President Truman's expansive Cold War secrecy, President Johnson through his mastery of the legislative process had managed to channel that sentiment into further affirmation that the president could keep secret many of the government's activities. Eight years later, compelling evidence that presidents, including Johnson, had abused that authority kept another president, Gerald Ford, from blocking the demands for a more open government.

6

Gerald Ford: A Time of Reckoning

Amid suspicions generated by the Vietnam War, the Watergate scandal, and revelations of a generation of misdeeds by secretive intelligence agencies, President Gerald Ford presided over a historic expansion of government openness and restraint of presidents' authority to act secretly and unilaterally. Known for his honesty and integrity, Ford engaged in open debate with Congress about the limits of executive secrecy and carried out new laws that subjected presidents' decisions and intelligence agencies' plans to congressional and court review. Ford's two and a half years in office ushered in a generation of more practical openness and more accountable secrecy.

"IN ALL MY PUBLIC AND PRIVATE ACTS as your president, I expect to follow my instincts of openness and candor." A few minutes after noon on August 9, 1974, Gerald R. Ford delivered a brief inaugural address. The sixty-one-year-old president stood in front of gold curtains in the formal East Room of the White House, before a seated group of congressional leaders, members of the diplomatic corps, and family members. He wore a dark blue suit and a red, white, and blue tie. His wife Betty wore a favorite light blue jersey dress dry-cleaned the night before. Their four children sat in the front row. Ford had just been sworn in as the nation's thirty-eighth president.

It was a hastily arranged affair. President Richard M. Nixon had told his vice president only the day before that he planned to resign. Until then, Ford—and the nation—had been uncertain whether Nixon would fight the House Judiciary Committee's impeachment charges for covering up his administration's role in the Watergate burglary. Nixon had tried to hide White House links to burglars caught breaking into the Democratic National Committee's offices during the 1972 presidential campaign. The burglars were trying to fix their illegal wiretap of the committee's phones.

Ford had emerged from his Alexandria home in his bathrobe at sunrise on the muggy inaugural morning to retrieve the morning newspapers, undeterred by the gaggle of reporters and photographers already gathered there. News reports said that he then cooked breakfast for himself and his son Steven while the rest of the family slept.

Ford aide Philip Buchen, his former law partner, had trouble persuading Chief Justice Warren Burger to return from Europe the night before: Burger couldn't believe that Nixon was resigning.[1]

Ford concluded his inaugural address: "Our Constitution works; our great Republic is a government of law and not of men. Here the people rule."

Stopping to greet congressional leaders, he walked briskly to the White House press room, where reporters crowded in for their first view of Ford as president. There he struck his usual conciliatory tone. He hoped for the kind of "rapport and friendship we've had in the past." He reassured them as well: "We will have an open . . . and candid Administration."[2]

That was what the American people wanted to hear. For more than two years, news stories and congressional hearings had revealed Nixon's secret intrigues. Nixon's own taping system had recorded his unsuccessful efforts to get CIA director Richard Helms to stop an FBI investigation of the Watergate burglary.[3]

Ford could not have predicted on August 9 that during his time in office an unlikely convergence of events would create the greatest expansion of government openness and the most formidable limits on presidential secrecy in the nation's history. In a cascade of suspicion that flowed from the Watergate scandal, Congress would grant courts the authority to second-guess presidents' closed decisions, and surround intelligence gathering with legal barricades to protect the rights of Americans. Torn between his commitments to openness and national security, Ford would try to contain Congress's disclosure of past intelligence abuses. And he would argue that the president alone should decide what information should remain confidential. But unlike Lyndon Johnson, he would make his arguments openly, contributing to a useful debate and a reasonable accommodation between openness and secrecy. The core idea that emerged

from Ford's years in office was that even when the nation's security was threatened, as it was during the ongoing Cold War, the secret activities of the president and his intelligence agencies would be subject to constitutional checks by
Congress and the courts.

In promising an open administration, Ford was not simply telling people what
they wanted to hear. He was known by Republicans and Democrats alike for his
candor. An Eagle Scout, a college football star at the University of Michigan,
and a Yale law school graduate, Ford remained, as people who knew him said
time and again, a man without guile. He listened to advice, laughed easily, and
cut through the pretensions of official Washington.

Ford also knew a great deal about the workings of government. The thirty-
eighth president had served as vice president for only eight months, appointed
by Nixon in October 1973 when Spiro Agnew had been forced to resign amid
allegations that he had accepted bribes as vice president and as governor of
Maryland. But Ford had represented Grand Rapids, Michigan, in the House of
Representatives for more than two decades, served on the committee that
approved intelligence spending from 1956 to 1965, and served as minority
leader from 1965 to 1973.

The American people knew more about Ford than they had ever known about
any president or vice president, thanks to a new constitutional requirement. He
was the first person to be subject to congressional investigation and approval
required under the terms of the Twenty-Fifth Amendment to the Constitution,
ratified in 1967. It was a new exercise in open government. FBI agents had
conducted more than a thousand interviews of his friends and colleagues, the
Internal Revenue Service had audited seven years of his tax returns, and
congressional staff members had reviewed twenty-four years of his votes and
statements in Congress. During two weeks of Senate hearings, he had assured
senators that he did not believe that the president was above the law. The president's authority to withhold information from Congress and the public was
limited. Presidents too often claimed secrecy "to cover up dishonesty, stupidity,
and failure of all kinds."[4]

But Ford's commitment to openness was matched by a fervent belief in a
strong national defense and the secrecy it required. After serving on an aircraft
carrier during World War II that was repeatedly bombed by the Japanese, Ford
came home an ardent internationalist. Lack of U.S. military preparedness had

encouraged German and Japanese aggression. Going forward, the U.S. military had to be stronger. Ford had supported Truman's Marshall Plan to help Europe recover after the war. He had supported Truman's decision to develop the hydrogen bomb in order to keep ahead of the Russians.[5]

National security required covert actions, he told Eric Sevareid in a television interview in 1975, when the CIA was under attack for violating its charter. "I can't imagine the United States saying we would not undertake any covert activities, and knowing at the same time that friends, as well as foes, are undertaking covert activity, not only in the United States but elsewhere. It would be like tying a President's hand behind his back."[6]

When Ford took the oath of office, the public knew little about the activities of the intelligence agencies created by President Truman. Besides the ambiguous terms of the National Security Act of 1949, a jumble of secret White House directives, internal regulations, and memos meant that agents operated on the basis of "a feel" for their job, Ford's CIA director William Colby wrote later. What the American people knew about intelligence agencies came mainly from chance revelations: a U-2 spy plane shot down over the Soviet Union in 1960, a CIA-sponsored invasion of Cuba in 1961, and now the CIA's links to the Watergate burglary.[7]

Ford aimed to govern from the center. He had a conservative's skepticism of government cures for the nation's social ills. But as a member of Congress, he had voted for federal aid to elementary and secondary schools, and for environmental measures. He favored gun control, affirmative action, and gay rights.[8]

The new president bucked conservatives to choose the liberal Republican and former New York governor Nelson Rockefeller as his vice president, and to offer limited clemency to men who evaded the draft during the Vietnam conflict. "I knew [limited clemency] wouldn't satisfy liberals . . . nor would it please conservatives," he wrote later. "Still, I thought it was fair."[9]

Cold War issues crowded the president's calendar. He had to oversee a desperate escape of U.S. officials and loyal Vietnamese as communist troops took over the South Vietnamese capital. He was preparing to meet Soviet premier Leonid Brezhnev in late November in order to reach agreement on reducing nuclear weapons. As a result of the arms race that began during Truman's presidency, both countries now had enough atomic weapons to destroy all of civilization. In May, India had tested an atomic bomb—becoming the sixth nuclear power.

The first Cold War president remained Ford's example. He viewed Truman as an independent-minded midwesterner who made tough decisions with confidence even when they were unpopular. On his first day as president, Ford asked that Theodore Roosevelt's and Woodrow Wilson's portraits in the cabinet room be replaced with Truman's and Lincoln's.[10]

Almost immediately, the president who promised openness became embroiled in issues of secrecy. Just four weeks after taking office, Ford was accused of making a secret deal to pardon Richard Nixon in exchange for Nixon's resignation. The former president had not yet been charged with any crime. But on September 8, Ford pardoned him of any offenses he might be charged with in the future. Ford tried to explain. A pardon would help to heal the nation. "Overriding almost everything else," he recalled in his memoir, "was the precipitous decline in the faith that Americans traditionally placed in their nation, their institutions and their leaders. . . . It upset me deeply that people were so down on their country."[11]

But instead of healing, the pardon stirred up a storm of protest that cast a pall over Ford's presidency. He was attacked by Republicans and Democrats alike. Republican senator Barry Goldwater argued that he had no authority to give Nixon a get-out-of-jail-free card. " 'Mr. President, you have no right and no power to do that. Nixon has never been charged or convicted of anything. So what are you pardoning him of? It doesn't make sense.' " Bob Woodward, who chronicled the events leading to the pardon in *Shadow,* concluded that there was no hard evidence of any quid pro quo. But Ford could not put to rest Democrats' repeated charges of a secret deal. The allegations made the usually even-tempered president furious. He pounded his fist on the table at a Senate hearing: "No deal."[12]

Weeks later, the president who promised candor faced a much larger question of executive secrecy. Energized by the Watergate scandal, the House and Senate had approved legislation that would finally give all Americans more effective access to most information held by the government.

The proposed law aimed to create what the Freedom of Information Act of 1966 had failed to provide—fast and inexpensive access to government policies, research, plans, and other documents. It narrowed law enforcement and national security exemptions, required agencies to respond quickly, and limited the amount they could charge.

The bill's lead sponsor in the Senate, Edward M. Kennedy, Congress's best-known Democrat, had studded his advocacy in the floor debate with references to secrecy as an incubator of corruption: "We have seen too much secrecy in the past few years, and the American people are tired of it. Secret bombing of Cambodia, secret wheat deals, secret campaign contributions, secret domestic intelligence operations, secret cost overruns, secret antitrust settlement negotiations, secret White House spying operations." The House and Senate approved the final bill by overwhelming majorities: the Senate by a vote of 64–17, the House by 349–2.[13]

But one provision troubled Ford. For the first time, courts could second-guess the president's judgment about what should be kept secret. When citizens were denied access to secret documents, they could appeal to federal judges to determine if the documents were in fact properly classified. By inserting that provision, Congress set an important new limit on presidential secrecy.[14]

Ford found the two values he cared about most to be at odds. Schooled in the importance of secret intelligence activities, he hesitated to let judges without national security expertise have the final word on secrecy. However, his life-long commitment to openness was authentic, and he had just reaffirmed that commitment to the American people in his inaugural address.

At his first cabinet meeting, on Saturday, August 10, the day after he was sworn in as president, his advisers argued about whether he should sign or veto the public information bill. Attorney General William Saxbe, a holdover from the Nixon administration, told the president that it was a bad bill and a veto could be sustained. The president's press secretary, Jerry terHorst, argued that Ford had to come down on the side of openness.[15]

Characteristically, Ford found a middle path. The administration would ask the congressional conferees to delay their work long enough for the White House to work out a compromise. After the meeting, the president sent a letter to congressional sponsors. He raised legitimate issues, and explained them with candor—a stark contrast to Lyndon Johnson's back-channel dealing. He simply could not accept a provision that would risk exposing military or intelligence secrets by allowing judges to decide whether documents were properly classified. "My great respect for the courts does not prevent me from observing that they do not ordinarily have the background and expertise to gauge the ramifications that a release of a document may have upon our national security," Ford wrote. "The Constitution commits this responsibility and authority to the President."

Negotiations began. Congressional conferees revised the bill. They could not give up the idea that courts could examine requested documents to determine whether they were properly classified. But courts could give "substantial weight" to agency views. Ford preferred a stronger presumption: the burden should be on the requester to convince the court that the document should be made public.[16]

If the Watergate scandal had reminded Congress of the importance of limiting executive secrecy, it had also reminded many in the executive branch of the need to limit disclosure of sensitive information to zealous representatives and a pliable public. Watergate allegations of a president's criminal conduct had shone a light on White House conversations and documents that would usually remain confidential. It was important to reestablish the president's authority.

This was one moment when large constitutional issues—in this instance the balance between openness and secrecy in democratic government—turned on the fine print of a proposed law. The result would determine to what extent presidential secrecy would remain unchecked.

Other concerns could be worked out. Congress would not require the disclosure of information provided by confidential sources in law enforcement investigations if disclosure might reveal their identity. Agency officials would not be held personally liable for improper withholding of documents. Corporations would not get documents free of charge.[17]

Kennedy hoped that the president would not veto the bill. "Openness is supposed to be the watchword of the present administration," he explained during the final Senate debate. "So far, however, it has been more of a slogan than a practice. A veto of this bill would reflect a hostility to just the kind of Government openness and accountability which the public must have to regain a full measure of confidence in our National Government."[18]

Both the president and members of Congress knew that the Freedom of Information Act was not working. President Johnson's strategy to cripple it had been successful. On paper, the law gave the American people the right to inquire into the business of government. In practice, that right was lost in a maze of exemptions, fees, and agency delays.

The government's own watchdogs had declared the law a failure. Its exemptions that allowed agencies to keep information secret were broad, vague, and applied inconsistently, the Administrative Conference of the United States concluded in 1971. Agencies required that people requesting documents be able to describe them even though the documents were secret. A special Library of Congress report in 1972 found that agencies withheld entire files when portions could have been released, took several months to produce information, and charged fees as high as ten dollars a page. The Civil Service Commission and other agencies kept no records "and apparently have no interest in implementing the law."[19]

For ordinary citizens, the barriers proved insurmountable. The Defense Department kept secret already published newspaper articles. The FBI would not release a file that contained John Lennon's published lyrics. Even members of Congress had trouble using the law. John Moss, who had shepherded it through Congress, could not get government officials to release information about fees doctors received for treating Medicare patients.[20]

The law proved useless to most journalists. Donald Rumsfeld, who had been a strong supporter of the law as a member of John Moss's House subcommittee, explained soon after the 1966 legislation was approved that "busy reporters . . . trying to dig out the news of the moment on a deadline" did not have time to use the cumbersome law.[21]

Judges found the law weak and ineffective. In a Supreme Court test in 1973, thirty-four members of Congress tried to gain access to agency memos that opposed a planned underground nuclear test at Amchitka Island, Alaska. Justice Potter Stewart observed that the law "provides no means to question an Executive decision to stamp a document 'secret,' however cynical, myopic, or even corrupt that decision might have been."[22]

The most frequent users turned out to be businesses seeking information from the government about their competitors. If information would improve their competitive position, it was sometimes worth the time and money to get it.[23]

Truman's well-intentioned system of classifying government secrets had spun out of control. No one believed that the millions of classified documents represented essential secrets. Classification "is noted more for its abuses than for its protection of legitimate Government secrets," Kennedy declared in the Senate floor debate. A recent congressional report had concluded that there was "widespread overclassification, abuses in the use of classification stamps, and other serious defects in the operation of the security classification system." Even the Nixon administration had declared that the classification system had failed to meet the standards of an open and democratic society, "allowing too many papers to be classified for too long a time . . . and . . . has frequently served to conceal bureaucratic mistakes or to prevent embarrassment to officials and administrations," Kennedy reminded his colleagues. Senator Edmund Muskie of Maine added that the government could stamp the Manhattan telephone directory top secret and no court could change it.[24]

Traditional advocates of openness like the American Civil Liberties Union and the American Society of Newspaper Editors were joined by newer organizations such as Common Cause and the Federation of American Scientists. Even General Motors became an involuntary contributor to the openness campaign. GM paid Ralph Nader $425,000 to settle his invasion of privacy suit against the auto company, and Nader used the money to launch consumer advocacy organizations that challenged government secrecy. Nader, the son of Lebanese immigrants and a Harvard Law School graduate, had come to Washington in 1964 to work as a part-time consultant on auto safety issues for Daniel Patrick Moynihan, then a Labor Department official. Chronicling the faulty design of the sporty GM Corvair in *Unsafe at Any Speed,* Nader was suddenly catapulted to prominence when press reports forced the company to admit to spying on him. The congressional investigation that followed revealed that GM had tapped Nader's phone and hired prostitutes to entrap him.[25]

Nearly a hundred "Nader's raiders" swarmed Washington during the summer of 1969, seeking documents and rating agencies on their openness. Nader compiled their findings into a report filled with dramatic examples of denied requests. Their report concluded that the public information law was being undercut by "a riptide of agency ingenuity." Pesticide files disappeared while students were researching them in the Department of Agriculture library. Highway safety officials denied students access to a report on auto accidents involving U.S. army personnel in Europe, even though the report had been given to General Motors. Airline regulators refused to provide information on public complaints about airlines, even though the information had been given to the airlines.[26]

In the end, Ford's concern for preserving presidents' authority trumped his commitment to openness. Defense Secretary James Schlesinger and congressional liaison William Timmons, another Nixon adviser, joined Attorney General Saxbe in recommending a veto. Schlesinger feared the bill would reveal national security secrets.[27] Ford's new chief of staff, Donald Rumsfeld, the former Illinois congressman who had led the Republican effort to strengthen the Freedom of Information Act in 1966 and served as Nixon's NATO ambassador, was still shuttling between Brussels and Washington and did not recall participating in the decision. Rumsfeld's thirty-three-year-old deputy, Richard Cheney, would later criticize congressional efforts to hem in presidents' authority and, as vice president to George W. Bush, would try to reverse the trend toward greater accountability.[28]

On October 17, five weeks after his inaugural promise of openness, Ford sent a veto message to the clerk of the House in a sealed envelope, along with the rejected bill. He hoped that his veto would lead to further negotiations after the November congressional elections. "The bill enrolled is unconstitutional and unworkable," the message said. The conduct of defense and foreign policy were entrusted to the president by the Constitution. The president still wanted language requiring courts to presume that secrecy classifications were correct. When publishers and editors met with Ford on October 25, he told them he expected Congress to pass a modified law that he could sign by Christmas.[29]

But the politics of the moment worked against the president. Democrats gained larger majorities in both houses in the November congressional elections—a majority of 61–39 in the Senate, and 291–144 in the House—and organized a national campaign to override the president's veto.[30]

A casual remark helped launch that campaign. "Who gives a damn except the *Washington Post* and the *New York Times* whether he vetoes [the bill]?" a White House aide asked a House subcommittee staffer. His question was quoted in a *New York Times* front-page story.[31]

In response, newspaper editors around the country set out to show who gave a damn. Editorials in big cities and small towns urged Congress to override the veto. The *Chicago Tribune* declared: "The proposed changes attack the notorious tendency in any bureaucracy to keep matters secret for the sheer joy of secrecy, a tendency which expresses itself in classifying many items of information more rigorously than necessary and for unreasonably long times."[32] A *Washington Post* article added: "The truth of the matter is that this legislation goes to the heart of what a free society is about. That's why we should all give a damn—especially those who are to cast their votes [to override Ford's veto]."[33]

The importance of the vote that followed was that the people's representatives voted to hold the president accountable to Congress and the courts, even as the fearful Cold War entered its fourth decade. The House voted 371–31 and the Senate voted 65–27 to override the president's veto. Their actions repudiated "the special antimedia, antipublic, anti-Congress secrecy of the Nixon administration," Senator Kennedy told his colleagues. Henceforth, courts would have the final word on presidents' secrets.[34]

Although the outcome was not what he wanted, Ford's character served the nation well. He defended executive authority forthrightly and encouraged a legitimate debate about whether the president, rather than the courts, should control government secrecy. The resulting open debate produced a lasting accommodation, even though Nixon's deception and Democratic control of Congress placed him at a disadvantage in that debate.

Once the Freedom of Information Act amendments became law, the president was straightforward in carrying out their new requirements. Unlike Lyndon Johnson, whose attorney general used his authority to undermine congressional intent, Ford's new attorney general, Edward H. Levi, a former president of the University of Chicago and a respected legal scholar, required agencies to change their ways to comply with the new law. The Justice Department's guidelines confirmed that officials could no longer simply deny requests for documents marked "secret." The new law required them to discern whether the information in fact needed to be classified. For the first time since President Truman created a framework of peacetime secrecy in 1947, those who stamped papers "top secret," "secret," or "confidential" had someone looking over their shoulders.

The new law had dramatic effects. Citizens got the information they requested in eleven days on average, instead of seventy days, and their appeals were denied 41 percent of the time, down from 72 percent. Many requests still came from businesses trying to learn more about their competitors. But citizens gained information about toxic wastes dumped in the Ohio River, CIA drug tests on unwitting human subjects, the Ford Pinto's exploding gas tank, and safety problems with infant formula.[35]

The law was still cumbersome. Requesting information with required specificity and appealing denials remained daunting tasks for citizens. Releasing information one request at a time remained a daunting task for agencies. And the law left too much room for presidents to widen or narrow openness by executive order. When Ronald Reagan took office in 1981, he increased secrecy by executive order. He told agency officials that they need not consider the public interest in deciding whether to release documents, broadened the national security exemption, abolished the requirement that agencies show identifiable damage from release of information, and allowed officials to classify documents after they were requested in order to keep them secret. He also asked Congress to exempt intelligence agencies, increase fees, and narrow court reviews.[36]

Later misdeeds demonstrated that no law could stop a president and his advisers from abusing their power by deceiving the public. Accountability usually came afterward. In what became known as the Iran-Contra affair, President Reagan's administration tried to use secrecy to thwart the will of Congress by funneling funds from weapons sales to Iran to finance anti-communist rebels who were trying to overthrow the Nicaraguan government. Congress had forbidden the use of federal funds to support the rebels. Eventually, eleven administration officials were convicted on various charges stemming from the scandal. President Bill Clinton was charged with giving false testimony under oath to hide his sexual exploits. He was impeached by the House of Representatives years later.[37]

Four months into Ford's presidency, a chance chain of events exposed intelligence agencies' earlier abuses of secrecy and triggered new limits on the president's authority. Congressional investigation and open debate made agencies more accountable to Congress and the courts. Ford vigorously defended executive authority, but he also diligently carried out Congress's new directives. The times and circumstances were different, but the nation was gradually returning to the culture of openness and limited secrecy that the founders had inaugurated.

On December 22, 1974, a month after Congress voted to override Ford's veto of the public information bill, Seymour Hersh, a Pulitzer Prize–winning reporter for the *New York Times* and one of journalism's most tenacious investigators, reported that Nixon's CIA had conducted secret surveillance of antiwar demonstrators and other dissidents, despite the prohibition in the National Security Act of 1947 against any "internal-security functions."[38]

Hersh's story became one link in a chain of events that began with the Watergate burglary and ended with new limits on presidents' secrets. E. Howard Hunt and James McCord, two of the Watergate burglars, had earlier worked for the CIA. That led Nixon's CIA director, James Schlesinger, to ask CIA employees in May 1973 to report to him any other agency links to the Watergate scandal, and any other activities that might have violated the agency's legal charter.

That last request turned out to be a large assignment. By the time William Colby replaced Schlesinger in September 1973, the CIA staff had produced a secret 702-page report describing seven hundred instances of questionable activities in the United States and abroad going back to the years after Truman created the agency.[39]

Colby issued orders to ensure that such transgressions would not reoccur. A seasoned intelligence officer in his mid-fifties who had parachuted behind enemy lines as an OSS agent during World War II, Colby had served in the CIA's clandestine division that planned covert activities, and had run the Phoenix Program of imprisonment and elimination of Viet Cong during the Vietnam War.

When Hersh's story broke, Colby phoned the president. He wrote later that he was amazed that Ford and other senior officials had never before been told about the agency's past activities. He reached the president on Air Force One, on his way to a Christmas ski vacation in Vail, Colorado, and promised a full report within forty-eight hours. By his own later account, Ford told Colby that he would not tolerate any violations of the law. Colby sent the report and provided details in a meeting in the Oval Office a week later. He briefed the acting attorney general and felt obliged to also brief members of Congress. When the story began to leak and congressional leaders launched investigations, he told his agents to put aside their sworn commitments to secrecy and testify openly.[40]

Among the CIA activities were assassination plots against foreign heads of state; surveillance of civil rights leaders, antiwar protesters, journalists, and members of Congress; twenty years of opening and photographing citizens' first-class mail; and experiments on uninformed individuals using LSD and other mind-altering drugs.[41]

Ford had to decide how much to reveal voluntarily. Some investigation was warranted, but he feared, as he told his advisers in a meeting on January 4, that the CIA would be destroyed if investigations revealed the agency's involvement in assassination attempts and other flagrant violations of the law.[42]

Any damage to the CIA's reputation would be devastating at the height of the Cold War. Ford needed foreign intelligence capabilities to manage a safe withdrawal by the United States from Vietnam, to understand the next moves of China's communist government, and to monitor the Soviet Union's development of nuclear weapons.

Ford also needed the domestic intelligence that a strong FBI could provide. The year 1975 proved to be a particularly violent one. The Weather Underground, a radical antiwar group, bombed the State Department in Washington and Defense Department offices in Oakland, California, and a bomb exploded at LaGuardia Airport in New York, killing eleven people. The president himself was the target of two assassination attempts.

As usual, Ford was honest about his reservations and tried to chart a middle course. First, he created a commission headed by the vice president, Nelson Rockefeller. It was a defensive measure. Rumsfeld's deputy Richard Cheney advised Ford that a presidential commission offered the best prospect for heading off efforts by Congress to encroach on the executive branch. Ford wrote later that he was concerned that publicity-seeking Democrats would conduct "sensational and irresponsible" hearings. He limited the investigation to the CIA's surveillance of American citizens.[43]

Next, Ford tried to persuade newspaper editors that full disclosure of the CIA's past transgressions would impair the agency's effectiveness. He invited the publisher and editors from the *New York Times* to lunch at the White House on January 16 to persuade them that revealing everything about the CIA's past would damage the nation and tarnish the reputation of every president since Harry Truman. During lunch, Ford let slip that the CIA had engaged in assassination plots. The *Times* editors honored the agreement they had made that the conversation was off the record, and did not print the president's admission.[44]

Finally, he asked members of Congress to limit the information about past misdeeds that investigators made public. In a dramatic appearance before a joint session of Congress on April 10, 1975, Ford warned that "in a world where information is power, a vital element of our national security lies in our intelligence services. . . . It is entirely proper that this system be subject to Congressional review. But a sensationalized public debate . . . is a disservice to this nation and a threat to our intelligence system."[45]

Nonetheless, the Senate and the House formed committees to investigate illegal or unethical activities by the nation's intelligence agencies. It would be the first thorough probe since Truman had created the CIA and the National Security Agency, and given the FBI new surveillance powers twenty-five years earlier.

The Senate chose Democratic senator Frank Church from Boise, Idaho, to chair its investigation. A Marine colonel and a World War II intelligence officer,

Church was elected to the Senate in 1952 as Truman left office, and had been a member of the Senate Foreign Relations Committee for more than fifteen years. Ford suspected he would use the investigation as a springboard for a presidential bid. (Church did in fact seek the Democratic nomination in 1976.)[46]

The Church Committee worked out ground rules with CIA director Colby to protect agents' identities and sensitive information. Colby found the committee's approach generally responsible and serious. Despite the president's appeal, the committee determined to make a full report to the American people.

The committee report explained that agency officials had initiated assassination plots against Fidel Castro of Cuba and Patrice Lumumba of the Congo (called Zaire at the time of the report), and assisted those planning the assassinations of Ngo Dinh Diem of South Vietnam, Rafael Leonidas Trujillo of the Dominican Republic, and General Rene Schneider of Chile.[47]

The NSA, barred by law from monitoring communications inside the United States, had routinely conducted electronic surveillance of Americans for the CIA, the Secret Service, the Defense Department, the Drug Enforcement Administration, and the FBI. The names of more than sixteen hundred Americans were on NSA watch lists, including government officials, civil rights leaders, and the antiwar protesters Jane Fonda and Dr. Benjamin Spock. The lists were discontinued only in 1973, the NSA director testified.

The NSA also contracted with three major communications companies to copy about 150,000 cables and telegrams each month between Americans and individuals abroad, and distributed the copies to other agencies. Former president Nixon admitted in a deposition that he had asked the NSA to intercept citizens' communications.[48]

In a television interview, committee chairman Frank Church warned that if the NSA's technical prowess was used against the American people, there would be no privacy left. "I know the capacity that is there to make tyranny total in America, and we must see to it that this agency and all agencies that possess this technology operate within the law and under proper supervision, so that we never cross over that abyss."[49]

As a result of these revelations, the president and Congress began the long process of surrounding intelligence gathering with layers of oversight and other legal limits. These measures were by no means perfect. Most relied on secretive oversight of secretive programs that would later prove flawed. And they remained controversial. But they inaugurated a new culture of accountability.

Ford renewed the bans on assassinations, CIA and NSA surveillance within the United States, mail opening, and agencies' examination of tax returns. FBI investigations would be limited to criminal cases, and wiretaps had to be approved by the attorney general. The Intelligence Oversight Board, composed of private citizens, would act as an independent auditor of proposed foreign intelligence activities.[50]

Congress made an effort to embed the legitimate activities of the nation's intelligence agencies within the constitutional framework of checks and balances that applied to the rest of the executive branch. A new law required a presidential finding that a covert action was important to national security before any funds were spent, and required the president to submit that finding to congressional committees within a limited time.[51] Any physical or electronic surveillance of Americans suspected of being foreign agents would henceforth require approval by a new Foreign Intelligence Surveillance Court.[52] Congress gave inspectors general within executive agencies new powers as independent auditors. Permanent House and Senate intelligence committees would approve annual budgets and conduct investigations. Agencies were required to keep those committees fully informed about current or planned activities.[53]

It is worth noting that this pivotal moment that began to constrain presidents' uses of secrecy occurred by chance. The unlikely circumstances included Richard Nixon's cover-up of a burglary linked to the White House and the CIA, questions posed by a CIA director to his staff, reporting by tenacious journalists, unusually rigorous congressional investigations, and the willingness of a new president to engage in open debate. Together these circumstances convinced Americans that unfettered executive secrecy created opportunities for abuse. Congress reversed President Truman's decision thirty years earlier to wall off intelligence gathering from the usual scrutiny by Congress and the courts. This new consensus would be tested by future presidents, most purposefully by George W. Bush after the terrorist attacks of 2001.

7

George W. Bush: A Test of the Limits

George W. Bush took office in 2001 committed to demonstrating that the president had broad authority to act unilaterally and secretly. After the terrorist attacks of September 11, commitment converged with crisis. Unlike the cautious George Washington who worried about exercising too much power, or the pragmatic Harry Truman who created intelligence agencies that simply got out of hand, Bush purposefully circled around settled law and practice to create new policies and institutions behind closed doors. But secrecy no longer worked for the president, the public, or the nation's security. Instead, Bush's actions produced chance revelations, an inflamed debate, and new limits on future presidents.

"WE'RE AT WAR." PRESIDENT GEORGE W. BUSH opened a teleconference with his advisers at 3:15 in the afternoon on September 11, 2001. With those three words, he made the most important decision of his presidency.

Bush had just arrived at the underground headquarters of the Defense Department's strategic command at Offutt Air Force Base in Nebraska after spending much of the day in the air. The Secret Service was searching for a secure location. It wasn't safe to return to the White House.

When a second plane smashed into New York's World Trade Center six hours earlier, the president had been listening to a class of second graders at Emma E. Booker Elementary School in Sarasota, Florida, read *The Pet Goat*. It was the beginning of a day when he planned to talk about improving public education, one of his highest domestic priorities. At 9:03 a.m., his chief of staff, Andrew Card, came up behind him and whispered: "A second plane hit the second tower. America is under attack." Bush at first did not react, then made a hasty exit. His motorcade sped to Angel, the code name for Air Force One. He flew to Barksdale Air Force Base in Louisiana, took off again, and flew to the Nebraska base, where there were more secure communications.

The president was not asking for advice. After earlier attacks on the World Trade Center in 1993 and on U.S. embassies in Kenya and Tanzania in 1998, the government had apprehended and prosecuted radical Islamic terrorists. President Clinton had ordered the bombing of their training camps in Afghanistan. Bush considered that a weak response. He would do more than put "a million-dollar missile on a five-dollar tent," he told his advisers.[1]

The world thought that America had gone soft, that the nation was self-satisfied, materialistic, and uninterested in fighting back. Bush would restore its stature. He would play a heroic role. "I was looking at a modern-day Pearl Harbor," he wrote in his memoir. "Just as Franklin Roosevelt had rallied the nation to defend freedom, it would be my responsibility to lead a new generation to protect America" in this first war of the twenty-first century.[2]

He had already decided that the war would be global. When Bush landed at the Offutt base, CIA director George Tenet had told him in a phone call that passenger information suggested that a specific group of Islamic terrorists, Al Qaeda, was responsible for the attacks. But Bush said the goal would be to defeat international terrorism everywhere. When he was finished, there would be no risk of future attacks. The war would not end, he explained days later to Congress, "until every terrorist group of global reach has been found, stopped, and defeated." Our responsibility to history is to "rid the world of evil." The global war on terror would now be the focus of his presidency.[3]

Senior officials questioned Bush's characterization of the nation's response as a war and pointed out the limitations of international law. Secretary of Defense Donald Rumsfeld urged the president to avoid calling the conflict a war on terror since it implied a campaign that could be won by bullets alone. Terror was a tactic, a choice of weapons. Bush should make it clear that the nation was fighting the people using those weapons. Senate majority leader Tom Daschle warned the president to be careful about employing the overused term when there might be no decisive victory.[4]

But the president had made up his mind. He did not need a declaration of war from Congress. He would exercise his wartime powers as commander in chief, the powers he believed were implicit in the Constitution. When Rumsfeld reminded him in an evening meeting on September 11 that international law allowed the United States to take action in self-defense but not to seek retribution, Bush responded impatiently, according to Richard Clarke, his counterterrorism adviser, "I don't care what the international lawyers say, we are going to kick some ass."[5]

Bush made a second decision that evening. Addressing the nation at 8:30 p.m. Eastern time, he announced, "We will make no distinction between the terrorists who committed these acts and those who harbor them."[6] It was a major change that became the core of Bush's foreign policy for the next eight years. He did not consult with his secretary of state, Colin Powell, or Donald Rumsfeld. National Security Advisor Condoleezza Rice wrote later that she read the line over the phone to Powell and Rumsfeld, and checked quickly with Vice President Dick Cheney.[7]

Before the day ended, Attorney General John Ashcroft executed a third decision. The FBI, with the president's support, began arresting Muslim men who seemed in some way suspicious, on the pretext that they might have violated immigration rules. Most were from Pakistan, Egypt, or Turkey. Following the usual procedures to protect suspects' rights would slow things down. The president's instructions were to stop the next attack, whatever it takes.[8]

In all, 762 men were caught in the FBI's secret net in the weeks after September 11, a later Justice Department investigation found. They were denied bond and imprisoned for an average of eighty days. Some were physically abused. Instead of the required notice of charges, open hearings, right to counsel, and court review, the FBI delayed charges, kept the prisoners' identities secret, made access to counsel difficult, and closed hearings to their families and the public. None of these men were ever charged with a terrorism offense.[9]

Within a week, Bush gave the nation's intelligence agencies orders that cast aside a generation of legal limits that had been constructed by Congress and earlier presidents, and that the American people relied on. There was no debate. The orders were secret. The CIA, whose covert activities had been circumscribed by law and practice, could now engage in secret activities anywhere in the world to counter Al Qaeda. "For us at the CIA," Tenet wrote later, "the new doctrine meant that the restraints were finally off."[10]

The National Security Agency, legally barred by the 1970s reforms from intercepting communications by citizens or residents without a court order, could now monitor calls and emails in and out of the country without a judge's approval. The FBI, barred by those reforms from conducting surveillance of political demonstrations and university events where there was no suspicion of a crime, was freed to engage in surveillance of groups that might be supporting violence.[11]

These were political decisions of consequence, made at a moment of crisis when the president's aims and instincts had overriding importance. President Bush made three choices—to fight a global war against terrorism, to treat nations that gave safe haven to terrorists as enemies, and to hold suspects in secret detention deprived of usual legal rights—without public debate and without hearing the views of his most knowledgeable advisers or members of Congress. Secrecy enabled the president to act quickly to protect the nation. Following the usual ground rules for consultation and approval could be slow, and the outcome uncertain. Secrecy also kept enemies in the dark. But the president's policies, lacking seasoned safeguards, inevitably led to mistakes and abuses. Excessive secrecy set up conflicts that opened the way for insiders to make piecemeal revelations, deprived Bush of leadership opportunities, diminished trust in the president and the presidency, fractured needed national unity, and ultimately undermined the nation's security.

On Tuesday, September 11, 2001, Americans had no reason to expect trouble. In the news that morning, Congress was working on tax cuts. The first case of mad cow disease was suspected in Japan. Iranian officials denied they had developed nuclear weapons. Consumer confidence was strong. Inflation was a manageable 3 percent, unemployment only 4 percent. The government was running the largest annual surplus in history, more than $200 billion.[12]

Eight months earlier, George W. Bush had celebrated the absence of threats to the nation in his inaugural address on the steps of the Capitol. Americans were living in a time of blessing. Outgoing president Bill Clinton had sounded the same theme: "Never before has our nation enjoyed . . . so much prosperity and social progress with so little internal crisis or so few external threats," he had declared in his last State of the Union address. Terrorism remained a distant concern. "We have to keep this inexorable march of technology from giving terrorists . . . the means to undermine our defenses," Clinton said. In ten or twenty years, "the major security threat this country will face will come from . . . the terrorists . . . with increasing access to ever more sophisticated chemical and biological weapons."[13]

Less than two years later, the images of planes crashing into New York's World Trade Center towers, the Defense Department's Pentagon headquarters in Washington, and a field in Pennsylvania were seared into the memories of Americans. In Chicago, Barack Obama, an Illinois state senator who had just turned forty, was evacuated from the legislature's chambers along with everyone else. "Up and down the streets," he wrote later, "people gathered, staring at the sky and at the Sears Tower," Chicago's tallest building.[14]

The attacks killed 2,977 individuals, more than the number killed in Japan's attack on Pearl Harbor in 1941 that had carried the United States into World War II. As Bush admitted later, "Before 9/11, most Americans had never heard of al Qaeda."[15]

The president did not inform the American people about imminent threats. Cold War habits of limiting and compartmentalizing information left citizens unable to use their eyes and ears to help prevent attacks, and intelligence agencies unable to share fragments of knowledge that might have stopped some of the terrorists.

The president himself had been briefed on Al Qaeda threats for nearly a year. CIA director George Tenet held sessions for Bush as a candidate and again as president-elect, giving him access to the same kinds of intelligence that President Clinton had, Tenet wrote later. Tenet's biggest concerns were terrorism, nuclear proliferation, and the growing power of China.[16]

As president, Bush received daily briefings. Six to eight short articles summarized the day's most important security threats. It was the kind of intelligence summary that Harry Truman had dreamed of when he created the CIA in 1947. On August 6, CIA briefer Michael Morell gave the president a detailed account of Al Qaeda threats in the living room of the president's ranch in Crawford, Texas, titled "Bin Laden Determined to Strike in US." In it the president read that "al-Qa'ida members—including some who are US citizens—have resided in or traveled to the US for years." There were unconfirmed reports that Al Qaeda's leader Osama Bin Laden planned to hijack airplanes and that individuals had recently been casing federal buildings in New York. However, as Morell wrote later, there was no specific indication of when, where, or how terrorists might strike.[17]

More than forty articles in earlier briefings focused on Bin Laden. The articles had titles like "Bin Laden Network's Plans Advancing" (May 26), "Bin Laden Planning High-Profile Attacks," and "Bin Laden Threats Are Real" (June

30). They suggested that there were terrorist cells in the United States plotting attacks, that Al Qaeda might be planning a "spectacular" attack with "high explosives," and that attacks could be "imminent." In July, Tenet told Rice that Al Qaeda was going to target the United States and the issue needed immediate attention. The intelligence system was "blinking red."[18]

Terrorist attacks had killed Americans nearly every year in the 1990s. In 1993, a Pakistani terrorist shot and killed two employees in front of CIA head-quarters in Virginia, and Al Qaeda set off explosives in the World Trade Center garage. In 1995, five Americans were killed by a bomb in Riyadh, Saudi Arabia, and the next year nineteen Americans were killed and 372 wounded by a bomb in the Khobar Towers apartment complex in Saudi Arabia that housed American troops. In 1996 and again in 1998 Bin Laden issued a declaration of war against the United States that urged Muslims to "kill the Americans" as a duty "for every Muslim who can do it in any country in which it is possible to do it." Al Qaeda agents killed 224 people and injured several thousand in attacks on American embassies in Kenya and Tanzania in 1998, and killed seventeen navy personnel by ramming the U.S.S. *Cole* in Yemen's Aden Harbor with a boat loaded with explosives two years later.[19]

Officials used a twentieth-century bromide to explain why they did not alert the public. Information was uncertain and people might panic. "If you scare the hell out of people too often, and nothing happens, that can also create problems," Vice President Cheney explained to *Washington Post* reporter Bob Woodward five weeks after the attacks, because people then don't pay attention when there is a real threat, adding, "if you create panic, the terrorist wins without ever doing anything." The government often "left its citizens to think what they chose about international threats for fear that they might find out the truth or react unpredictably," Daniel Patrick Moynihan wrote in *Secrecy* three years earlier, after he had chaired a congressional commission charged with reexamining Cold War secrecy.[20]

Excluding the public was a mistake, Presidents Bush and Obama later concluded. The public could be the government's most important security partner. Citizens might provide tips, jumpstart preemptive action, activate social networks, and perhaps spot terrorists before they did harm. Properly prepared, they did not panic. Americans had long been accustomed to respond-ing to uncertain and potentially catastrophic risks, including tornados, hurri-canes, earthquakes, wildfires, and epidemics of infectious disease. Bush eventually created a well-intentioned but dysfunctional terrorist threat warning system.

In 2001, Cold War intelligence agencies still hoarded information. The Defense Department's NSA, the CIA, and the FBI each held fragments of information that, if shared with other agencies, could have stopped some or all of the hijackers, as many pointed out with the benefit of hindsight. The 9/11 Commission concluded in 2004 that the failure of intelligence agencies to share information among themselves contributed to the nation's vulnerability. One problem was neglect. The NSA had lost a third of its resources and people in the 1990s, and could no longer keep up with new technology and new priorities. The agency tracked two messages among possible terrorists on September 10: "The match is about to begin" and "Tomorrow is zero hour." They were not translated until September 12.[21]

Bush explained later that he thought intelligence pointed to an attack overseas. Without more specifics, the administration increased security at embassies, alerted foreign intelligence services and U.S. troops abroad, and informed airline regulators about possible hijackings of international flights. The FBI warned field offices, federal agencies, and state and local governments that the threat of an attack in the United States should not be discounted.[22]

But the agencies that could have protected Americans never mobilized, the 9/11 Commission concluded. "They did not have direction. . . . The borders were not hardened. Transportation systems were not fortified. Electronic surveillance was not targeted against a domestic threat. . . . The public was not warned."[23]

The attacks "should not have come as a surprise," the commission concluded after reviewing classified information. "Islamist extremists had given plenty of warning that they meant to kill Americans indiscriminately and in large numbers. The intelligence reporting consistently described the upcoming attacks as occurring on a calamitous level."[24] The commission noted that voters might have forced faster responses to terrorism if they had had access to the government's knowledge about the threats.[25]

For the president, secrecy was more than a Cold War habit. It was an expedient way to expand presidential power. "Bush has rarely leveled with the public to explain what he was doing and what should be expected," reporter Bob Woodward concluded in *The War Within* after interviews with the president and his senior advisers. Among the lessons of the Bush presidency, Woodward wrote, was "trust the public with the truth, in all its pain and uncertainty."[26]

Their own secrecy also gave terrorists power out of proportion with their small numbers. In the past, hostile nations with well-understood aims had employed known weapons against American soldiers fighting in foreign lands. On September 11, a shadowy network of religious extremists hijacked commercial aircraft to carry out large-scale, coordinated attacks against civilians on American soil. They had been living among ordinary citizens in American cities and suburbs. Their stealth tactics created waves of fear and uncertainty that encouraged extreme measures. The president expressed his frustration: "I'm fighting an enemy I can't see."[27]

"My immediate concern," Bush wrote later, "was that there could be more Al Qaeda operatives in the United States."[28] On September 11, the government grounded four thousand commercial flights in two hours. Fighter jets flew in formation over the nation's capital. More than eight thousand federal buildings across the country sent home most of their one million workers. NASA sent twelve thousand employees home and closed the Kennedy Space Center. Nuclear power plants added security. The navy sent a ship to guard the entrance to Seattle's harbor. Cities guarded bridges, tunnels, and downtown buildings. The Sears Tower in Chicago, the Gateway Arch in St. Louis, the Space Needle in Seattle, and the Trans-America Pyramid in San Francisco all closed, as did landmarks like the Liberty Bell and Mount Rushmore.[29]

If nineteen religious fanatics armed with box cutters could hijack planes and kill nearly three thousand people, then volatile chemicals stored at factories, the web of underground oil and natural gas pipelines that crisscrossed the nation, and public water reservoirs could also become weapons.

New scares kept everyone on edge. At 11:00 p.m. on September 11, agents hustled President and Mrs. Bush and their two dogs and a cat to the secure bunker three floors beneath the East Wing of the White House, the president in running shorts, a t-shirt, and bare feet and Mrs. Bush in her robe. A plane headed down the Potomac River had not made radio contact. It turned out that the pilot had used the wrong radio frequency.[30] The next day, there was a bomb scare at the White House.[31] On October 7, Osama Bin Laden declared that "God has blessed a group of vanguard Muslims . . . to destroy America."[32]

A week later, a letter containing the deadly bacteria anthrax arrived in the office of the Senate majority leader, Tom Daschle. This was the first of several such letters sent to prominent individuals and organizations, including Tom Brokaw of NBC News, the *New York Post,* and Senator Patrick Leahy. At least twenty-two individuals contracted anthrax and five people died. On October 18, an alarm from White House sensors that suggested there was something toxic in the air turned out to be a false alarm. Then, on December 22, Richard Reid, a British citizen who had converted to Islam while in prison for petty crimes and trained at Al Qaeda camps in Afghanistan, attempted to ignite explosives packed in his shoe during a flight from Paris to Miami. At the time, it seemed possible that all these events were connected. Every morning, CIA briefers brought the president a threat matrix, often fifty or sixty items that reflected the increased threat reporting after the attacks.

The president took charge and showed personal courage. On September 11, he returned to the White House against Secret Service advice in order to address the nation from a familiar setting. On September 12, he visited the Pentagon, talked with the morgue team, and visited badly burned victims in the hospital. He flew to the scene of the attacks in New York and made an impromptu speech to rescue workers. Back in Washington, he personally chaired National Security Council meetings, rejecting Cheney's suggestion that he, the vice president, should do that.[33]

Secretary of Defense Rumsfeld emphasized later that the administration was improvising. There was no longer any road map for keeping Americans safe.[34]

The circumstances were indeed new, but by 2001 a generation of law and practice told presidents a great deal about how to respond to unexpected emergencies while protecting democratic values. A generation of national and international law governed the detention, interrogation, and trial of suspects; protected citizens against unreasonable intrusions into their daily lives; encouraged consultation within the executive branch; and provided oversight by Congress and the courts. Some rules dated from reforms introduced in the 1970s when an improbable chain of events revealed how secrecy had enabled presidents' abuses of power. Others reflected a growing determination by Congress, the courts, the legal community, and the media to provide oversight of the president's security judgments, and to protect civil liberties. Officials had taken new rules to heart, built in standards, trained staff, and hired lawyers to vet proposed actions. The spirit as well as the letter of accountability had become embedded in the culture of national security agencies. The leaders of the intelligence community had lived through the humiliation of exposed abuses twenty-five years earlier. When national security required secrecy, secrecy now required accountability.

National and international law provided settled answers to detention, trial, and interrogation of prisoners in times of war and peace. Individuals charged with committing federal crimes, whether citizens or noncitizens, were tried in criminal courts where they had a right to a lawyer, to be informed of the charges against them, to confront and question their accusers, and to be treated as innocent until proven guilty beyond a reasonable doubt. Soldiers charged with violating the laws of war could be tried before established military commissions. A uniform code of military justice required that such commissions provide most of the protections given to suspects in civilian courts.[35]

Under international law, nations could imprison fighters captured during armed conflicts without trial until hostilities ended, in order to keep them from returning to battle. Such prisoners, the Geneva Conventions stated, "must at all times be humanely treated . . . and protected, particularly against acts of violence or intimidation and against insults and public curiosity." In addition, "no physical or mental torture, nor any other form of coercion, may be inflicted on prisoners of war to secure from them information of any kind whatever. [They] may not be threatened, insulted," or exposed to other unpleasant treatment. Torture was defined as "any act by which severe pain or suffering, whether physical or mental, is intentionally inflicted on a person" to obtain information, punish, or coerce, when instigated or acquiesced in by a public official.

The Geneva Conventions, ratified by the Senate, had the force of law in the United States. Nearly two hundred countries, including Afghanistan, Iraq, Pakistan, and other members of the United Nations, had signed the agreements in the 1950s in response to the horrors of Nazi and Japanese abuses of prisoners during World War II. In 1994, Congress had added an anti-torture statute that made it a crime to inflict "physical or mental pain or suffering" on prisoners.[36]

In the past, most suspected terrorists had been tried in the nation's open criminal justice system and accorded the usual rights of defendants. The men accused of bombing the World Trade Center in 1993 had been found guilty of conspiracy, using a destructive device resulting in death, and other charges, and sentenced to 240 years in federal prison. They remained behind bars, several in a maximum security prison in Florence, Colorado.

Rules constructed in the 1970s protected Americans against secret government wiretapping, bugging, and physical searches that were not related to crimes and approved by the courts. They translated the Constitution's promise that "the right of the people to be secure in their persons, houses, papers, and effects, against unreasonable searches and seizures, shall not be violated" into practical restraints that protected Americans' privacy in their homes and daily activities. Respect for personal privacy from government intrusion was something Americans counted on. It supported creative work, useful protests, religious freedom, individual choices in everyday life, and freedom from racial or ethnic discrimination.

Intrusions, whether by police officers or wiretaps, required a court order confirming that there was a reasonable belief (in legal language, "a probable cause") that a suspect had committed a specific crime, and there were limits on a search's duration and scope. Congress had legislated special privacy protection for bank records, credit reports, phone records, and Internet use.

After Congress exposed intelligence agencies' political spying in the 1970s, Congress and President Ford had blocked the CIA and NSA from secretly collecting information about Americans, and limited the FBI's searches to criminal investigations. Agents could no longer improvise programs to spy on Americans as they had in earlier times. "Secrecy should no longer be allowed to shield . . . constitutional, legal or moral problems from the scrutiny of the three branches of government or from the American people themselves," Congress's Church Committee investigation of government secrecy had concluded in 1976.[37]

The Foreign Intelligence Surveillance Act (FISA) Court, created as part of those reforms, provided one institutional means of preserving essential secrecy while protecting citizens' constitutional rights. Its judges issued constitutionally required warrants for foreign-intelligence surveillance within the United States based on probable cause that the target was a foreign agent. To protect national security, the court generally met behind closed doors and issued confidential rulings. Congress built in layers of oversight by the attorney general and Congress.

Like other reforms, the court was not perfect. It lacked civil liberties advocates, sometimes responded slowly in emergencies, approved virtually all government requests, and operated behind closed doors as a rule rather than as an exception.

Rules from the 1970s held the president and senior officials responsible for the actions of government agents. Covert actions that once left CIA agents operating in foreign lands, free to improvise, now required formal presidential approval and reporting to Congress. FBI wiretaps once secretly ordered by J. Edgar Hoover or his agents now required a signoff by the attorney general. Such oversight meant many stops at lawyers' offices and policy shops on the way to the Oval Office—stops where questions could be asked.

But President Bush also inherited the remnants of dysfunctional Cold War secrecy. Everyone agreed that the broken classification system no longer protected either essential secrets or the public's right to know what the government was doing. As Justice Potter Stewart had noted in a concurring opinion in the Pentagon Papers case in 1971, "When everything is classified, then nothing is classified, and the system becomes one to be disregarded by the cynical or the careless, and to be manipulated by those intent on self-protection or self-promotion. . . . The hallmark of a truly effective internal security system would be the maximum possible disclosure, recognizing that secrecy can best be preserved only when credibility is truly maintained."[38]

Senator Moynihan's commission found that no one in or out of government any longer understood the classification of secrets. National security officials had added scores of categories to the simple "confidential," "secret," and "top secret" designations.[39] The commission recommended that this culture of secrecy be countered by a renewed "culture of openness," including laws that set time limits on classification, balanced public versus security needs, and required annual reporting of the dimensions of the nation's vast store of secrets.[40]

Actions by Congress and the Clinton administration had strengthened public access to government information. The Electronic Freedom of Information Act (E-FOIA) of 1996 required agencies to place policy statements, final opinions, and frequently requested documents in digital reading rooms. In an effort led by Vice President Al Gore, the administration declassified old spy-satellite footage and other valuable data, and directed agencies to provide information citizens needed without waiting for specific requests.[41]

During his peaceful early months in office, Bush assembled an experienced national security team and made plans to strengthen the presidency and expand government secrecy.

Most of the senior advisers he chose had lived through the embarrassing exposure of the intelligence abuses of the 1960s and 1970s, and had participated in the reforms that followed. His secretary of defense, Donald Rumsfeld, had championed the Freedom of Information Act in the 1960s and served under President Ford, who instituted restraints on secret security measures. Secretary of State Colin Powell had served as a White House fellow during the Nixon administration, and as national security adviser and chairman of the joint chiefs of staff during the 1980s. CIA director George Tenet had served on the staff of the Senate Intelligence Committee and as deputy director and then director of the CIA in the Clinton administration. Attorney General John Ashcroft, a former Missouri senator and governor, was less experienced in national security matters.

Michael Hayden, a four-star general who had risen through the ranks of the air force during the Cold War, would continue to head the NSA. He hoped to run a more open agency, revamp its computer technology, make more use of outside contractors, and convince the American people that agents were not the ruthless spies that Hollywood portrayed. "We couldn't survive with the popular impression of this agency being formed by the last Will Smith movie," he told CNN national security correspondent David Ensor in 2005.[42]

In the White House, Condoleezza Rice, a former provost of Stanford University and an expert on Europe and Russia after the Cold War, would serve as national security adviser. Richard A. Clarke, who had coordinated counterterrorism for eight years, would continue in the role of senior counterterrorism adviser.

Most of the president's team took away lessons of restraint from the abuses and reforms of their earlier years of public service. James Comey, who would serve as Bush's deputy attorney general and later as President Obama's FBI director, kept on his desk a copy of a threatening letter an FBI official sent to the civil rights leader Martin Luther King in 1964 as a reminder of past wrongdoing.

Vice President Cheney took away instead a determination to increase the power of the presidency and to demonstrate the president's authority to make decisions secretly and unilaterally, especially during times of emergency. He told reporter Cokie Roberts his main worry. "In 34 years, I have repeatedly seen an erosion of the powers and the ability of the president . . . to do his job."[43] "I am a firm believer in protecting the president's prerogatives," he wrote in his memoir, "especially when it comes to the conduct of national security policy." A foreign power could attack the United States with chemical, biological, or nuclear weapons. The president needed the authority to respond.[44]

Bush chose Cheney as his vice president in part because of Cheney's understanding of the military and international affairs, and gave him extraordinary responsibilities to oversee intelligence and national security matters. Cheney had represented Wyoming in Congress, served as President Ford's chief of staff, as Bush's father's secretary of defense, and had most recently run Halliburton, an international oil company. It was Cheney who would propose the president's most controversial secret measures, including the president's domestic surveillance program and new military commissions that did not provide terrorist suspects with the usual rights of criminal defendants.[45]

Bush and Cheney made an odd couple. The taciturn Cheney, age sixty, was analytical, rarely showed emotion, and had suffered four heart attacks.[46] Bush, fifty-five, liked action, was a garrulous master of meeting and greeting, showed flashes of temper, had limited patience with detail, and was relentless in his exercise routine.

"I'm not a textbook player. I'm a gut player," Bush told *Washington Post* reporter Bob Woodward during one of several interviews. Like Harry Truman, whom he admired, Bush trusted his instincts, made decisions quickly, and rarely looked back. Like Truman, he got along with almost everybody, used humor to deflect controversy, and tried to seem confident even when he was not. "If I weaken, the whole team weakens." Bush liked structure and tangible results. "I'm a baseball fan. I want a scorecard." After the attacks of September 11, Bush kept in his desk drawer in the Oval Office photos of the most wanted terrorists. He drew an X through the photo when the person was killed or captured.[47]

Bush had his father's political ambitions. George H. W. Bush had served as director of the Central Intelligence Agency, vice president, and president. But the younger Bush would say that he got his "mouth" from his outspoken mother.[48]

As a young man, Bush became a heavy drinker. He could not say for sure if he was an alcoholic. "I do know I have a habitual personality," he wrote in his memoir.[49] But as he matured, he also showed extraordinary discipline. He stopped drinking the day after his fortieth birthday party, became a devout Christian, read the bible every morning, and aimed to run seven-minute miles.[50]

In 2000, he campaigned for president as a "compassionate conservative" who would restore "honor and dignity" to the presidency after the scandals that led to President Clinton's impeachment. He cared about improving public education and helping working people gain financial security.

Bush came to office without foreign policy experience, and without a popular mandate. His Democratic opponent, Al Gore, had won the popular vote, and Bush had carried Florida by only 537 votes in the initial tally. In a controversial decision, the Supreme Court confirmed Bush's election. Both houses of Congress, too, were nearly evenly divided between the two parties: 223 Republicans, 211 Democrats, and 2 independents in the House, and 50 Republicans and 50 Democrats in the Senate, where Bush's vice president could cast the deciding vote. (On June 6, 2001, Democrats gained marginal control of the Senate when Republican James Jeffords of Vermont declared himself an independent.)[51]

But he did come to office with a plan to increase the power of the presidency, an agenda shared by some other conservatives who talked and wrote about a "unitary presidency." Bush and Cheney believed that sunshine laws and congressional checks had crippled the office. Cheney held the extreme view that neither Congress nor the courts had constitutional authority to examine information that the president wanted to keep secret. The president had the inherent power to act unilaterally and secretly, and should not share power that was rightfully his. The president could respond to emergencies unconstrained by Congress or courts. Cheney liked to invoke Alexander Hamilton's statement about the need for the president to act with "secrecy and dispatch." Others pointed out that early presidents used secrecy rarely and reluctantly, and only to protect sensitive negotiations and the government's agents. Bush and Cheney invoked secrecy as a matter of principle.[52]

Delivering an opening volley, Cheney provoked a constitutional crisis. He refused to provide congressional committees with information about a task force he chaired to create a new national energy policy. Openness would deprive the president of candid advice. The task force involved hundreds of government employees and held closed consultations with energy executives and lobbyists, including executives of Chevron, the National Mining Association, and the National Petrochemical and Refiners Association. It had been structured by Cheney's staff to avoid disclosure requirements, Peter Baker reported in *Days of Fire*. Cheney would not release even the names of its members.[53] The vice president's office told Congress's investigative arm, the General Accounting

Office (GAO), that the office "lacked statutory authority to examine [the task force's] activities." For the first time in its history, the GAO sued the executive branch. When a federal judge asked Cheney to provide documents to the court confidentially, Cheney argued in legal documents that the courts too lacked authority to review task force records.[54]

Cheney also showed an early inclination to skirt customary consultation within the administration. In March, he got the president to sign a four-page memo backing off from his campaign commitment to reduce carbon emissions, without informing either the head of the Environmental Protection Agency or the secretary of state, according to Barton Gellman in *Angler,* his account of the Cheney vice presidency.[55]

Over the still-peaceful summer, Ashcroft's staff went to work on a broader mission: to change the presumption of government openness to a presumption of confidentiality. When Bush took office, Clinton's order required agencies to provide information to the public unless they could show "foreseeable harm." Ashcroft's new policy allowed agencies to keep government information secret as long as there was a "sound legal basis" for doing so. Bush also issued an executive order allowing any current or future president to block the release of presidential records.[56]

These plans were well under way when two planes hit the World Trade Center towers on September 11. Responding to a national sense of urgency and his own commitment to increasing presidential power, Bush created new secret machinery to track down, capture, interrogate, and imprison terrorist suspects, to keep terrorists from getting information about vulnerabilities they might exploit, and to uncover terrorist networks in the United States and abroad. He believed he had the authority to do so as commander in chief and under Congress's general resolution to fight Al Qaeda. Actions addressed urgent problems. But the president limited not only public debate but also consultation with his knowledgeable advisers. Ultimately, secrecy failed to strengthen the presidency. Instead, reactions to secrecy led to new restraints, and Bush paid a high political price for ignoring time-tested policies.

Within twenty-four hours after the 2001 attacks, the Bush administration began removing from government websites public information about health and safety vulnerabilities that might be useful to terrorists. During the Cold War, the government had kept secret information about the location of missiles, the identities of intelligence agents, their means of gathering information, military plans, code-breaking technology, and spy satellite capabilities. There wasn't much direct conflict between these security measures and what the American people needed to know. But now almost anything could become a terrorist weapon. The same information that helped Americans avoid risks in their daily lives might help terrorists plan attacks.

The Department of Transportation removed from its websites maps of the nation's 2.2 million miles of oil and gas pipelines, maps that had been posted to keep construction crews and home owners from digging where ruptures might cause explosions. The Environmental Protection Agency removed information about past accidents and future risks at factories that handled dangerous chemicals. Energy regulators removed safety reports on power plants and on the transportation of hazardous materials. Airline regulators took down information about airport security breaches. The U.S. Geological Survey asked libraries to destroy information it had distributed about the characteristics of reservoirs. By one estimate, more than six thousand public documents were removed by March 2002.[57]

Ashcroft instructed agencies to restrict more broadly the release of information. Any documents should be made public only "after full . . . consideration of the institutional, commercial, and personal privacy interests." Bush's chief of staff urged agencies to consider keeping "sensitive" information secret even if it wasn't classified. Agencies could decide for themselves what was sensitive.[58]

Sweeping presidential orders gave many more officials authority to classify information as confidential, secret, or top secret. Bush added the Environmental Protection Agency, and the Departments of Health and Human Services and Agriculture, and, significantly, the vice president's office to the agencies that could classify information. He provided steps to reclassify open information, and delayed Clinton's order to declassify historically important documents.[59]

In May 2002, Ashcroft eliminated President Ford's restrictions that kept the FBI from engaging in political eavesdropping. His new guidelines allowed the FBI to secretly monitor political or advocacy groups for security threats without evidence of criminal conduct.[60]

Over time, Congress and international authorities had settled on legal processes to search for, interrogate, try, and imprison terrorist suspects, and those measures had been employed in earlier crises.

Instead of adapting them to the current emergency, Bush created entirely new rules. In the process, he abridged long-standing privacy protections without informing the public and without consulting with senior advisers. On October 4, 2001, the president signed a secret order drafted by the vice president's staff that allowed the NSA to monitor communications between individuals inside and outside the United States without the usual court review if there was a reasonable belief that one of the individuals had links to terrorism. Initially, Bush did not inform the intelligence court. The order had to be renewed every forty-five days, and officials would alert the FBI whenever Americans were swept up in the surveillance net. Congress had authorized the judges to issue individual warrants. But those procedures were ill suited to the scans of cellphones and emails that might uncover terrorist networks.

The NSA's director, Lieutenant General Michael Hayden, questioned whether the order was a good idea. Hayden pointed out that his agency could not afford to take many close pitches after the exposure of its abuses in the 1970s. Bush took the time to personally reassure Hayden in an Oval Office meeting. "I understand your concerns," the president said, "but . . . if there are things we could be doing, we ought to be doing them," *New York Times* reporter Peter Baker reported in *Days of Fire*. The president didn't need Congress's approval. He was the commander in chief, and Congress had given him authority to fight terrorism. Hayden introduced some limits. After consulting with NSA lawyer Bob Deitz, he asked that Congress be notified, and he limited new surveillance to exclude calls and emails when both parties were located inside the United States.[61]

Bush did not inform his secretary of state or his secretary of homeland security about this new surveillance program. He did not involve the lawyers in the national security agencies who would normally review the legality of new orders. Even Rumsfeld, to whom the NSA reported, was not told right away. Ashcroft was sworn to secrecy and asked to sign off on the program's legality the same day he was informed about it. The Foreign Intelligence Surveillance Court did not rule on the program until 2004.[62]

Cheney briefed eight congressional leaders, barring them from discussing the program with colleagues or aides. Senator Bob Graham, a Florida Democrat who chaired the Senate Intelligence Committee in 2001 and 2002, wrote later that such limited briefings gave senators no opportunity to prepare, consult with staff, take notes, or debate the issues. It would have been better, NSA director Hayden wrote later, to brief the full committees and some staff members.[63]

But secrecy didn't work as the president intended. His silence left the way open for troubled officials, civil liberties groups, and the media to seize the initiative. The public would learn about the government's surveillance of international communications four years later, but not from the president. James Risen and Eric Lichtblau reported in the *New York Times* in 2005 that "President Bush secretly authorized the National Security Agency to eavesdrop on Americans." The NSA, an agency banned from domestic spying, monitored "the international telephone calls and international e-mail messages of hundreds, perhaps thousands, of people inside the United States without the court-approved warrants." The NSA tapped directly into "some of the American telecommunication system's main arteries . . . [with] the cooperation of American telecommunications companies to obtain backdoor access to streams of domestic and international communications."[64]

The White House had warned the *Times* that publishing the article would endanger national security. Reporters and editors met multiple times with national security officials, and finally with the president himself in the Oval Office, Eric Lichtblau of the *New York Times* explained in *Bush's Law.* Bush wrote in his memoirs that he told them that the story would increase the danger to the nation. After fourteen months of meetings, additional reporting, and the prospect that the story would be published in Risen's book, the *Times* removed sensitive details and published the story.[65]

Next Bush had to decide how and where terrorist suspects would be held, what their rights were, whether and how to put them on trial, and how to find out what they knew. Again, these difficult issues had been resolved in established national and international frameworks. But, once again, the president circled around those frameworks to make new decisions behind closed doors, often without the advice of cabinet officials. He chose to hide suspects' identities, trials, imprisonment, transport, and interrogation.

Two months after the September 11 terrorist attacks, the president signed a secret order creating a new kind of military commission to try terrorists, without the advice of his national security or legal experts. The vice president's staff drafted the order hastily. Bush signed it as he prepared to board a helicopter on the south lawn of the White House on his way to his ranch in Crawford, Texas.

The president's military commissions would not follow the established code of military justice. Instead, the government could use classified information as evidence to convict suspects without telling them what the evidence was. It could use information from coerced confessions. Suspects would not have a right to know or confront their accusers. Commissions could hand out death sentences. There would be no court review.[66]

Condoleezza Rice, the president's national security adviser, wrote later that she had not seen the order and that Secretary of State Powell first heard about it on CNN. The president also had not asked his National Security Council for advice. Members of Congress and federal judges likewise were taken by surprise. Briefed on the order by the vice president shortly before Bush signed it, Attorney General Ashcroft argued unsuccessfully that the Justice Department, not the vice president's office, should be determining how prisoners would be tried.[67]

As the CIA began covert operations in Afghanistan, agents captured and interrogated hundreds of men suspected of links to Al Qaeda. The president often referred to those captured as if they had already been tried and convicted. Terrorists did not deserve the rights of common criminals.

In fact, some suspects did have religious commitments to Al Qaeda. But others had taken jobs with radical Muslim groups as drivers or farmers in order to make money. Still others had simply been in the wrong place at the wrong time. Many were in their twenties. The youngest were fifteen.[68] Naqib Ullah, one of the fifteen-year-olds, had no links to terrorism. Kidnapped in Afghanistan by a warring tribe affiliated with the Taliban while running an errand for his father, he was captured by U.S. forces and held at the Guantánamo Bay prison in Cuba for eight months "because of his possible knowledge of the Taliban resistance efforts and local leaders," according to the Defense Department transfer order. By 2014, five prisoners had died while in custody at Guantánamo. Four of those had committed suicide. Human Rights Watch estimated that fifteen suspects held there since the prison opened were under the age of eighteen.[69]

The president also authorized secret prisons that would operate outside the bounds of national and international law. With his support, the CIA sent suspects to prisons in Eastern European countries, Thailand, Morocco, and other locations. Again, key administration officials and members of Congress were not told about the program in advance or asked for their advice. Troubled officials talked to reporters, and the prisons became an odd kind of public secret. When Dana Priest of the *Washington Post* began reporting about them in 2005, the CIA still would not admit that they existed.[70]

Secrecy backfired. Unplanned revelations forced the president to change his detention policy. In a speech on September 6, 2006, five years after the first suspects were detained, Bush acknowledged that a small number of suspected terrorist leaders had been held and questioned by the Central Intelligence Agency in foreign lands. Many would now be transferred to the Guantánamo Bay detention center. Established in January 2002, the offshore prison was not intended to be subject to U.S. criminal laws. Prisoners could not question their detention and were not given the protections of the Geneva Conventions. More than seven hundred terrorist suspects would be imprisoned at Guantánamo over time.[71]

Bush also secretly approved harsh interrogation methods. They were justified, he wrote later, because there was a great risk that the country would be attacked without the information that suspects could provide. Again, he decided that the protections of the Geneva Conventions and anti-torture laws did not apply, based on secret Justice Department legal opinions. Bush believed that Richard Reid, the English citizen linked to Al Qaeda who attempted to light explosives hidden in his shoes on a commercial flight in December 2001, should have been interrogated instead of being given the traditional protections of criminal suspects. House and Senate intelligence committees were not briefed on the interrogation methods until September 2002.[72]

Even Bush's massive reorganization and expansion of the government's security apparatus was designed behind closed doors. The president sent five staff members to the emergency bunker three stories under the East Wing of the White House and told them they could not talk with anyone while they drafted plans for a new agency to oversee the nation's security, Peter Baker reported. They sketched on poster board a Department of Homeland Security that combined drug enforcement, aviation regulation, border patrol, the Secret Service, and emergency response officials.

Security was not at stake. Secrecy was expedient. The president needed to move quickly and wanted to avoid lobbying. He did not tell even his cabinet until the department plan was complete, months later. Bush's chief of staff called Rumsfeld the night before the announcement to give him a heads up that the Defense Department would be losing several agencies, according to Baker.[73]

The president's acceptance of inaccurate intelligence about Iraq's possession of nuclear and biological weapons dealt the most devastating blow to the administration's credibility. Compartmentalized information contributed to Bush's conclusion that President Saddam Hussein was using aluminum tubes to enrich uranium for nuclear weapons. Intelligence leaders did not give credence to nuclear scientists' statements and a secret Energy Department report in 2001 that the tubes were probably being used for other purposes. They were not persuaded by United Nations weapons inspectors' confirmation in December 2002, four months before the U.S. invasion, that suspected nuclear weapons sites hid only conventional artillery. The president himself had doubts. When briefed on the intelligence by CIA director George Tenet and his deputy on December 21, 2002, according to *Washington Post* reporter Bob Woodward's later account, Bush responded: "Nice try . . . it's not something that Joe Public would understand or would gain a lot of confidence from. . . . Is that the best we've got?" Tenet, who knew the most about the intelligence, then made the famous remark, "Don't worry, it's a slam dunk." He explained later that he had meant that improving the proposed public presentation of the intelligence was a sure thing.[74]

The Republican-led Senate Intelligence Committee concluded in 2004 that intelligence leaders did not explain to the president the many uncertainties about the programs. The committee found no indication that Iraq's government supported Al Qaeda. The committee vice chairman, Senator Jay Rockefeller, believed that Congress would not have supported the use of force in Iraq if members had known the truth. The nation's credibility among allies and its reputation among Muslims were damaged. Presidential briefer Michael Morell wrote later that a CIA analysis in June 2002 concluded that there was no evidence of any working relationship between Iraqi leadership and Al Qaeda before, during, or after the September 11 attacks, and that the president was aware of that analysis. But the National Intelligence Estimate in 2002 concluded that Iraq had active chemical and biological weapons programs and was reviving its nuclear weapons program. Bush wrote later that he believed the intelligence pointed overwhelmingly to the conclusion that the Iraq government was hiding nuclear or biological weapons. Looking back, Morell observed that the Iraq War supported the Al Qaeda narrative and helped spread the group's ideology.[75]

No nuclear, biological, or chemical weapons were ever found. The secrecy and deception surrounding the invasion of Iraq created an atmosphere of suspicion when the president most needed the nation's support. Suspicion, in turn, helped spur future probes by Congress and the media of the president's secretive programs, including his detention and interrogation of terrorist suspects and his electronic surveillance of Americans.

By the time Bush left office, it was clear that the president's attempts to hide fundamental policy changes had been counterproductive. Secrecy impaired consultation among advisers, deprived the president of opportunities to lead, and reduced the lasting legitimacy of his actions. Secrecy gave leakers, the media, and political opponents an opportunity to choose what, when, and how to make policies public, and to gain the public's attention. Without intending to, the president ceded power to government officials who took their opposition public, to the media that reported the stories, to members of Congress who investigated, to lawyers who brought suits, and to the courts that questioned his actions. When revelations were made without full understanding of their consequences, they could create new risks or bury serious security issues in partisan politics.

The president's secrecy added needless acrimony to important debates, left a trail of distrust, and staked out new limits on future presidents' emergency actions. Presidents could not unilaterally create new military commissions. They could not decree harsh interrogation methods. They could not deprive prisoners of their right to challenge their detention. As Supreme Court justice Sandra Day O'Connor wrote in a statement that resonated, a national emergency does not give the president a blank check when it comes to individual rights.[76]

It was the uncoordinated actions of individuals rather than an orderly process that led to these restraints. Government watchdogs, troubled officials, members of Congress, investigative reporters, lawyers in private practice, and liberal and conservative rights advocates revealed the president's secrets and challenged his authority. This ad hoc rebalancing was not automatic, and it had limits. By the time the president's actions were deemed improper, lives had been changed.

Glenn A. Fine, a college basketball star, Rhodes scholar, Washington lawyer, former prosecutor, and the Justice Department's inspector general, made public in June 2003 his detailed account of the mistreatment of the hundreds of Muslim men who were detained after the terrorist attacks. His 198-page report found that even those who were detained by chance were treated as if they had links to terrorism. The FBI made judgments about such links with little information and no court guidance. Individuals were held for an average of eighty days, and often were not informed of the charges against them for more than a month.

Some were subjected to physical and verbal abuse by corrections officers. In later investigations, Fine and his staff of four hundred probed the department's approval of harsh interrogation practices, the accuracy of FBI watch lists, methods used to collect personal information under the USA Patriot Act, and charges of civil liberties' violations.[77]

Congress had strengthened the independence of agencies' inspectors general in 1978 to guard against fraud and abuse of power. These officials were confirmed by the Senate, they reported to Congress as well as to agency heads, they had access to classified documents, they had court-enforced subpoena power, they could conduct searches and make arrests, and they could not easily be fired.[78]

John Helgerson, a political scientist and longtime CIA analyst who was the CIA's inspector general, began an investigation of the president's secret detention and interrogation practices in January 2003, after the CIA's general counsel told him that agents were using unauthorized interrogation methods, according to Jack Goldsmith, a senior Justice Department official. Helgerson's 109-page report in 2004, portions of which were declassified by President Obama five years later, confirmed that Bush had used "improvised, inhumane, and undocumented detention and interrogation." Helgerson referred more than a dozen CIA employees or contractors to the Justice Department for possible prosecution. Others received administrative reprimands or left the agency.[79]

Inspectors general from the Defense Department, the Justice Department, the NSA, the CIA, and the office of the Director of National Intelligence teamed up to review Bush's electronic surveillance programs. Their report in 2009 chronicled the legal questions raised by the Justice Department and the president's eventual agreement to limit the program.[80] In a now well-known story, acting attorney general James Comey, Justice Department attorney Patrick Philbin, and the new head of the Office of Legal Counsel, Jack Goldsmith, questioned the legality of a portion of the surveillance program in 2004. When they refused to reauthorize it, White House officials raced to the bedside of Attorney General Ashcroft, who was recovering from a life-threatening bout with pancreatitis at George Washington University Hospital, in an unsuccessful attempt to get him to approve the program's legality. When that didn't work, Bush signed the renewal anyway, Justice Department lawyers and FBI director Robert Mueller threatened mass resignations, and the president was forced to revise the program to satisfy the lawyers' objections.

Other Bush appointees questioned the president's secret programs when they tripped across them. Eric Lichtblau of the *New York Times* recounts some of these stories in *Bush's Law.* Senior lawyers in the Justice Department were not told about Bush's order in October 2001 that allowed the NSA to collect the phone and Internet records of Americans. When FBI agents discovered evidence that the NSA was conducting surveillance without the usual court orders, they questioned Mueller, who refused to provide information. When Bush's deputy attorney general, Lawrence Thompson, tripped across the NSA surveillance program, he was told he could not be informed about it. He simply stopped signing surveillance orders when he could not verify the source of information. Lichtblau wrote that James Ziglar, head of the Justice Department's Immigration and Naturalization Service, could not get the FBI to listen to his objections to secret detention of Muslim men without charges or lawyers after September 11. He resigned.[81]

By the beginning of Bush's second term, even the president's closest advisers had begun to see excessive secrecy as a problem. Condoleezza Rice, by then secretary of state, saw that the president's unacknowledged imprisonment and interrogation programs were creating problems with allies. "Ironically, one of the most debilitating aspects of these programs was the secrecy surrounding them," she wrote in a later memoir. "It was difficult to explain what we were doing and the protections that were in place if we couldn't acknowledge the basic facts." Bush's secret prisons were "having a corrosive effect on the nation's ability to secure intelligence cooperation."

Both Rice and Michael Hayden, who had recently become director of the CIA, wanted Bush to close the foreign prisons. Cheney objected. Bush finally rejected the vice president's view and announced in September 2006 that the prisons would be closed and suspects transferred to the Guantánamo Bay facility, but only after officials had leaked their existence and suspected interrogation techniques to the press. Rice's State Department staff also drafted a nine-page memo arguing that the Geneva Conventions' rules for humane treatment of prisoners should represent a minimum standard for terrorist suspects. She further proposed that the president seek congressional approval for detention policies.[82]

Given the opportunity, Congress showed that new terrorism policies could be arrived at through open debate. In the fearful days and weeks immediately after the September 11 attacks, Congress trimmed back the broad scope and unlimited resources the president asked for to fight a global war on terror, but granted the president much of what he had requested. Bush wanted authority to fight terrorism and aggression against the United States anywhere in the world, and asked for an open-ended financial commitment. Instead, on September 14, a bipartisan majority granted the president limited authority. He could use force only against "nations, organizations or persons he determines planned, authorized, committed or aided the terrorist attacks that occurred on September 11, 2001," with an initial appropriation of $40 billion.[83]

Days later, the president proposed the Patriot Act, to make it easier for the FBI to initiate investigations related to foreign espionage, and for officials to deport noncitizens for participating in suspect organizations. A sweeping provision required private organizations, including universities, bookstores, retailers, libraries, and charities, to secretly turn over customer records to government investigators when they were sought for a terrorist investigation, without probable cause and without opportunity for appeal. House and Senate leaders negotiated sunset provisions for the most controversial sections.[84]

Congress also approved a broad exception to open government that kept secret company-provided information about the risks and vulnerabilities of critical infrastructure to terrorist attacks, information that communities also needed. Critical infrastructure included communications, transportation, water supply, energy, or any other system when its destruction would have a debilitating impact on security, the economy, health, or safety. Senator Patrick Leahy of Vermont, a champion of government openness, called it "the most severe weakening of the FOIA [Freedom of Information Act] in its 36-year history."[85]

These laws expanded the president's authority, but they were policies that were openly arrived at. Debate about their terms fostered checks on their execution, and set off a decade of constructive modifications that provided increasing protection for individual rights during times of emergency.

Even when the president created new policies behind closed doors, Congress sometimes found ways to provide checks through its power to investigate and to control government spending. In November 2002, Congress created a bipartisan commission chaired by Republican Thomas Kean, former governor of New Jersey, and Democrat Lee Hamilton, a longtime member of the House, to probe the causes of the September 11 attacks and the president's responses. The commission staff reviewed more than two million documents, many of them

classified, interviewed more than one thousand individuals—virtually all of the
participants in national security decisions before and after the attacks—and
held nineteen days of public hearings. Its report described the specific intelligence flaws that made the September 11 attacks possible, asked that the intelligence budget be made public, and recommended that Bush's unilateral actions
be replaced with a common approach among allies for detention and treatment
of terrorism suspects based on the Geneva Conventions' requirements for
humane treatment. Less than three years after the 2001 attacks, Congress
outlined some midcourse corrections.[86]

Two early congressional actions suggested that the people's representatives
had limited tolerance for secret surveillance of Americans. In 2002, Congress
canceled Ashcroft's plan to recruit a million private volunteers—utility workers,
postal employees, and other public service workers—who would secretly report
to the Justice Department any suspicious behavior they observed, known as
Operation TIPS (Terrorist Information and Prevention System). Members
complained that the government was promoting citizen spying. Republican
House majority leader Dick Armey of Texas included language in the government's Homeland Security Act of 2002 to block the government's use of such
tipsters.

A year later, when Defense Secretary Rumsfeld launched a program to use
digital technology to combine information about credit card use, web browsing,
banking, drug prescriptions, medical records, and other government data in one
giant database to help identify terrorist networks, Democrats and Republicans
united to kill what Senator Ron Wyden of Oregon called "the biggest surveillance program in the history of the United States."[87]

Then, in 2005, when stories about secret prisons and inhumane treatment of
prisoners leaked out, a bipartisan majority led by Republican senator John
McCain of Arizona, himself a prisoner of war during the Vietnam conflict,
limited the president's secret interrogation techniques, banned torture, and
provided for court review of prisoners' status. An angry president considered
vetoing the bill despite a veto-proof majority in Congress. Instead, he issued a
cryptic signing statement. He would construe the act's requirements "in a
manner consistent with the constitutional authority of the president . . . and . . .
the constitutional limitations on judicial power."[88]

A later Senate investigation suggested that harsh interrogations amounting to
torture had contributed little or no essential information to stop future attacks.

Senate Intelligence Committee chairwoman Dianne Feinstein, a Democrat from California, released in December 2014 a summary report that disputed the president's claims that interrogation was humane and legal, and that extreme interrogation methods produced "unique, otherwise unobtainable information to stop terrorist attacks." The report remained controversial. John O. Brennan, the CIA director, argued that the agency had not misled the White House or Congress and that harsh interrogation had produced valuable intelligence. Critics pointed out that the investigation lacked interviews with participants and that Republican committee members did not participate.[89]

By 2001, federal courts had a long track record of reviewing executive decisions in order to protect civil liberties. In a series of rulings beginning in 2004, the Supreme Court limited the president's power to make secret and unilateral decisions about how to imprison and interrogate suspected terrorists. Justice Stephen Breyer discussed these cases in his 2015 book *The Court and the World*.[90]

The Court ruled that both citizens and noncitizens could challenge the government's claim that they were enemy combatants, something the Bush administration had resisted.[91] The justices then ruled that the president could not unilaterally create military commissions to try terrorists. The Constitution gave that authority to Congress. Requiring congressional action "does not weaken our Nation's ability to deal with danger," Justice Breyer wrote. "To the contrary, that insistence strengthens the Nation's ability to determine—through democratic means—how best to do so." The Court also ruled that Al Qaeda suspects were protected by the provision of the Geneva Conventions requiring humane treatment of prisoners—a momentous decision. Again, open deliberation forced policy change. The president sought congressional authorization for his unconventional military commissions, and the CIA and Defense Department made new rules to eliminate now-prohibited practices.[92]

After Congress authorized new military commissions, giving the president much of what he wanted, the Court ruled that even these new commissions were not valid, because they did not give suspects imprisoned at Guantánamo Bay an opportunity to challenge the commission's judgments in federal court.[93]

By constitutional design, courts usually act slowly. Judges have to await a case or controversy.[94] Often it takes many years for important issues to reach the Supreme Court. But in this instance, the actions of skeptical journalists, pro bono lawyers, advocacy groups, and lower court judges brought cases to the Supreme Court quickly, and the Court reaffirmed the importance of protecting civil liberties in times of trouble.

Secrecy also empowered the media. Within weeks of the September 11 attacks, senior members of the Bush administration were talking with reporters about the president's controversial actions. Officials have all sorts of reasons for talking about what they know, *Washington Post* national security reporter Dana Priest wrote with co-author William M. Arkin in *Top Secret America.* "Pride, angst, guilt, a need for praise, a desire to correct the record or to explain away something that sounds evil, or to save the agency from itself, or to stop wrongdoing."[95]

In October 2001, only a week after Bush signed a secret order, Bob Woodward was reporting in the *Washington Post* that the president had freed the CIA to undertake covert actions anywhere in the world in order to destroy Al Qaeda. Senior government officials told Woodward that "the gloves are off. The president has given the agency the green light to do whatever is necessary."[96]

At about the same time, reporter Seymour M. Hersh revealed in the *New Yorker* that an unmanned Predator drone armed with two Hellfire missiles had targeted a Taliban leader, Mullah Omar, in Afghanistan, but he had gotten away. It was the first reporting of the government's targeted killing with drones, a weapon that was ready for deployment only a few months before the September 11 attacks.[97]

A few months later, the *Washington Post* began to report on the secret transport of suspected terrorists to countries known for torture, and in 2003 investigative reporter Stephen Grey reported in the *New Statesman* and the Sunday *Times* of London about planes that flew suspects to far-off lands. Dana Priest revealed the CIA's network of secret prisons more fully in 2005.[98]

Journalists were embarrassed that they had not more closely questioned the administration's rationale for invading Iraq. In a retrospective note to its readers, *New York Times* editors said, "We wish we had been more aggressive in re-examining the claims as new evidence emerged. . . . Editors . . . were perhaps too intent on rushing scoops into the paper." The paper would continue "setting the record straight."[99]

In April 2004, the CBS television show *60 Minutes II* showed shocking photos of prisoner abuse at the Defense Department's Abu Ghraib prison in

Iraq. It was another instance of ad hoc accountability. Sergeant Joseph Darby of the 372nd Military Police Company, which provided prison guards, had seen the photos by chance on a compact disc given to him by another M.P., Charles Graner, who was later convicted of abusing prisoners and sentenced to ten years in prison. After agonizing about turning in his friends, Darby finally made copies of the photos and gave them to the army's criminal investigation unit. As the photos circulated more widely, a relative of one of the accused guards apparently provided them to CBS.

President Bush himself knew about the abuses at Abu Ghraib at least by March, when the army had completed an investigation. But they remained concealed until the photos became public on April 28. After the television broadcast, Bush attributed the mistreatment of prisoners to "a few people" rather than to more general problems of supervision or oversight. Eleven rank-and-file soldiers were convicted of various charges. The government did not prosecute senior officers or senior private contractors.[100]

Journalists benefit from the fact that a democratic government never speaks with a single voice. But revealing classified information is always controversial. The conflict between government secrecy and the free press that is built into the Constitution intensifies during times of emergency when the public needs to know about new dangers and the president's responses, and the government needs to keep secret information that might aid the enemy. There remained with each story the danger of revealing important facts that could increase risks to individuals or to the nation. Reporters worked "with sources who may be scared, who probably know only part of the story, who may have their own agendas that need to be taken into account," New York Times editor Bill Keller wrote in 2012. Reluctant to explain the specific need for concealment that might reveal more secrets, security officials often told reporters that disclosure of any classified information threatened national security, an answer that satisfied no one. Documents classified as top secret could be more important to public debate than to national security, as the Supreme Court had found in the 1971 Pentagon Papers case. Courts would remain the final arbiters of official secrecy versus free and independent reporting.[101]

We elect presidents to respond to the unexpected. In national emergencies, the president's unique aims and instincts matter. President Bush acted quickly during a time of fear and uncertainty in order to prevent more terrorist attacks.

His secrecy was not motivated by personal gain. He believed that the measures he adopted were essential to protect the nation. To circumstances that called for action, he added his inclination to make quick decisions, his impatience with debate and cumbersome reviews, and his personal determination to increase presidential dominance.

An enduring lesson of the Bush years was that the president could no longer hide unilateral actions for decades, as presidents had sometimes done during the Cold War. Everything was speeded up in the digital age. Secrecy led to abuses, as it had in the past. But this time senior officials, Congress, the courts, the media, and liberal and conservative advocates quickly revealed and challenged hidden decisions. Open debate made secret prisons untenable, brought interrogation under legal restraints, and reduced the conflicts between surveillance and privacy. Individually, revelations were idiosyncratic, sometimes created new risks, and often occurred too late to prevent harm. But collectively, they continued the process of re-embedding the president's secret actions in the constitutional framework of checks and balances.

Excessive secrecy exposed the president to unpredictable revelations, deprived him of opportunities for leadership, and imposed a high political cost. Bush left office believing that his proudest accomplishment was the prevention of more large-scale terrorist attacks. He also left office with a final approval rating of 22 percent. Secrecy had deprived him of the nation's most powerful aid to security—the trust and assistance of the American people. Bush himself came around to the view that he could have avoided some of the controversy and legal setbacks if he had sought legislation at the outset for military commissions, new surveillance, and interrogation methods.[102]

By any measure, secret programs had expanded rapidly during Bush's time in office. In 2009, it remained uncertain whether Congress and the courts could oversee the new generation of security programs that operated behind iron gates and locked doors. The CIA had become a paramilitary organization that assisted foreign anti-terrorist operations and targeted suspects with armed drones. The Defense Department operated military commissions to try terrorists and maintained the prison at Guantánamo Bay, where nearly three hundred suspected terrorists remained in legal limbo. The department's National Security Agency monitored digital communications and developed cyber-weapons. The FBI exercised broad investigative powers. In all, something like 265,000 contractors did intelligence work. Reporter Dana Priest called the institutions and programs "a parallel top secret government."[103]

President Barack Obama inherited the struggle against terrorism and Bush's policies. He would have to decide what to keep, what to discard, and what to tell the American people.

8

Barack Obama: A Twenty-First-Century Bargain?

Eight years after the terrorist attacks of 2001, Barack Obama became the first president to fully confront the challenges of openness and secrecy in the digital age. As threats evolved and technology advanced, he promised to anchor counterterrorism policies in law and ensure oversight by Congress and the courts. But secretive oversight of secretive policies was no longer enough. When fragments of information leaked out about targeted killing with armed drones, the deployment of offensive cyberweapons, and myriad programs of electronic surveillance, secrecy itself became the issue. Belatedly, Obama showed how a president can lead an open debate about stealth programs without revealing operational secrets.

ON JANUARY 20, 2009, SHORTLY AFTER NOON on a frigid, sunny Tuesday, Barack Hussein Obama delivered his inaugural address to a crowd of nearly two million from the steps of the Capitol. Another 38 million Americans watched at home. The nation was still in crisis, threatened by "a far-reaching network of violence and hatred." But the new president rejected "the false choice between our safety and our ideals." Obama reminded his audience that the Constitution, adopted during a time of "perils we can scarcely imagine," nonetheless upheld "the rule of law and the rights of man." Even in times of emergency, government must respect Americans' rights.[1]

It was a theme he would return to often. Four months later, on May 21, he delivered his first major national security address from the rotunda of the National Archives in Washington, D.C., where copies of the Constitution and the Declaration of Independence were displayed in glass cases.[2] He promised that his administration would protect both security and liberty, both essential secrets and open government, in a time when "technology gives a handful of terrorists the potential to do us great harm."

He distanced himself from the hasty decisions of the past that were based on fear. "I've studied the Constitution as a student, I've taught it as a teacher, I've been bound by it as a lawyer and a legislator. I took an oath to preserve, protect, and defend the Constitution as Commander-in-Chief. . . . I believe with every fiber of my being that in the long run we also cannot keep this country safe unless we enlist the power of our most fundamental values."

He promised that "whenever possible, my administration will make all information available to the American people so that they can make informed judgments and hold us accountable. But the most sensitive national security measures—defending our troops at war, protecting sources and methods, safeguarding confidential actions to keep the American people safe—cannot simply be an open book. . . . Whenever we cannot release certain information to the public for valid national security reasons, I will insist that there is oversight of my actions—by Congress or by the courts. . . . When I release something publicly or keep something secret, I will tell you why."[3]

Here was a clear statement that extended the 1970s oversight of presidents' security policies, and affirmed that the unfettered secrecy that characterized much of the Cold War and that President Bush found expedient had indeed come to an end. Instead of hidden executive action based on public ignorance, secrecy, when it was essential, would be based on oversight by the people's elected representatives and by independent judges sworn to uphold the law. But as Obama took office, oversight often remained a matter of closed hearings, secret court proceedings, classified assessments, and reflexive deference to executive action. Many of the controversies of the next eight years would test whether oversight could be made more fair, open, and independent.

However, Obama did not address in his speech what would become the most consequential secrecy issue during his years in office: whether presidents in the twenty-first century were obliged to lead an open debate about proposed policies that affected Americans' rights and expectations—however secretive those policies' operational details might be. As Obama and his advisers would learn by trial and error, failure to foster a consensus about such policies in advance led to political trouble later. Better-educated, more skeptical, more information-savvy citizens expected new surveillance programs and new weapons to be grounded in public understanding, not in an assumption that the American people could be kept in the dark.

For a while, these issues were obscured by immediate crises. In addition to terrorism threats and digital challenges, Obama inherited a collapsing domestic economy; armed conflicts in Iraq and Afghanistan; the threat of nuclear weapons programs in Iran, North Korea, and Pakistan; the prospect of war in the Middle East; and aggressive moves by nationalistic regimes in Russia and China. "It is hard to think of a president who entered office facing more challenges of historic magnitude than Obama," Robert M. Gates, secretary of defense, wrote in *Duty,* his 2014 memoir.[4]

The financial crisis only increased Americans' sense of helplessness and distrust of government. To many, the economic crisis looked like another case of decisions made behind closed doors that adversely affected their everyday lives. It made little difference whether the closed doors were those of big government or big banks. The president acknowledged that it was both. Irresponsible decisions by Wall Street executives, little government oversight, and thoughtless government spending led to a crisis "largely of our own making."[5]

Two weeks after he took office, Obama's new director of national intelligence, Dennis Blair, told the Senate intelligence committee that the growing economic crisis had become "the primary near-term security concern" for the United States—more urgent than terrorism.[6]

Fourteen million people were unemployed. The nation's credit markets were failing. A million families had lost their homes in 2008, and another two million were threatened with foreclosure. The government surplus of $200 billion at the start of the Bush administration had become a deficit of more than $1 trillion, as Bush had waged wars in Iraq and Afghanistan and spent nearly $3 trillion responding to terrorist attacks.[7]

Obama also inherited a terrorism threat that had become more complicated. Bush's actions had disrupted Al Qaeda's leadership. Of the twenty-two suspects whose photos Bush kept in his desk drawer in the Oval Office, five had been killed and three had been captured. Al Qaeda's core remained small, perhaps a few hundred zealots. But there were now thousands of loosely affiliated Islamic militants. A new generation of young men, some of them radicalized by the American bombs, missiles, or prison abuses, hid in Afghanistan, Pakistan, and Yemen, perhaps in Nigeria, Libya, Syria, Mali, and Iraq, and perhaps also in the

United States. Obama suggested that "Guantánamo likely created more terror-ists around the world than it ever detained."[8]

A threat at the inauguration itself provided a reminder that the government still viewed Americans as passive recipients of, instead of participants in, their security. Intelligence indicated that a group of radical Somali terrorists entering the United States from Canada might be planning to set off explosives during the ceremony. It turned out to be a false alarm—perhaps one radical Somali group inventing information about a rival group, officials concluded. Spectators at the inauguration, who could have been at risk or could have provided useful information if the threat had been real, were told nothing.[9]

In times of tumultuous change, the president's aims and instincts take on outsized importance. The most important differences between George W. Bush and Barack Obama were not in their age, their background, their race, or their political party. The most important differences were in the way they approached problems, and in their views of presidential power and presidential secrecy.

Bush was a man of action, impatient with debate and inclined toward secrecy. His unusual determination to increase the president's power was reinforced by his vice president, Richard Cheney. Obama was deliberative, inclined to seek opposing views, and committed to anchoring policies in law. His professors at Harvard Law School remembered a confident, centered student who listened and found common ground, his biographer David Remnick wrote in The Bridge. He talked about law as a long-running conversation, a nation arguing with itself. After working as a community organizer, he taught constitutional law at the University of Chicago, and served as a state senator and then a U.S. senator from Illinois. He would be criticized for his intellectual approach to problems, for taking too long to ponder decisions, for perpetuating some of his predeces-sor's policies, and for his own acceptance of traditional secrecy.[10]

Virtually all of the new president's national security team had participated in the reforms of the 1970s that limited presidents' secrets. General Robert Gates, who continued as secretary of defense, had served in the CIA and then joined the National Security Council staff in 1974. Leon Panetta, Obama's CIA director and then secretary of defense, had served in the House of Representatives as a Democrat from California when Congress placed legal limits on secrecy in the 1970s. General Keith B. Alexander, who would continue as head of the NSA, was a four-star general with a long career in army intelligence. Attorney

General Eric Holder had prosecuted government officials for corruption as a Justice Department attorney in the 1970s and 1980s. FBI director Robert Mueller, who led a rifle platoon in Vietnam, had prosecuted fraud and corruption cases as a U.S. attorney and had headed the Justice Department's criminal division. John Brennan, a twenty-five-year CIA official who had headed Bush's national counterterrorism center, became Obama's counterterrorism adviser. The director of national intelligence, James Clapper, was a longtime air force intelligence officer who had also served in the Bush administration.

Faced with multiple crises, the president chose to spend his first full day in office emphasizing his commitment to open government. He directed agencies to presume openness when responding to requests for government information under the Freedom of Information Act, reversing Bush's presumption of secrecy.[11] He sent a memo to federal agencies committing his administration to an unprecedented level of openness. He ordered government-wide steps to put information online in user-friendly ways, create new opportunities for the public to participate in policy making, and develop digital tools for collaboration within government and with the private sector. He followed up with instructions to agencies that led to the release of hundreds of thousands of digital data sets.[12]

On his second day in office, he announced a variety of measures to anchor counterterrorism policies in national and international laws. He declared the United States would be bound by the international Geneva Conventions that required the humane treatment of terrorist suspects, limited interrogations to army field manual rules, gave the Red Cross access to jailed suspects, and suspended Bush's special military commissions that had reduced suspects' rights.[13]

He exposed one of the secrets Bush had tried hardest to protect. He declassified Justice Department memos that had provided legal arguments to justify harsh interrogation of terrorist suspects. He did so, he said, in order to anchor the inflammatory debate about torture with facts, provide closure to a painful episode, and preempt a court order. He also created a national declassification center to systematically open documents twenty-five years old or older, ordered agencies to review their classification guidance to employees and contractors, and set in motion practices that substantially reduced new classifications.[14]

Openness did not always produce the results the president wanted. Obama affirmed Bush's decision to close the CIA's secret prisons, promised to review the status of captured suspects, and proposed trying as many prisoners as possible in federal courts, where they would have the usual rights of criminal defendants. By transferring others to maximum security prisons in the United States that held earlier terrorists, it would be possible to close the Guantánamo Bay prison within a year.[15]

But now that detention policies could be openly debated, Congress stopped the president from transferring suspected terrorists to federal prisons in the United States, effectively frustrating his plans to close the Guantánamo Bay facility. In July 2016, more than four hundred persons tried and convicted of crimes related to terrorism were held in federal prisons around the country, and seventy-six suspects remained imprisoned at Guantánamo Bay, of whom twenty-seven were eligible to be transferred.[16]

Then, on Christmas Day of 2009, an unsuccessful terrorist attack provided a reminder of the difficulty of changing old secrecy habits within the government. Intelligence agencies had updated technology to track millions of leads. Computer programs could sort through them. But the sheer volume of information was daunting, the Cold War practice of compartmentalizing incoming intelligence was hard to break, and human judgment still trumped technology.

A twenty-three-year-old Nigerian, Umar Farouk Abdulmutallab, boarded Northwest Airlines flight 253 from Amsterdam to Detroit with 290 people aboard. As the plane approached Detroit, he tried to ignite explosives hidden in his underwear. They malfunctioned and caused a small fire. He was tackled by a vigilant passenger and restrained by flight attendants.

The incident underscored the difficulty of piecing together any meaningful fragments of intelligence to prevent future large-scale attacks. Intelligence agencies had not shared shards of information that could have prevented the attack. Umar's father, a prominent banker, had phoned the American embassy in Abuja, Nigeria, to report that his son might have joined a radical Islamic group, but the son's name had not been added to the FBI database for no-fly lists, and immigration authorities had not revoked his U.S. visa.[17]

Informed while vacationing with his family in a rented beachfront house in Kailua near Honolulu during the Christmas holidays, the president did not try to hide the intelligence failure. He told the press: "There were bits of information available within the intelligence community that could have and should have been pieced together. . . . A systemic failure has occurred, and I consider that totally unacceptable."[18]

Abdulmutallab's conviction did show that the openness and customary protections of the criminal justice system could be applied to terrorists. He pleaded guilty in federal court to conspiracy to commit an act of terror and attempted use of a weapon of mass destruction, was sentenced to life in prison, and was transferred to the maximum security prison in Florence, Colorado, where other convicted terrorists were serving their sentences.[19]

Digital technology made it easier for intelligence agencies to share information, at least in principle. But it also made it easier to steal secrets. The same advances that enabled government officials to obtain and process gigabytes of data to search for terrorists also made it possible for disgruntled officials, hackers, spies, or criminals anywhere in the world to copy gigabytes of government secrets. Digital theft proved particularly hard to trace and hard to stop.

It became a frequent event. The Defense Department was attacked many times a day, Gates wrote in his memoir. Attacks on the government's computers to steal data provided no warning. The department had protected its networks. But "the country remains dangerously vulnerable to cyberattack."[20]

In 2015, digital thieves repeatedly broke through the government's shields. The White House disclosed that Russian agents had gained access to some of the president's unclassified emails as well as those of the White House staff. Hackers with suspected links to the Chinese government stole the Social Security numbers, addresses, and health and financial records of 19.7 million individuals who had received government background checks in the past fifteen years, along with the records of 1.8 million of their spouses and friends. A separate theft targeted 4.2 million government employees. U.S. officials expressed concern that records could reveal the identities of intelligence agents posted in China over the years. Sony Corporation, JPMorgan Chase, and other companies also were targeted with massive attacks. In 2016, hackers stole from a law firm in Panama more than 11 million files that revealed the secret offshore bank accounts of more than 14,000 private clients, including more than a hundred public officials around the world.[21]

The Internet also connected violent extremists around the world. Loosely organized groups routinely used digital technology to recruit followers who launched attacks in Middle Eastern and North African countries, and in the United States. Al Qaeda had long featured an Internet presence to promote its cause. But ISIS, or the Islamic State, became more expert in using digital messages and videos to inspire extremists and frighten potential victims. In October 2014, a man inspired by ISIS attacked four police officers in Queens, New York. In May 2015, two men linked to ISIS through social media shot at police officers in Garland, Texas. In June, an ISIS recruit who planned to attack police officers was killed in a confrontation with Boston police. In July, an electrical engineer with ties to extremists killed five people at two military bases in Chattanooga, Tennessee. In August, an ISIS-affiliated organization published a spreadsheet targeting 1,400 U.S. marines as well as State Department, air force, FBI, and other government personnel. In December, a young husband and wife inspired by ISIS killed fourteen people and seriously injured twenty-one at a public health department holiday party in San Bernardino, California. Breaking its code of silence about offensive cyberweapons in 2016, the administration announced the use of such weapons against ISIS.[22]

Experts feared that in future scenarios, terrorists or hostile nations could spread false information or shut down power grids, air traffic control systems, or other infrastructure. In a small preview, hackers tied to Islamic extremists briefly commandeered the social media accounts of the U.S. Central Command in January 2015, sent out their own tweets, and replaced the Command's Twitter banner with "I love you ISIS." In December, a cyberattack perhaps planned in Russia cut off electrical power to 225,000 Ukrainians, leading the Obama administration to warn that such attacks could be launched against the U.S. electrical grid, water supply systems, or transportation controls.[23]

Advances in the collection, storage, and communication of data also disrupted the customary formal and informal means of resolving conflicts between media and government. Digital technology made it easy for government employees or contractors to steal large quantities of documents, and to instantly self-publish to an international audience. The usual restraints imposed by officials, editors, and courts didn't work anymore.

In the past, it took a lot of work to copy secret documents. Daniel Ellsberg, a government contractor who sought to expose a top-secret history of the Vietnam War in 1970, began copying and collating forty-seven volumes of the Pentagon Papers one page at a time. When he used commercial copiers, he sat in a coffee shop, cut off the top-secret heading from each page, and paid ten cents a page for photocopying. In order to reach a large audience, Ellsberg had to convince others—members of Congress, newspaper editors, and ultimately the Supreme

Court—that the public value of those top-secret documents outweighed national security concerns.[24]

Traditionally, courts were the final arbiters of clashes between national security secrecy and press freedom. Media organizations had their own processes for weighing the harm that might be caused by publishing classified information, sometimes meeting with government officials, removing sensitive details, or delaying publication. But the government could also ask a judge to stop publication. The Nixon administration had done that in 1971 when the *New York Times* prepared to publish the Pentagon Papers. In that case, when the Supreme Court denied the government's request to block publication, Justice Potter Stewart suggested that only "direct, immediate, and irreparable damage to our nation or its people" could justify such prior restraint.[25]

But none of these accommodations work in a world where insiders can self-publish top-secret information on the Internet with no filters and no advance notice, and can operate beyond U.S. borders—and beyond U.S. laws. In 2010, army private Bradley Manning (later Chelsea Manning), stationed in Iraq, copied more than 250,000 State Department cables, airstrike videos, and soldiers' reports from Afghanistan and Iraq over a six-month period. Manning came to work with music on CDs, he explained later, then erased the music and replaced it with secret documents. He said at trial that he was revealing the true cost of war.[26]

Manning provided the documents to WikiLeaks, itself a secretive organization that claimed to expose oppressive regimes and to reveal alleged unethical behavior by governments, led by an eccentric computer programmer from Australia. WikiLeaks in turn gave some of the documents to the mainstream international press, *Der Spiegel, El País,* and the *Guardian* (whose editors shared them with the *New York Times*), all media organizations accustomed to vetting classified documents before publishing stories.

New York Times editor Bill Keller explained that reporters removed names of ordinary citizens, local officials, activists, academics, and others who had spoken to American soldiers or diplomats and took out any information about intelligence-gathering methods, weapons, or tactics.[27]

WikiLeaks, however, also posted directly on its website documents that created threats to security and privacy. Reports from Afghanistan and Iraq included the names, villages, or relatives of dozens of Afghan informants who were cooperating with American troops. That information became instantly available to terrorist groups and hostile governments.[28]

Some disclosures were simply embarrassing. Hillary Clinton asked diplomats to find out if Argentina's president took pills for her mood swings. Prince Andrew made rude remarks about Americans. But the disruption of confidential communications could interfere with allies' cooperation. "Individually, the disclosures are trivial. . . . But collectively, they are corrosive," the *Economist* concluded.[29]

Turned in by an online acquaintance, Manning pleaded guilty and was convicted in a military court-martial on multiple charges of theft and disclosure of classified documents. He was sentenced to thirty-five years in prison, eligible for parole in seven years, and imprisoned at Fort Leavenworth in Kansas.

Three years later, in 2013, an NSA contractor, working as a computer system administrator for Booz Allen Hamilton in an office building in Honolulu, Hawaii, used widely available software to copy nearly two million classified NSA documents. They revealed secret government surveillance programs, a United States role in a cyberattack against an Iranian nuclear facility, and the budgets of sixteen U.S. intelligence agencies. They also revealed 160,000 personal communications in emails and instant messages, among them medical records and photos of children.[30]

Edward Snowden, twenty-nine, the son of a Coast Guard officer and a federal court clerk who grew up in a Washington, D.C., suburb, said his purpose was to inform the public about what was done in their name. He provided the documents to Glenn Greenwald, a columnist for the London-based *Guardian* newspaper; Laura Poitras, a documentary filmmaker; and Bart Gellman, a journalist who wrote articles for the *Washington Post* based on the documents. Snowden then revealed that he was the source of the leak, was charged with theft and espionage, and fled, eventually becoming stranded in Russia when his passport was revoked.[31]

Faced with these new threats to security, the Obama administration took six steps. Each raised questions about the future of open government in the digital age. The administration issued new transparency principles for the intelligence community, limited employees' and contractors' access to secret information, encouraged whistleblowers to report to officials rather than the press, instituted insider-threat measures to identify likely leakers, searched for reporters' sources, and prosecuted officials who disclosed classified information. Each step exposed conflicts among enduring values.

Honing digital tools to limit employees' access to secret information clashed with the administration's broader information-sharing objectives. Encouraging troubled officials to report complaints to their bosses collided with the public interest in exposing illicit activities. The insider threat program to identify potential leakers interfered with employees' privacy and invited abuse. The president's order told employees to watch one another for "high-risk behavior." Agencies' follow-up instructions could be exploited by overzealous officials to unjustly target workers. The Education Department, for example, asked employees to watch for signs of stress, including financial or marital problems, that might turn a loyal employee into a threat. The Defense Department's strategy explained that leaking was tantamount to siding with the enemy.[32]

Finally, the administration's use of digital tools to identify and prosecute reporters' sources set off new controversies. In 2013, Justice Department officials admitted obtaining an order to secretly search the phone records of Associated Press (AP) reporters in order to find the source of a leak. Reporters had written that the government was analyzing an explosive device taken from terrorists in Yemen who were planning to blow up a commercial airliner. Officials feared the leak would expose to those terrorists intelligence sources and methods. A White House spokesman said the president had no knowledge of the search of AP's records. In an unrelated action, the Justice Department named a Fox News reporter as a co-conspirator to gain court approval to search his communications related to reporting of North Korea's nuclear tests.[33]

Criticized by journalists and free-speech advocates, President Obama and Attorney General Holder backtracked. "I'm troubled by the possibility that leak investigations may chill the investigative journalism that holds government accountable," Obama said in a speech at the National Defense University in May 2013.[34] Holder issued new guidelines that promised advance notice of searches of journalists' phone or Internet records, and limited those searches to criminal cases. He also promised that no reporter doing his or her job would go to jail. The Justice Department also dropped a controversial effort to order *New York Times* reporter and book author James Risen to reveal sources. In 2015, the House signaled bipartisan concern by appending to an appropriations bill a provision to prevent courts from compelling any reporter to testify about confidential sources. Forty-nine states already had some kind of shield law.[35]

During Obama's two terms in office, the Justice Department charged nine individuals with violating anti-theft laws, including Woodrow Wilson's outdated Espionage Act, which had been intended to punish traitors. Two related to investigations left over from the Bush administration. Two more related to the massive digital theft of documents by Manning and Snowden. The disparity in sentences, ranging from probation and community service to thirty-five years in prison, underscored the need for new laws and better calibrated penalties.[36]

Meanwhile, a double standard hurt the government's credibility. In 2013, senior officials' old habit of themselves providing information to the media when it served their interests created an absurd scenario that highlighted the broken system of classifying secrets. Congress tried to stop such "authorized disclosure of national intelligence" by requiring officials to tell the intelligence committees each time they gave classified information to the media. The NSA refused because, the agency said, the list of authorized leaks was classified. Revealing it would do "exceptionally grave damage to national security."[37]

Controversies surrounding President Obama's attempt to keep hidden three momentous policies provided dramatic evidence of the clash between traditional secrecy and the public's new expectations about open debate. The president followed his predecessor's lead in remaining silent about ground rules for targeted killings with unmanned drones, deployment of offensive cyberweapons, and the government's storage and search of Americans' phone records.

The resolution of these controversies suggested possible elements of a new consensus. First, it became clear that protection of operational secrets was becoming both more important and more difficult. Second, amid acrimony and partisan politics, congressional and court oversight was generally becoming more open, fair, and rigorous as secretive programs grew and flaws in accountability were revealed. Finally, secrecy about policy changes simply didn't work—for the president, for the Congress, for the courts, or for the public. Each time the president attempted secrecy, he lost opportunities for leadership, sacrificed public trust, and ceded the timing and substance of revelations to insiders and outsiders who had an imperfect understanding of both facts and consequences. The legitimacy of new initiatives that altered Americans' rights or the nation's safety depended on public debate, however secretive their operations.

Step by step, Obama expanded and legitimized Bush's program of targeted killing of suspected terrorists with missiles launched from unmanned drones. The CIA and the Defense Department deployed these weapons in nations with which the United States was not at war, without fostering a debate among

Americans or in the international community about when and how they should be used, or accounting for their consequences. By 2016, China, Iran, Iraq, Israel, Nigeria, Pakistan, Somalia, South Africa, United Arab Emirates, and the United Kingdom all had armed drones. France, Greece, India, Italy, Russia, Spain, Sweden, Switzerland, Taiwan, and Turkey were developing them. In essence, the president had taken the lead in changing the terms of international conflicts without revealing what the new terms were.

When Bush urged the president-elect to continue the program, Obama learned exactly how the CIA and the Defense Department were using a new and controversial weapon. A "pilot" sitting at a console in the CIA's headquarters in Langley, Virginia, or at an air force base could kill an unarmed terrorist suspect anywhere in the world with a missile fired from an unmanned drone. Predator drones looked like small, windowless airplanes that could travel more than seven hundred miles to a target, hover overhead for twenty hours or more, and fire two Hellfire missiles. Drones were not new to the military. They had been used for reconnaissance during the Clinton administration, but President Bush had inaugurated their deployment for targeted killing shortly before the September 2001 terrorist attacks.[38]

He ordered targeted strikes in Yemen, in military actions in Iraq and Afghanistan, and, after a secret agreement in 2004 with Pakistan's president, in that country as well. Such attacks were classified by the CIA as covert actions. Covert actions required secrecy. Only congressional leaders were informed. By the time he left office, Bush had ordered more than forty strikes outside military zones in Iraq and Afghanistan, virtually all in Pakistan. Michael Hayden, director of the NSA and then the CIA, wrote later that targeted killing had become a core part of the American way of war.[39]

Obama expanded strikes in Pakistan, Yemen, Afghanistan, Somalia, Iraq, and Syria, without disclosing the criteria for choosing individuals to kill, the effectiveness of strikes, or civilian casualties. He also authorized strikes to disrupt terrorist activities when the identities of those on the ground were unknown. By 2016, the CIA and the air force had conducted more than a thousand strikes. By one estimate, 2,378 militants, 293 civilians, and 233 persons of unknown affiliations had been killed by U.S. drones in Pakistan through March 2016, and 992 militants, 90 civilians, and 44 persons of unknown affiliation in Yemen, meaning that 16 percent were either civilians or of unknown affiliation, if those numbers are correct.[40]

Former officials and allies questioned both the program and its secrecy. Richard Haass, president of the Council on Foreign Relations and a former State Department official, predicted that "dozens of governments as well as militias, gangs, cartels and terrorist groups will come to possess them." Drone policy should be based on "public discussion, not ... classified memorandums."[41] Former secretary of defense Robert Gates wrote that "war has become for too many ... a kind of arcade video game ... bloodless, painless, and odorless."[42] A former CIA chief legal officer noted that it was ironic that it was "far less legally risky ... to stalk and kill a dangerous terrorist than ... to capture and aggressively interrogate one."[43] The European Parliament condemned the United States' targeted killing.[44]

But secrecy blocked debate. Congressional leaders were informed confidentially about the CIA's strikes, as required by law for covert actions, but without meaningful opportunities to question the ground rules. When Americans had openly debated targeted killing in the 1970s, President Ford had ordered that "no employee of the United States Government shall engage in, or conspire to engage in, political assassinations." Americans needed to hear the president's rationale for distinguishing drone strikes from assassinations.[45]

The issue became more complicated in 2011 when Obama authorized a drone strike to kill an American citizen, Anwar Al-Awlaki, in Yemen. Officials said that Al-Awlaki led operations for Al Qaeda in the Arabian Peninsula and helped plan attacks, including the December 2009 attempt by a young Nigerian to set off explosives on a Detroit-bound commercial flight. Within the administration, a robust debate continued. But the White House did not release the Justice Department's legal justification for the strike for another three years.[46]

Drone attacks became a strange kind of public secret. Reporters wrote about them. Members of Congress talked about them. Citizens debated their use. Watchdog organizations attempted to track civilian casualties. But the president and his national security advisers did not acknowledge the strikes, and provided no accounting of targeted suspects or civilians killed. The upshot was a crippled public debate that lacked both reliable information and the president's leadership at a time when it was needed.[47]

Only when leaks forced him to address the issue did Obama begin to provide public guidelines, oversight, and accountability for this new weapon, and to belatedly affirm the value of open debate. In a speech in May 2013 at the National Defense University at Fort McNair in the nation's capital, he demonstrated that the president could level with the American people while still protecting security secrets. He conceded the issue's public importance. "This new technology raises profound questions—about who is targeted, and why; about civilian casualties, and the risk of creating new enemies; about the legality of such strikes under U.S. and international law; about accountability and morality." Attacks were limited to Al Qaeda and allied forces that posed a "continuing and imminent threat to the American people," instances where capture was not possible, where there is "near-certainty that no civilians will be killed or injured," and where nations in which attacks took place had been consulted. Nonetheless, there were civilian casualties. But putting boots on the ground would invite far more carnage. Congress should consider a special court or other independent group to monitor such killings. Obama's speech opened the way for a better-informed debate without revealing operational secrets. In 2016, he issued a summary of guidelines and data on casualties. But whether an open debate would continue and create effective oversight remained issues for the next president.[48]

President Obama authorized the development and use of another digital-age weapon, without explaining the change. Cyberweapons could jam the computer systems of hostile nations or terrorist groups. But they could also shut down hospitals, police departments, or water systems by replacing legitimate code with malware. Whether they were used by the United States or against the United States, they could cause deaths, injuries, and massive economic damage. Like armed drones, they altered the terms of international conflicts.

As Americans learned from media reports, but not from the president, Obama launched the first major cyberattack on a nation's infrastructure soon after he took office. When President Bush briefed Obama at the White House a few days before his inauguration, he told the president-elect about a secret plan to launch a cyberattack on Iran's nuclear facility at Natanz. Bush viewed it as a limited measure that might provide an alternative to military action by Israel against Iran's suspected development of nuclear weapons.

Remarkably, the Bush administration had concluded in 2004 and 2005 that it was not legally necessary even to inform Congress that the nation was developing cyberweapons, although NSA director Hayden briefed leaders anyway. He wrote later that restricting information about such weapons within the administration hampered the development of effective policy.[49]

President Obama carried out the plan Bush had approved. In 2010, a computer worm that became known as Stuxnet temporarily disabled most of the uranium enrichment centrifuges at the nuclear facility in Iran in a secret U.S. operation code-named Olympic Games. But when an Iranian scientist signed on to the Internet, the worm escaped. It circled the globe, giving hackers everywhere code for a successful cyberattack. Iran retaliated, escalating cyberattacks on U.S. companies, including several major banks. To former NSA director Hayden, the cyberattack on Iran felt a bit like August 1945, when Truman had ordered the world's first use of atomic weapons. We were in a new military age, he wrote later, and now we would have to live with the consequences.[50]

But controversial secrets could not hold. Investigative reporters began to piece together information from leaks. The *New York Times* reported in 2009 that Bush had authorized the cyberattack on Iran and reported in June 2012 that it had taken place. The British *Guardian* posted on its website a secret 2012 presidential order setting out criteria for cyberattacks and asking agencies to identify possible targets. Classified documents revealed by Edward Snowden in 2013 confirmed that the worm was engineered by the United States and Israel.[51]

President Obama maintained his silence. He told his advisers that admitting the development and use of cyberweapons would help hostile nations or terrorist networks justify their own attacks, David Sanger of the *New York Times* reported in 2012.[52]

Security officials referred to such weapons obliquely. In March 2013, General Keith Alexander, head of the Defense Department's new cybercommand, acknowledged in his confirmation hearing that the group was forming teams of computer experts to develop both offensive and defensive weapons. When Admiral Michael S. Rogers replaced General Alexander, he told a Senate committee that the army, navy, air force, and marines would each have cyberattack forces and predicted that these would be part of any future crisis. In 2016, after the cyberattack that cut off electrical power in Ukraine, the president warned that U.S. power, water, and transportation systems could be attacked by hostile nations or individuals. He issued a cybersecurity action plan that addressed only defensive measures, and appointed a commission to recommend ways to improve public and private security, and to deter, disrupt, and recover from incidents.[53]

Still, the public debate about deployment of offensive cyberweapons remained stunted from lack of information and presidential leadership. In 1950, another president ordered the peacetime development of a devastating new weapon that changed the character of international conflicts. Like Truman, who authorized development of the hydrogen bomb, Obama tried unsuccessfully to avoid public debate. Like Truman, he paid a political price by ceding the timing and terms of that debate to enterprising journalists, political opponents, and imperfectly informed commentators. In both instances, the public learned too little too late to participate in decisions. But the hydrogen bomb was never used and would have been impossible to hide. Cyberattacks were deployed in peacetime and were hidden from public view even after they occurred. Americans were excluded from understanding or legitimizing a new form of aggression as a president who made transparency his credo tried unsuccessfully to maintain secrecy.

The secrets that created the most dramatic clashes between presidents' traditional habits and Americans' new expectations were programs that stored and scanned personal communication records in order to search for terrorist networks. Most of these programs targeted mainly foreign communications. But Obama also continued Bush's collection and storage of Americans' phone metadata, including the date, time, length, and phone identification of cell and landline calls, without obtaining individual warrants. He did not invite debate, and he did not make public the legal authority for such surveillance. He acknowledged the phone records program only after media reports in 2013, twelve years after President Bush initiated it. Only then did government evaluators conclude that the program rested on a shaky legal foundation. Only then did the president propose revising it to minimize conflicts with Americans' privacy.

Bush had created the phone records program in a secret presidential authorization, without any provision for the usual court approval of surveillance. He based his action on his executive authority, later claiming additional authority under a section of the Patriot Act that allowed collection of business records for foreign intelligence investigations.[54]

At first, Bush intended such surveillance as a temporary measure. One of the 9/11 hijackers had made calls from San Diego to Al Qaeda bosses back in Yemen, but the NSA could not legally trace the domestic end of those calls, and did not provide the information to the FBI.[55]

A temporary measure grew into a lasting policy change. The government aimed to store the phone records of all Americans, including the date, time, phone number, length, and phone identification for every cellphone or landline call, without the usual requirement in criminal law that a judge confirm probable cause based on a reasonable expectation that a crime had been committed. In this program, the government did not store the content of domestic calls and emails, although, NSA director Michael Hayden wrote later, if you had enough metadata "you could pretty much determine what the owner of a device was up to." Officials withheld knowledge of the collection of phone records from the American public for fear that terrorists would change their code words or stop using networks if they knew about it.[56]

Phone companies submitted daily records to the NSA, queried by analysts only under strict rules, when there was "a reasonable, articulable suspicion" of terrorism. Computers then did most of the work. The NSA held the phone data for as long as five years and sometimes shared it with other agencies. Both presidents had approved the briefing of congressional leaders.[57]

When the program was leaked in 2013, Obama was finally forced to explain it. He observed that the government could not prevent terrorist attacks without some capability to penetrate digital communications. Congress and the courts had authorized modest encroachments on privacy to help prevent such attacks. He had increased oversight when he took office. He declassified documents that described internal controls. But he was fighting an uphill battle by trying to reassure the public after having kept the program secret for so long.[58]

Meanwhile, civil liberties groups filed lawsuits and federal judges divided on whether such a large surveillance program violated the Constitution's prohibition against unreasonable searches, or Congress's authorizations. The Second Circuit Court of Appeals ruled it illegal in May 2015, the judges noting that collection was not related to investigations, as required by the law, and was particularly troubling because it was kept secret.[59]

In the end, debate proved useful to the president as well as the public. In January 2014, the congressionally authorized Privacy and Civil Liberties Oversight Board found that the program produced minimal benefits, lacked "a viable legal foundation," and raised constitutional issues concerning free expression and freedom from unreasonable searches. The board recommended that the government end it. Private companies could continue their current practice under Federal Communications Commission rules of storing phone records for eighteen months. Intelligence agencies could query those records only when approved by a FISA judge. A separate five-member review group appointed by the president agreed that the government should end the program and instead query phone companies for records when national security required it and only under court order.[60]

This sequence of events demonstrated that secretive approval of secretive programs was no longer enough. Angered by the secret program, Democrats and Republicans formed an alliance to oppose stealth intrusions of privacy. Representative Jim Sensenbrenner, a member of the House Judiciary Committee and a sponsor of the Patriot Act, said that such collection was not what Congress had intended.

In January 2014, in a speech at the Justice Department, Obama accepted review groups' recommendations and belatedly asked Congress for legislation. A congressional compromise in June 2015 ended government bulk collection of phone data. The USA Freedom Act required the government to request records from phone companies for foreign intelligence purposes under court order. It created expert privacy and technology advisers for the court and required the court's legal interpretations to be made public. Phone companies rather than the government would store records for the same eighteen months that the FCC currently required for customer complaints and billing issues. The NSA could access data only with a court order and could search only the individuals the target communicated with, and those individuals' communications, but no further.[61]

The phone records program was only one of an array of post-9/11 surveillance initiatives. They were so many and so varied that it was hard for Americans to understand them or trust that surveillance had limits. Each had its own authority, targets, safeguards, and impact on the privacy of Americans or citizens of other countries. The so-called PRISM program focused on the content of communications outside the United States or between individuals in the United States and those in foreign countries. It collected information through Internet companies' servers when the NSA decided that communication was relevant to a terrorist investigation. Content included emails, videos, chat room conversations, photos, file transfers, video conferencing, and login data. Leaked documents seemed to show that the government had secret arrangements with Microsoft, Yahoo, Google, Facebook, YouTube, Skype, AOL, Apple, and other tech companies for them to provide information without disclosing the requests. Several companies later denied that they had cooperated, though. The *Washington Post* reported that Americans' emails and other communications could be swept into the NSA's net because the agency had to be only 51 percent certain that it was not targeting Americans. Any information about American citizens was supposed to be turned over to the FBI. Congress provided general authority for this program in 2008 amendments to the Foreign Intelligence Surveillance Act, but the American people were told nothing about it.[62]

Another NSA program tapped into overseas fiber-optic cables owned by tele-communications companies such as Verizon and Level 3 that connected data centers around the world. The agency siphoned off Google, Yahoo, and other Internet data that companies did not provide directly, in what was known as the MUSCULAR program.[63] Apparently taken by surprise when the program was disclosed in 2013, technology companies including Apple, Google, Microsoft, Facebook, and Twitter submitted their own plan to limit government surveil-lance and create more oversight. They proposed an end to all bulk collection of personal data, strong and public oversight by courts, agreements on cross-border requests for information, and prompt disclosure of government orders to companies for user information.[64]

These programs created new kinds of conflicts with powerful technology companies that would determine the scope and limits of surveillance in the twenty-first century. Apple and Google introduced customer encryption of data for new operating systems beginning in 2014 and 2015 in order to regain consumer confidence, a step opposed by intelligence officials. Both companies explained that this technological change meant that they would be unable to provide any encrypted phone data to law enforcement or intelligence agencies. Encryption became a topic of heated public debate when the FBI sought a court order in 2016 to force Apple to develop software to defeat password protection on a phone used by one of the alleged terrorists who killed fourteen people in San Bernardino, California. The FBI's announcement that a private expert had provided a way around encryption tabled the issue for the time being.[65]

Leaks also revealed that the government collected the phone conversations and emails of senior United Nations officials, foreign energy company execu-tives, and perhaps thirty-five heads of state, including the Israeli prime minister, the president of Brazil, and German chancellor Angela Merkel. The NSA had spied on a climate change conference in Bali in 2007. The agency had inter-cepted the talking points of the United Nations secretary general before a White House meeting. With the assistance of an Australian intelligence agency, it had spied on conversations of an American law firm that was representing Indonesia in trade talks in 2013, the *New York Times* reported.[66]

These revelations triggered a diplomatic crisis. Chancellor Merkel told the president that interception of her private communications represented a grave breach of trust. In perhaps the most surprising revelation of all, a senior official said that Obama apparently was unaware of the electronic eavesdropping on friendly heads of state. "These decisions are made at NSA. . . . The president doesn't sign off on this stuff," the *Wall Street Journal* reported.[67]

By the time President Obama left office, a moment of national emergency had become a seemingly endless period of troubled peace when security threats continued to change in unpredictable ways. It was the kind of time when, in the past, secret activities had grown out of control amid fear and uncertainty. Obama had narrowed the nation's aims in the struggle against terrorism. Bush's impromptu promise to defeat international terrorism everywhere became a sustained effort to defeat specific networks of violent extremists that threatened the United States. The more limited aim was to prevent massive attacks and minimize smaller ones. Americans would live with the tragedies of occasional shootings and bombings by politically motivated individuals as they had long lived with the more frequent mass murders by angry or mentally ill individuals. When such crimes were committed by lone attackers, whatever their motive, they would remain difficult to prevent.

Two presidents with different approaches to the democratic process led the nation in the years after the 2001 terrorist attacks. From their steps and missteps came the tentative beginnings of a new bargain between openness and secrecy. Like past resets of the role of closed doors in open government, these changes emerged from ad hoc responses to unexpected crises, inevitable mistakes, agency scuffles, passionate advocacy, legislative compromises, thoughtful reports, and narrow court decisions.

Oversight improved and became more open. Obama's commitment to congressional and court review of all of the president's secret policies extended the reforms of the 1970s and set a useful precedent. But both presidents found that secretive oversight of secretive actions no longer gained the public's trust. Too often that oversight had proved ineffective. Only nine percent of those polled had a lot of confidence in Congress. The American people still expected the president to protect critical secrets. But they also expected the president, Congress, and the courts to provide enough public information to assure them of the fairness and independence of checks on sensitive programs.

More transformative were growing signs that it was in the interest of the presidents as well as the public to provide advance information about initiatives that changed rights or values, however secretive their operations. Obama and his intelligence leaders demonstrated that open debate was possible while still protecting essential secrets, although they did so only after being challenged by leaks.

These new ideas coexisted with old ways, and could be nurtured or disabled by future presidents. Secretive oversight still featured summary briefings of a few congressional leaders. The intelligence court continued to approve virtually all surveillance requests. The classification system was still broken. And Congress, judges, and citizens had not yet gained the specialized understanding of technology and security challenges to play a more active role in resolving issues.

Technology alone did not change entrenched habits. The promise of digital advances began to be realized in Obama's order to make public large data archives at data.gov, and in White House leadership of digital innovations to advance health, safety, and other national priorities. But technology did not erase the cumbersome and time-consuming processes of the fifty-year-old Freedom of Information Act that left each president too much discretion to alter the openness-secrecy balance, despite amendments in 2016. Nor did technology provide a secure space for intelligence gathering that the public, the media, and would-be leakers understood and respected.

Legislation did settle for the time being the terms under which the government could search Americans' phone records to locate terrorist networks, but there was as yet no bright line that reassured ordinary citizens that the government would not eavesdrop on their private lives in other ways, or that promised that limited authority would not be abused.

If responsible secrecy remained elusive, responsible openness remained contentious. In conflicts built into the Constitution, national and international media continued to seek out and publish government secrets, and officials continued to try to stop them. New Justice Department ground rules provided some clarity. Searches of reporters' communications in criminal investigations required disclosure and court review. And no twenty-first-century president attempted censorship, as Wilson did, or asked a court to stop publication, as Nixon did. More problematic were digital data dumps by insiders or hackers that circled around government persuasion, media self-restraint, and judicial authority. It remained for the next president to complete the task of stopping data theft that was truly damaging to security and privacy.

On January 12, 2016, President Obama stood before members of both houses of Congress in the House chamber to describe for the last time the state of the union. The nation was stronger than when he took office. The United States spent more on its military than the next eight nations combined. Sixty-five partners had joined the fight against terrorism. But there was a need to rebuild trust at home, for more debate, because democracy withers when people feel their voices don't matter. And "too many people feel that way right now."[68]

Conclusion

TWENTY-FIVE YEARS AFTER THE END OF THE Cold War, the United States is engaged in a new kind of seemingly endless struggle. Like the earlier Cold War, this conflict is characterized by uncertain threats, secretive enemies, and an extraordinary need for both secrecy and openness. The president needs stealth tactics to identify terrorist networks and stop attacks before they happen. The American people need information to stay out of harm's way, to understand and approve new policies, and to judge the president's performance.

But this twenty-first-century cold war is also different. The threat is not of nuclear holocaust but of attacks in cafes, at concerts, on busy streets, and on trains and airplanes. It comes not from missiles but from suicide vests, truck bombs, or the release of chemical, biological, or nuclear poisons. The secretive enemy is not a nation subject to diplomacy but disparate groups and individuals driven by ideology who hide among ordinary citizens and target civilians.

There are reasons for optimism. Despite missteps, the nation continues on a path toward more open government, greater tolerance, more robust freedom of expression, stronger protection of individual rights, and greater accountability. The Internet and computer power create opportunities to renew participatory democracy and international cooperation. These days, officials, journalists, advocates, and people around the world watch the president's every move and demand more information faster. Citizens expect that their voices will be heard on matters large and small.

There are signs that the growth of stealth activities may be balanced with greater openness in policymaking and oversight. Controversies surrounding presidents' actions to alter Americans' rights or expectations behind closed doors suggest that there is now a high political price attached to such secrecy. Oversight institutions have gained strength. The Foreign Intelligence Surveillance Court has added public advocates and makes more decisions public. The Supreme Court questioned President Bush's security policies. The inspectors general embedded in government agencies have gained resources and independence. Congress has engaged in exhaustive investigations of executive actions and required that privacy and civil liberties be weighed in national security decisions.

Leaders have begun to talk about this change. Belatedly, President Obama acknowledged that debate about secretive surveillance made the nation stronger. Bush's NSA and CIA director, Michael Hayden, noted in *Playing to the Edge* that the nation is in the midst of "a broad cultural shift that is redefining legitimate secrecy, necessary transparency, and what constitutes consent of the governed."[1]

Nonetheless, it is a dangerous time. Presidents have not been able to protect secrets from digital theft. They do not yet provide voluntarily the information that Americans now expect about security policies. Employed with skill and restraint, presidential secrecy remains an essential tool of governance. Abused or neglected, it keeps democracy from working. Secrecy blocks checks on abuses of power. It is the invisible enemy of individual rights. It takes over the healthy workings of government. It undermines security by squelching debate, encouraging information hoarding, and leaving officials uncertain about what they can and can't do. It eats away at public trust and drains the confidence of allies. A confused and distrustful nation cannot respond to new threats with its full strength. As Senator Moynihan wrote about the twentieth-century Cold War, secrecy poisons American politics.

Earlier crises demonstrate how secrecy can get out of hand. Sometimes it has escaped restraint when presidents have hidden their personal failings. Woodrow Wilson kept his incapacitating stroke hidden in order to stay in office when he could no longer do the job. Bill Clinton was impeached for lying and encouraging others to lie in order to escape the consequences of his sexual indulgences.

More often, secrecy has thrived because presidents were preoccupied with giving officials sufficient power to counter immediate threats without balancing civil liberties or other enduring values. Wilson, who had little tolerance for dissent, was intent on rallying a reluctant public to support a distant war. To do so, he stirred up fears of conspiracy; empowered officials to detain immigrants, labor organizers, and protesters; and fostered what became a long government practice of tapping into international communications and opening private mail. Faced with a wartime ally that suddenly became a peacetime aggressor, Harry Truman supported covert operations and secret surveillance. Lyndon Johnson mixed politics with national security to monitor the private communications of civil rights leaders and antiwar protesters, and to hide his expansion of the Vietnam War.

Occasionally, ideology has driven excessive secrecy. George W. Bush and Richard Cheney sought to protect the nation in a time of crisis. But they also came to office intent on proving a point. Opposed to earlier limitations on presidential authority, Bush approved secret prisons and interrogation programs that countered international law, and launched unprecedented surveillance of Americans and foreigners that bypassed judicial restraints.

But usually, secrecy has simply grown from neglect. Well-intentioned presidents created stealth enterprises without effective limits or oversight. Operating outside domestic and foreign laws became a habit for Harry Truman's Central Intelligence Agency, a habit sanctioned by the nation's leaders. His National Security Agency could ignore its charter because the charter was secret and no one knew what the agency was doing.

Finally, secrets have metastasized in the dark because presidents have found it difficult to talk openly about programs that alter Americans' rights or expectations but that also require a measure of confidentiality. President Bush and President Obama kept from the American people the government's scanning of their phone records because the specifics could have tipped off terrorists. For similar reasons, neither president would talk about when and how the United States initiated attacks with drones or cyberweapons in nations where there was no armed conflict, even though those new weapons could someday be used against Americans. Citizens did not need to know the operational details of these secretive programs, but they did need to know enough to judge for themselves whether the public benefits outweighed their risks. After information leaked, President Obama provided an example of the benefits of such debate. When he explained the storing of Americans' phone records in a major speech, critics quickly came up with alternatives that were less intrusive, alternatives that the president endorsed and Congress affirmed in law.

Secret government has always thrived on the politics of fear. A state of emergency that never ends creates an ambiguous space between war and peace in which there is uncertainty about which rules apply. Fear favors zealots who use secrecy to gain power. Wilson's attorney general, hoping to run for president, rounded up immigrants and labor organizers in what became known as the Palmer raids. FBI director J. Edgar Hoover used the fear of communism to conduct secret investigations for and against presidents, members of Congress, and private citizens and to stay in power for nearly half a century.

Much depends on leadership. No law or sensible process can stop a president from engaging in illegal or unethical conduct behind closed doors. Presidents who are handicapped by inexperience, driven by ideology, preoccupied with the politics of the moment, or motivated by personal gain can degrade democracy. Even if their secrets are later revealed, the damage has been done. In the last Cold War, presidents' ad hoc decisions behind closed doors triggered decades of abuses. Fighting secretive enemies, the nation itself became more secretive, and presidents lost the public's trust.

A brighter future is possible. Presidents can anchor emergency authority in legislation, streamline consultations for today's high-speed decision making, and champion laws that reassure citizens that their personal information is safe. They can jettison outdated Cold War practices and replace them with laws that narrowly circumscribe essential secrets, provide practical penalties for revealing them, and spell out oversight. And they can insist on public debate about every new proposal that clashes with Americans' prevailing understanding of their rights and values, even when those proposals require operational secrecy.

There continues to be a broad consensus about the need to protect security information from terrorists and hostile nations. Most security secrets do not clash with cherished values or established rights. Missile launch codes, weapons' technologies, military strategies, the identity of undercover agents, and steps taken to protect the president are secrets that few would dispute. Likewise, Americans do not question the necessity of confidential diplomatic negotiations or private consultations between the president and his advisers.

And there have always been moments when presidents' actions create a lasting legacy of openness. George Washington, who had a high tolerance for dissent and feared accusations of monarchical power, established a presumption of openness and narrowly circumscribed secrecy, providing sensitive information to Congress, affirming congressional authority to investigate executive mismanagement, and creating cabinet government to ensure a diversity of views. After revelations of abuses created a national crisis in the 1970s, President Ford, known for his candor, approved new rules that staked out boundaries to presidents' hidden programs and provided oversight, and joined Congress in inaugurating a culture of accountability. President Obama worked to bring counterterrorism policies under the rule of domestic and international law, promised that his secret actions would always be subject to congressional and court review, and used digital technology to increase government transparency.

We elect presidents to deal with the unexpected. Managing secrecy and openness is part of the job. Experience has shown how much presidents differ in their interest in engaging the public in debate, their inclination toward unilateral actions, their tolerance of dissent, their interpretation of the Constitution, and their honesty. But experience has also shown that there is nothing inevitable about the sacrifice of openness during times of crisis, the sacrifice of privacy for national security, or the sacrifice of press freedom for official secrecy. These are political choices that rest first with the president and members of Congress, and ultimately with the American people.

The framers of the Constitution acknowledged the need for limited secrecy in military and diplomatic affairs. But they also expected that public debate would provide reasonable checks on presidents' actions and give those actions legitimacy. Concurring in the Supreme Court's denial of President Richard M. Nixon's request to stop publication of a top-secret assessment of the Vietnam War, Justice Potter Stewart argued for such open debate: "The only effective restraint upon executive policy and power . . . may lie in an enlightened citizenry –in an informed and critical public opinion which alone can here protect the values of democratic government."[2]

NOTES

Introduction

1. Mary Madden and Lee Rainie, "Americans' Attitudes About Privacy, Security and Surveillance," Pew Research Center, May 20, 2015, available at www.pewinternet.org; "Public Trust in Government: 1958–2014," Pew Research Center, November 13, 2014, available at www.pewresearch.org.
2. Stephen Breyer, *The Court and the World* (Knopf, 2015), 13.
3. Mary Graham, "The Information Wars: Terrorism Has Become a Pretext for a New Culture of Secrecy," *The Atlantic,* September 2002. The work of the Transparency Policy Project can be accessed at transparencypolicy.net.

Chapter 1. The Constitutional Convention

1. *The Records of the Federal Convention of 1787*, ed. Max Farrand (Yale University Press, 1911), 3:86–87 [hereafter *Records of the Federal Convention*]. According to Farrand, there is no date that can be given to this anecdote by William Pierce.
2. Entry of October 4, 1784, in *George Washington's Diaries,* ed. Dorothy Twohig (University of Virginia Press, abr., 1999), 265–66 [hereafter Washington, *Diaries*].
3. *Records of the Federal Convention,* 3:31.
4. *Journals of the Continental Congress, 1774–1789,* ed. Worthington C. Ford et al. (Government Printing Office, 1904–37), 32 (February 21, 1787): 74.
5. *Madison's Journal of the Convention,* ed. E. H. Scott (Scott, Foresman, 1898), 1:55–58 [hereafter Madison, *Journal*]. The record suggests that the delegates' decision to close the Convention's doors, like many in the meeting's early days, was made informally. It seems likely that at least some delegates had reached a consensus in their boardinghouse conversations during their first weekend together. On Sunday, May 27, two days before they voted to conduct secret deliberations, George Mason wrote to his son George Mason, Jr.: "It is expected our doors will be shut, and communications upon the business of the Convention be forbidden during its sitting. This I think myself a proper precaution

to prevent mistakes and misrepresentation until the business shall have been completed, when the whole may have a very different complexion from that in which the several crude and indigested parts might in their first shape appear if submitted to the public eye." *Records of the Constitutional Convention,* 3:28.

6. Washington, *Diaries,* 318.

7. Erskine May, *Treatise on the Law, Privileges, Proceedings and Use of Parliament,* 21st ed. (Butterworths, 1989), 170–71; Daniel N. Hoffman, *Governmental Secrecy and the Founding Fathers: A Study in Constitutional Controls* (Greenwood, 1981), 13. The Articles of Confederation provided: "The Congress . . . shall publish the Journal of their proceedings monthly, except such parts thereof relating to treaties, alliances, or military operations, as in their judgment require secrecy; and the yeas and nays of the delegates of each State, on any question, shall be entered on the Journal, when it is desired by any delegate; and the delegates of a State, or any of them, at his or their request, shall be furnished with a transcript of the said journal, except such parts as are above excepted, to lay before the legislatures of the several States." Articles of Confederation of 1781, art. IX, para. 7.

8. Thomas Jefferson, letter to John Adams, August 30, 1787, available from the National Archives and Record Administration's Founders Online website, founders.archives.gov [hereafter Founders Online].

9. *Records of the Constitutional Convention,* 3:173–74, 191 (emphasis in original).

10. Patrick Henry, statement, June 4, 1788, in *Documentary History of the Ratification of the Constitution* 9 (1976): 930 [hereafter *DHRC*].

11. Alexander Dallas, *Pennsylvania Evening Herald,* June 2, 1787.

12. Henry Knox, letter to George Washington, New York, February 22, 1787; George Washington, *Writings,* selected and with notes by John H. Rhodehamel (Penguin, 1997), 630, 635, 643.

13. *Records of the Constitutional Convention,* 1:10; Max Farrand, *The Fathers of the Constitution* (Yale University Press, 1921), 132.

14. *Records of the Constitutional Convention,* 3:368.

15. James Madison, letter to James Monroe, June 10, 1787, available at Founders Online.

16. Madison, *Journal,* 2:717.

17. *Records of the Constitutional Convention,* 1:xii. In a letter to James Madison, historian Jared Sparks later wrote, "It seems to me that your secretary of the Convention was a very stupid secretary, not to take care of those things [notes and votes] better, and to make a better journal than the dry bones which now go by that name." Jared Sparks, letter to James Madison, November 14, 1831, in *Records of the Constitutional Convention,* 3:514.

18. *Records of the Constitutional Convention,* 1:xv–xxii.

19. James Madison, letter to Thomas Jefferson, June 6, 1787, available at Founders Online.

20. *Records of the Constitutional Convention,* 3:64.

21. *New York Daily Advertiser,* August 18, 1787; *Records of the Constitutional Convention,* 3:73–74; Ron Chernow, *Washington: A Life* (Penguin, 2010), 237.

22. *Records of the Constitutional Convention,* 4:74; 1:xiv.

23. *Records of the Constitutional Convention,* 3:59.

24. *DHRC,* 8: 9.

25. Farrand, *Records of the Constitutional Convention,* 3:76.
26. Washington, *Writings,* 630; *New York Daily Advertiser,* March 24, 1787.
27. *Records of the Constitutional Convention,* 3:77–78.
28. Federalist nos. 48, 51 (James Madison).
29. U.S. Const., art. II, § 3.
30. Hoffman, *Secrecy,* 35–37.
31. Hoffman, *Secrecy,* 32–33.
32. James Madison, letter to Thomas Jefferson, September 6, 1787, available at Founders Online.
33. *Records of the Constitutional Convention,* 1:2 n. 1.
34. *Records of the Constitutional Convention,* 2:631–46.
35. Washington, *Writings,* 633, 658–59.
36. *Records of the Constitutional Convention,* 2:646–50.
37. *Records of the Constitutional Convention,* 1:xi; Washington, *Diaries,* 325.
38. Washington, *Writings,* 655.
39. Chernow, *Washington,* 540.
40. *DHRC,* 9:1067.
41. Chernow, *Washington,* 267; *Records of the Constitutional Convention,* 3:432 (citing *Memoirs of John Quincy Adams,* ed. Charles Francis Adams [J. B. Lippincott, 1875], 4:363–87).
42. *DHRC,* 13:277–78; Pauline Maier, *Ratification: The People Debate the Constitution, 1787–1788* (Simon & Schuster, 2010), 69; George Washington, letter to David Humphries, December 26, 1786, available at Founders Online.
43. Maier, *Ratification,* 63–64.
44. Maier, *Ratification,* 216–25.
45. Jack Rakove, *James Madison and the Creation of the American Republic,* 3rd ed. (Pearson/Longman, 2007), 19.
46. Maier, *Ratification,* 448–49.
47. Federalist no. 69.
48. *Records of the Constitutional Convention,* 2:618, see n. 15; Pinckney's speech is quoted in *Records of the Constitutional Convention,* Appendix CLXXIII.
49. Federalist no. 48 (James Madison).
50. Rakove, *Madison,* 90–96.
51. Herbert Friedenwald, "A Letter of Jonas Phillips to the Federal Convention," in *Publications of the American Jewish Historical Society* 2 (1894): 107. The letter was brought to Dr. Friedenwald's attention by S. M. Hamilton, who worked for the State Department and came upon the letter when preparing papers of the Federal Convention for publication.
52. 31 Annals of Cong. 799–800 (January 22, 1818); Jonathan Eliot, *The Debates in the Several State Conventions on the Adoption of the Federal Constitution* (Sayer, 1987), 122; Lee H. Burke, *Homes of the Department of State, 1774–1976: The Buildings Occupied by the Department of State and Its Predecessors* (Historical Office, Bureau of Public Affairs, Department of State, 1977), 21.
53. John Quincy Adams, memoirs, November 19, 1818, available at www.consource.org.
54. *Records of the Constitutional Convention,* 3:425–34.

55. *Records of the Constitutional Convention,* 1:xv.
56. U.S. Const., preamble.

Chapter 2. George Washington

1. General St. Clair, letter to President Washington, *The St. Clair Papers,* ed. William Henry Smith (Robert Clarke, 1882), November 9, 1791, 2:262; "From George Washington to the United States Senate and House of Representatives," December 12, 1791, National Archives and Records Administration, available at Founders Online, founders.archives.gov [hereafter Founders Online]; Ron Chernow, *Washington: A Life* (Penguin, 2010), 667.
2. House Documents, 266: 531–32 (1871).
3. Letter from George Washington to James Madison, May 5, 1789, available at Founders Online; *George Washington's Papers: Presidential Series,* ed. Dorothy Twohig (University Press of Virginia, 1987), 10:169 [hereafter Washington, *Papers*]; Andrew A. Lipscomb, ed., *The Writings of Thomas Jefferson* (Thomas Jefferson Memorial Association of the United States, 1905), 1:303–5 [hereafter Jefferson, *Writings*].
4. Jefferson, *Writings,* 1:303–5.
5. Jefferson, *Writings,* 1:303–5.
6. President Richard Nixon, who would unsuccessfully claim executive privilege for taped conversations related to the Watergate scandal, explained that "the doctrine of executive privilege . . . was first invoked by President Washington." "Statement about Executive Privilege," March 12, *Public Papers of the President* 1973: 184.
7. *The Papers of James Madison Digital Edition,* ed. J. C. A. Stagg (University of Virginia Press, 2010), 12:120–21. Washington, *Papers,* 2:232,153–54, 314.
8. Gordon S. Wood, *Empire of Liberty* (Oxford University Press, 2009), 58; Robert V. Remini, *The House: A History of the House of Representatives* (HarperCollins, 2006), 9–19.
9. On May 28, 1789, Congress required both the Senate and the House to secure printing contracts. Printers made 600 copies of approved legislation and 700 copies of the House and Senate Journals. J. H. Powell, *The Books of a New Nation: United States Government, 1774–1814* (University of Pennsylvania Press, 1957), 85–88. See also Aimee C. Quinn, "Keeping the Citizenry Informed: Early Congressional Printing and 21st Century Information Policy," *Congressional Information Quarterly* 20 (2003): 281, 285.
10. George Washington, letter to David Stuart, July 26, 1789, available at Founders Online; Kenneth R. Bowling and Donald R. Kennon, *The House and the Senate in the 1790s* (Ohio University Press, 2002), 33.
11. Elaine K. Swift, *The Making of an American Senate* (University of Michigan Press, 2002), 58 (quoting Condorcet, "To the Editor").
12. George Washington, letter to John Adams, May 10, 1789, in Washington, *Writings,* 737–38.
13. Stephen Decatur, Jr., *Private Affairs of George Washington* (Riverside, 1933), 83–85, 200–202; Chernow, *Washington,* 609–13.
14. Decatur, *Private Affairs,* 92.
15. Chernow, *Washington,* 586–87, 625; Decatur, *Private Affairs,* 133.

16. Debt figures from John C. Miller, *The Federalist Era, 1789–1801* (Waveland, 1960), 38.

17. Hamilton proposed that the Bank of the United States issue bank notes as a national currency, and manage the government's credit and debt transactions. It would be a public-private institution, with most of its stock and most of its directorships reserved for private investors.

18. Daniel N. Hoffman, *Governmental Secrecy and the Founding Fathers: A Study in Constitutional Controls* (Greenwood, 1981), 52.

19. In 1817 Madison recalled in a memorandum Washington's quandary, writing, "The constitutionality of the national Bank, was a question on which his mind was greatly perplexed." See George Washington, letter to James Madison, February 21, 1791, available at Founders Online; "Final Version of an Opinion on the Constitutionality of an Act to Establish a Bank [February 23, 1791]," in *The Papers of Alexander Hamilton*, vol. 8, ed. Harold H. Syrett et al. (Columbia University Press, 1961), 100–111. Hamilton's view of implied powers, validated by the Supreme Court in John Marshall's opinion in *McCulloch v. Maryland* (1819), helped to promote a powerful presidency.

20. Jeffrey L. Pasley, *The Tyranny of Printers* (University of Virginia Press, 2001), 51–66, 70; Frank Luther Mott, *American Journalism* (MacMillan, 1968), 122–23.

21. Thomas Jefferson, letter to Thomas Mann Randolph, Jr., May 15, 1791, available at Founders Online; Pasley, *Tyranny,* 63–78.

22. "The Difficulties of the Editor of a Daily Paper," *General Advertiser,* October 23, 1790.

23. Letter to the editor, *General Advertiser,* January 23, 1793.

24. George Washington, *Writings,* selected and with notes by John H. Rhodehamel (Penguin, 1997), 842; George Washington, letters to Edmund Randolph, Mount Vernon, August 26, 1792, available at Founders Online; Mott, *American Journalism,* 126.

25. "From George Washington to the United States Senate and House of Representatives," January 8, 1790, available at Founders Online.

26. "From George Washington to the United States Senate and House of Representatives," October 25, 1791, available at Founders Online; James Madison, *National Gazette,* December 19, 1791 (emphasis in original).

27. Paul Starr, *Creation of the Media: Political Origins of Modern Communications* (Basic, 2004), 88. Subscribers paid one cent postage for delivery within one hundred miles and one and a half cents for greater distances. Richard R. John, *Spreading the News* (Harvard University Press, 1996), 36.

28. An Act to Establish the Post-Office and Post Roads of the United States, ch. 23, §1, Stat. 232, 238 (1792). Recreational mail-opening continued, however. Envelopes did not come into common use for another fifty years, and wax seals were easily broken. Visitors to taverns and boarding houses that sometimes served as local post offices sometimes could not resist the temptation to peruse the letters in transit. Ron Chernow, *Alexander Hamilton* (Penguin, 2004), 680.

29. George Washington, letter to Alexander Hamilton (private and confidential), July 29, 1792, available at Founders Online.

30. Thomas Jefferson, "Notes of a Conversation with George Washington, October 1, 1792," in *The Papers of Thomas Jefferson,* ed. John Catanzariti (Princeton University Press, 1990), 24:434–36; Alexander Hamilton, letter to George Washington, July 30–August 3, 1792, available at Founders Online.

31. 4 Annals of Cong. 151–52 (December 26, 1793).

32. Letter to the editor, *General Advertiser,* December 30, 1793.

33. Morris, who had served in the Continental Congress and written the preamble to the Constitution, apparently was suspect because he had joined efforts to prevent execution of the king and nobles. Mark J. Rozell, *Executive Privilege: The Dilemma of Secrecy and Democratic Accountability* (Johns Hopkins University Press, 2010), 34–35; Hoffman, *Secrecy,* 104–16, 236.

34. "Proclamation 4—Neutrality of the United States in the War Involving Austria, Prussia, Sardinia, Great Britain, and the United Netherlands Against France," April 22, 1793, American Presidency Project, www.presidency.ucsb.edu.

35. Pasley, *Tyranny,* 92–94; Stanley Elkins and Eric McKitrick, *The Age of Federalism* (Oxford University Press, 1993), 416–21.

36. Pasley, *Tyranny,* 92; *The Papers of Alexander Hamilton,* ed. Harold C. Syrett (Columbia University Press, 1973), 18:487.

37. George Washington, letter to Alexander Hamilton, July 3, 1795, available at Founders Online.

38. Pasley, *Tyranny,* 88–92; Hoffman, *Secrecy,* 151.

39. Elkins and McKitrick, *Federalism,* 420.

40. George Washington, letter to Alexander Hamilton, September 28 and 29, 1795, available at Founders Online; George Washington, letter to Thomas Jefferson, July 6, 1796, quoted in Chernow, *Washington,* 743.

41. Hamilton, former secretary of the treasury, was now a private citizen whose advice Washington still sought. George Washington, letter to Alexander Hamilton, March 7, 1796, available at Founders Online.

42. George Washington, memorandum to the United States House of Representatives, March 30, 1796, available at Founders Online.

43. Hoffman, *Secrecy,* 168–71.

44. Washington, *Writings,* 942–47; James Thomas Flexner, *George Washington: Anguish and Farewell, 1793–1799* (Little, Brown, 1972), 303.

45. John C. Hamilton, *History of the Republic of the United States of America: as Traced in the Writings of Alexander Hamilton and His Contemporaries* (Appleton, 1857–65), 510. See also "Transcript of George Washington's Farewell Address (1796)," available at National Records and Archives Administration, www.ourdocuments.gov/doc.php?doc=15&page=transcript.

Chapter 3. Woodrow Wilson

1. Accounts differ slightly concerning the details. Ike Hoover, *Forty-Two Years in the White House* (Houghton Mifflin, 1934), 101–3; Dr. Grayson and Dr. Dercum's accounts in *The Papers of Woodrow Wilson,* ed. Arthur S. Link et al. (Princeton University Press, 1966) [hereafter *PWW*], vol. 64; John Milton Cooper, Jr., *Woodrow Wilson: A Biography* (Alfred A. Knopf, 2009), 520–30.

2. U.S. Const. art. II, § 1; August Heckscher, *Woodrow Wilson* (Scribners, 1991), 613.

3. William B. McAllister, Joshua Botts, Peter Cozzens, and Aaron W. Marrs, *Toward "Thorough, Accurate, and Reliable": A History of the* Foreign Relations of the United

States *Series* (U.S. Department of State, Office of the Historian, Bureau of Public Affairs, 2015), chapter 2.

4. Philip H. Melanson, *Secret Service* (Basic, 2002), 10–32.

5. Captain Wyman H. Packard, *A Century of U.S. Naval Intelligence* (Department of the Navy, 1996), 9; G. J. A. O'Toole, *Honorable Treachery* (Grove, 2014), 127–28; Sean Wilentz, *The Rise of American Democracy* (W. W. Norton, 2005), 708; Matthew Algeo, *The President Is a Sick Man* (Chicago Review Press, 2011).

6. U.S. Congress, *Report of the Commission on Protecting and Reducing Government Secrecy* [hereafter the Moynihan Commission], March 3, 1997, A-12.

7. Woodrow Wilson, Third Annual Message to Congress, December 7, 1915, American Presidency Project, available at www.presidency.ucsb.edu [hereafter American Presidency Project]; 1916 Democratic Party Platform, June 14, 1916, American Presidency Project.

8. The Black Tom blast embedded fragments in the Statue of Liberty, required the evacuation of immigrants at Ellis Island, shattered windows in Times Square, and caused $20 million in damage, equivalent to nearly $500 million today. Margo Nash, "Explosion by the Hudson, Foreign Espionage, Local Fear: 1916," *New York Times*, September 23, 2001.

9. "Joint Address to Congress Leading to a Declaration of War Against Germany," April 2, 1917, National Archives, available at www.archives.gov.

10. Woodrow Wilson, "Address on Flag Day," June 14, 1917, American Presidency Project.

11. Daniel Patrick Moynihan, *Secrecy: The American Experience* (Yale University Press, 1998), 99.

12. "On the Eve of War: A Recollection," in John L. Heaton, compiler, *Cobb of the World: A Leader in Liberalis: Compiled from His Editorial Articles and Public Addresses* (Press Publishing, 1924), 270.

13. Exec. Order No. 2587A, Federal Employees Removal on Security Grounds (April 7, 1917); Paul L. Murphy, *World War I and the Origin of Civil Liberties in the United States* (W. W. Norton, 1979), 74.

14. Exec. Order No. 2604 (April 28, 1917).

15. Geoffrey R. Stone, *Perilous Times: Free Speech in Wartime, from the Sedition Act of 1798 to the War on Terrorism* (W. W. Norton, 2004), 156–57.

16. Murphy, *World War I*, 98–102; Stone, *Perilous Times*, 153–58.

17. Espionage Act, June 15, 1917, ch. 30, 40 Stat. 217; Stone, *Perilous Times*, 185.

18. Stone, *Perilous Times*, 149; Moynihan, *Secrecy*, 96.

19. Woodrow Wilson, letter to Chairman Webb of the House Judiciary Committee, May 22, 1917, in *President Wilson's Great Speeches and Other History Making Documents* (Stanton and Van Vliet, 1917), 204; Stone, *Perilous Times*, 149; Moynihan, *Secrecy*, 92–96.

20. John Milton Cooper, Jr., *Pivotal Decades: The United States, 1900–1920* (W. W. Norton, 1990), 299–300; "Eugene V. Debs Foundation," debsfoundation.org (accessed July 24, 2016).

21. Schenck v. U.S., 249 U.S. 47 (1919), Debs v. U.S., 249 U.S. 211 (1919).

22. Murphy, *World War I*; Samuel Walker, *Presidents and Civil Liberties from Wilson to Obama: A Story of Poor Custodians* (Cambridge University Press, 2012), 30.

23. Harold C. Relyea, "Security Classified and Controlled Information: History, Status, and Emerging Management Issues," Congressional Research Service, RL 33494, updated

February 11, 2008, Federation of American Scientists, available at www.fas.org; Alvin S. Quist, *Security Classification of Information,* vol. 1, 9–43 (revised 2002), Federation of American Scientists, available at www.fas.org/sgp/library/quist/chap_2.pdf.

24. Murphy, *World War I,* 270–71; William E. Leuchtenburg, *The Perils of Prosperity, 1914–1932* (University of Chicago Press, 1958), 70–75, 85, 125.

25. Harry N. Scheiber, *The Wilson Administration and Civil Liberties, 1917–1921* (Cornell University Press, 1960), 41–42, 66–67.

26. Scheiber, *Civil Liberties,* 65–66; Curt Gentry, *J. Edgar Hoover* (Norton, 1991), 81–83, 104.

27. Albert W. Fox, " 'Very Sick Man,' Says Grayson of President in Late Night Bulletin," *Washington Post,* October 3, 1919; "President Is Improved Slightly, Late Report by Dr. Grayson Says," October 4, 1919; "Wilson's Mind Is 'Clear' and He Can Act, but Grayson Says Cure Requires Time; Senators Discuss Disability; Won't Act," *New York Times,* October 14, 1919.

28. Link, "Grayson's Predicament," 292–93.

29. Grayson had excelled in medical studies at the Medical College in Richmond, Virginia, and Johns Hopkins University. He was a thirty-year-old navy doctor on the presidential yacht *Mayflower* when President Theodore Roosevelt chose him as his personal physician. President William Howard Taft asked him to continue in that role. Arthur T. Link, "Dr. Grayson's Predicament," *Proceedings of the American Philosophical Society,* December 1994, 488.

30. Cooper, *Woodrow Wilson,* 563; Hoover, *Forty-Two Years,* 102; E. Wilson, *Memoir,* 284.

31. *PWW,* 64:498, 64:510.

32. Joseph Patrick Tumulty, *Woodrow Wilson as I Know Him* (Doubleday, Page, 1921), 443–44; *PWW,* 63:547, 64:456–57; Link, "Dr. Grayson's Predicament," 492; Heckscher, *Woodrow Wilson,* 613.

33. Hoover, *Forty-Two Years,* 102–3.

34. "Details of Illness Kept from Cabinet: Members Get Reports on Wilson only Through the Press, Says Palmer," *New York Times,* October 14, 1919; Heckscher, *Woodrow Wilson,* 613.

35. J. Frederick Essary, *Covering Washington* (Houghton Mifflin, 1927), 49; Josephus Daniels, *The Wilson Era: Years of War and After, 1917–1923* (University of North Carolina at Chapel Hill Press, 1946), 513.

36. Quoted in John D. Feerick, *From Failing Hands: The Story of Presidential Succession* (Fordham University Press, 1965), 176; John Milton Cooper, *Breaking the Heart of the World* (Cambridge University Press, 2001), 210 (citing Charles M. Thomas, *Thomas Riley Marshall: Hoosier Statesman* [Mississippi Valley Press, 1939], 207).

37. Phyllis Lee Levin, *Edith and Woodrow: The Wilson White House* (Scribner, 2001), 76 (citing Edith Bolling Galt Wilson to Woodrow Wilson, June 10, 1915).

38. William Seale, *The President's House: A History,* 2nd ed. (Johns Hopkins University Press, in association with White House Historical Association, 2008), 59, 101–3.

39. Kristie Miller, *Ellen and Edith: Woodrow Wilson's First Ladies* (University Press of Kansas, 2010), 119.

40. Edith Bolling Wilson, *My Memoir* (Bobbs-Merrill, 1939), 64.

41. Levin, *Edith and Woodrow,* 87.

42. "How 'Woman's Sphere' Is Being Enlarged: Representative Women of America Set New Standard of Service and Culture for Femininity of World," *Atlanta Constitution,* October 12, 1919.

43. Wilson, *Memoir,* 289.

44. Levin, *Edith and Woodrow,* 352.

45. Ray Stannard Baker, "Inside Story of Wilson's Fight at Paris Peace Conference," *Springfield Weekly Republican,* October 30, 1919.

46. *PWW,* 55:486–89, 58:636, 58:613; Dr. Bert E. Park, "Wilson's Neurologic Illness During the Summer of 1919," in *PWW,* 62:629–31.

47. "Reports Wilson Suffered Shock: Senator Moses Writes Friends That President Had a Cerebral Lesion," *New York Times,* October 12, 1919.

48. *PWW,* 64:510–11.

49. Daniels, *Wilson Era, 1917–1923,* 512; *PWW,* 64:512.

50. Cooper, *Pivotal,* 351; *PWW,* 64:135–39.

51. "Belgian Royalties See the President," *New York Times,* October 31, 1919, "President Enjoys Chat with Prince," *New York Times,* November 13, 1919.

52. *PWW,* 64:vii; Wilson, *Memoir,* 289.

53. *PWW,* 63:600–602 nn. 1 and 3.

54. Albert W. Fox, "Has Grasp, Senators Find, on Nation's Vital Needs: Read Fall's Resolution," *Washington Post,* December 6, 1919.

55. Hoover, *Forty-Two Years,* 634–35.

56. Hoover, *Forty-Two Years,* 636–37; Park, "Wilson's Neurologic Illness," 646.

57. Link, "Predicament," 493–94.

58. Dr. Bert E. Park, "Woodrow Wilson's Stroke of October 2, 1919," in *PWW,* 63:645. Dr. Park's notes are Appendix II.

59. Heckscher, *Woodrow Wilson,* 627.

60. "A Draft of a Public Letter," December 17, 1919, in *PWW,* 64:199–202.

61. "Wilson's Last Mad Act," *Los Angeles Times,* February 15, 1920.

62. *Defining Article II, Section I, Clause 5, of the Constitution, Relative to Disability, Removal from Office, etc., of the President of the U.S., Hearings Before the Committee on the Judiciary on H.R. 12609, 12629. 12647 and H.J. Res. 297* (February 26, 1920, and March 1, 1920) [hereafter *Hearings*].

63. Stone, *Perilous Times,* 222–24; Gentry, *Hoover,* 76–77; *To the American People: Report Upon the Illegal Practices of the United States Department of Justice* (National Popular Government League, 1920), available at archive.org/details/toamericanpeople00natiuoft.

64. *To the American People.*

65. Cooper, *Pivotal,* 313, 345.

66. *Treaty of Peace with Germany: Report of the Conference Between Members of the Senate Committee on Foreign Relations and the President of the United States,* S. Doc. No. 66–76, at 6 (1919).

67. Memorandum of President Woodrow Wilson, September 3, 1919, in *PWW,* 62:621.

68. Heckscher, *Woodrow Wilson,* 618–19; Weinstein, "Wilson's Neurological Illness," 363; "Senator Hitchcock's Interview with the President, November 17, 1919," *PWW,* 64:43–45.

69. "Text of Statement Issued at the White House Announcing President's Stand on the Treaty," *New York Times,* December 15, 1919.

70. *PWW,* 64:258–59; 59 Cong. Rec. 1,249 (1920).

71. *PWW,* 64:vii; Link, "Grayson's Predicament," 494.

72. "Text of President's Note on Treaty," *New York Tribune,* March 9, 1920; Carter Field, "Wilson Refuses to Compromise," *New York Tribune,* March 9, 1920.

73. *PWW,* 65:71n.

74. "Nation's Press Regrets Fate of Treaty," *Chicago Daily Tribune,* March 20, 1920.

75. *PWW,* 65:108–9.

76. *PWW,* 65:561–64.

77. *PWW,* 65:110–49.

78. "A Memorandum by Cary Travers Grayson," April 13, 1920, *PWW,* 65:179–80.

79. *PWW,* 65:186n.; see also Hoover, *Forty-Two Years,* 637.

80. *PWW,* 65:567.

81. Cooper, *Breaking the Heart,* 386.

82. Donald Bruce Johnson and Kirk H. Porter, compilers, *National Party Platforms, 1840–1972* (University of Illinois Press, 1973), 213.

83. *Address of Warren G. Harding, President of the United States, Delivered at a Joint Session of the Two Houses of Congress, April 12, 1921* (Government Printing Office, 1921).

84. *PWW,* 67:320.

85. Cary T. Grayson, statement, February 3, 1924, *PWW,* 68:567.

86. Gentry, *Hoover,* 126–41.

87. Theodore Kornweibel, Jr., *Seeing Red: Federal Campaigns Against Black Militancy, 1919–1925* (Indiana University Press, 1999), 176 (citing David Williams, " 'They Never Stopped Watching Us': FBI Political Surveillance, 1924–1936," *UCLA Historical Journal* 2 (1981): 5–17; Select Committee to Study Governmental Operations with Respect to Intelligence Activities [Church Committee], *Final Report, Book II: Supplementary Detailed Reports on Intelligence Activities and the Rights of Americans,* S. Rep. 94-755 (U.S. Government Printing Office, 1976), 3 (quoting Mary Jo Cook, testimony, December 2, 1975, *Hearings,* 6:111; James B. Adams, testimony, December 2, 1975, *Hearings,* 6:135).

88. Gentry, *Hoover,* 204–29.

89. Thomas H. Neale, "Presidential Disability: An Overview," Congressional Research Service, RS20260, July 12, 1999, 2–3; Richard E. Neustadt, "The Twenty-Fifth Amendment and Its Achilles Heel: The Speech," *Wake Forest Law Review* 30 (1995): 427–35.

90. U.S. Const., amend. XXV.

91. Herbert L. Abrams, "Can the Twenty-Fifth Amendment Deal with a Disabled President? Preventing Future White House Cover-Ups," *Presidential Studies Quarterly* 29, no. 1 (1999): 115.

92. Arthur S. Link, "Woodrow Wilson: A Cautionary Tale," *Wake Forest Law Review* 30 (1995): 591.

93. Birch Bayh, "The Twenty-Fifth Amendment: Dealing with Presidential Disability," *Wake Forest Law Review* 30 (1995): 437.

94. Bayh, "The Twenty-Fifth Amendment," 224, 437; Judith Havermann and David Hoffman, "Presidential Disability Discussed," *Washington Post,* April 28, 1989; John D.

Feerick, *The Twenty-Fifth Amendment*, 3rd ed. (Fordham University Press, 2013), 202. At the 2010 conference on presidential succession, Birch Bayh said that he had spoken to Valerie Jarrett and that he was allowed to say that the Obama administration had a very comprehensive plan. He stated that she had said, "Hopefully we never have to use it." Feerick, *Twenty-Fifth Amendment*, 224 (quoting "Transcript of Symposium: Panel and Response on Interpreting Ambiguities in Current Constitutional Arrangements," 71 [April 16, 2010]).

95. Lawrence K. Altman and Jeff Zeleny, "Obama's Doctor, Praising His Health, Sees No Obstacles to Service," *New York Times*, May 30, 2008; Lawrence K. Altman, "Many Holes in Disclosure of Nominees' Health," *New York Times*, October 20, 2008. Obama's doctor released six paragraphs covering the most recent twenty-one years of his life. Lawrence K. Altman, "The 1992 Campaign: Candidate's Health; Clinton, Citing Privacy Issues, Tells Little About His Health," *New York Times*, October 10, 1992. "Despite repeated requests, Mr. Clinton's staff has refused to give permission for interviews with the doctors and Mr. Clinton."

96. Link, "Cautionary Tale," 592.

Chapter 4. Harry Truman

1. Robert H. Ferrell, ed., *Truman in the White House: The Diary of Eben A. Ayers* (University of Missouri Press, 1991), 122–24; Admiral William Leahy, diary entry for January 24, 1946, William D. Leahy Papers, Library of Congress, Washington, D.C.

2. *Memoirs by Harry S. Truman* (Doubleday, 1955), 1:98–99 [hereafter Truman, *Memoirs*].

3. Colonel Richard J. Park, Report to the President, Rose A. Conway Files, Box 9, Harry S. Truman Library & Museum (HSTL), Independence, Missouri; Christopher M. Andrew, *For the President's Eyes Only: Secret Intelligence and the American Presidency from Washington to Bush* (HarperCollins, 1995), 156; Louis Menand, "Wild Thing," *New Yorker*, March 14, 2011.

4. Quoted in David F. Rudgers, *Creating the Secret State: The Origins of the Central Intelligence Agency, 1943–1947* (University Press of Kansas, 2000), 194.

5. Walter Trohan, "New Deal Plans Super Spy System: Sleuths Would Snoop on U.S. and the World," *Chicago Tribune*, February 9, 1945; Rudgers, *Creating the Secret State*, 29.

6. "Memorandum from the Director of the Office of Strategic Services (Donovan) to President Truman, August 25, 1945," *Foreign Relations of the United States, 1945–1950: Emergence of the Intelligence Establishment* (U.S. Government Printing Office, 1996) [hereafter *FRUS: Emergence of the Intelligence Establishment*].

7. Exec. Order No. 9621, Termination of the Office of Strategic Services and Disposition of Its Functions (September 20, 1945); "Truman Ends OSS, Shifts Functions," *New York Times*, September 21, 1945.

8. "Directive on Coordination of Foreign Intelligence Activities," January 22, 1946, HSTL; "The President's News Conference," January 24, 1946, HSTL.

9. Select Committee to Study Governmental Operations with Respect to Intelligence Activities [Church Committee], *Final Report, Book IV: Supplementary Detailed Staff Reports on Foreign and Military Intelligence*, S. Rep. No. 94-755 (U.S. Government Printing Office, 1976), 28; Wilson Andrews and Todd Lindeman, "Funding the

Intelligence Program," *Washington Post,* August 29, 2013; Tim Weiner, *Legacy of Ashes: The History of the CIA* (Doubleday, 2007), 3, quoting a letter from Truman to David M. Noyes, a Truman adviser, December 1, 1963, David M. Noyes Papers, HSTL.

10. John H. Crider, "President's Health 'Satisfactory,'" *New York Times,* April 5, 1944; "Roosevelt Is Well, His Physician Says," *New York Times,* October 13, 1944; Clayton Knowles, "Wife Says Doctors Cleared Roosevelt," *New York Times,* August 9, 1956; "Election of 1944," American Presidency Project, available at www.presidency.ucsb.edu [hereafter American Presidency Project].

11. Truman, *Memoirs,* 1:5. The White House daily log for August 18, 1944, says that Roosevelt and Truman had lunch with Roosevelt's daughter, Anna Roosevelt Boettiger, under a magnolia tree. "August 18th, 1944," White House Day by Day, A Project of the Pare Lorentz Center at the Franklin D. Roosevelt Presidential Library & Museum (FDRL), available at www.fdrlibrary.marist.edu/daybyday; "Vice Presidential Candidate Harry S. Truman at Lunch with President Franklin D. Roosevelt," photograph 66-2610, HSTL.

12. Truman, *Memoirs,* 1:4–5; Alonzo L. Hamby, *Man of the People: A Life of Harry S. Truman* (Oxford University Press, 1995), 290. Other accounts differ slightly. Arthur Krock of the *New York Times* reported Mrs. Roosevelt's statement this way: "Tell us what we can do. Is there any way we can help you?" Arthur Krock, "End Comes Suddenly at Warm Springs: Even His Family Unaware of Condition as Cerebral Stroke Brings Death to Nation's Leader at 63," *New York Times,* April 13, 1945.

13. Collection Historical Note, Lucy Mercer Rutherfurd Papers, FDRL. Eleanor had been summoned from a thrift shop benefit at the Sulgrave Club, where Woodrow Wilson's widow, Edith, was also in attendance. Eleanor Roosevelt, *This I Remember* (n.p., 1949), 344.

14. Krock, "End Comes Suddenly at Warm Springs"; "Harry S. Truman Taking the Oath of Office," photograph 73-1909, and "Vice-President Harry S. Truman Preparing to Take Oath of Office," photograph 73-1916, April 12, 1945, HSTL.

15. Truman, *Memoirs,* 1:192.

16. James T. Patterson, *Grand Expectations: The United States, 1945–1974* (Oxford University Press, 1996), 93. Quote from Churchill's radio address, October 1, 1939, cited in Winston Churchill, *Churchill: The Power of Words,* ed. Martin Gilbert (Da Capo, 2012), 233.

17. Truman, *Memoirs,* 1:122–24. In Truman's physical examination papers from World War I, "blind" is written next to 20/400 for his left eye, "Report of Physical Examination of Harry S. Truman," August 9, 1917, Military Personnel File, HSTL. He had escaped farm work by enlisting during World War I, memorizing the eye chart to hide his poor vision and becoming a popular lieutenant and then captain of an artillery battery (in France). The HSTL chronology notes that Truman was "assigned command of Battery D, 129th Field Artillery regiment, 35th Division. Battery was composed of 188 men, 167 horses, and a complement of French-designed 75mm guns." Chronology of Harry S. Truman's Life and Presidency, 1840s–1945, HSTL.

18. Truman chaired a committee whose findings saved the government millions of dollars and led President Roosevelt to create a War Production Board to oversee spending. Robert H. Ferrell, *Harry S. Truman: A Life* (University of Missouri Press, 1994), 156–65.

19. Hamby, *Man of the People,* 467–70; Truman, *Memoirs,* 2:272.
20. There were approximately 17 million men ages eighteen to thirty-four in 1945. *Sixteenth Census of the United States—1940, Population, Characteristics of the Population,* vol. 2, United States Summary, Section 2, available at www2.census.gov/prod2/decennial/documents/33973538v2p1ch2.pdf.
21. C. P. Trussell, "Food 'Coordination' Urged on Truman," *New York Times,* May 3, 1945.
22. Truman, *Memoirs,* 2:1; Truman, letter to his mother, Martha Ellen Truman, and his sister, Mary Jane Truman, October 23, 1945, HSTL.
23. Truman had known something was going on. He had been denied access to the research sites when he was leading the Senate investigation about waste and corruption in military construction. And Roosevelt may have mentioned the project at the same lunch on the White House lawn when the two planned campaign strategy. Ferrell, *Harry S. Truman,* 172, 418; Sean L. Malloy, *Atomic Tragedy: Henry L. Stimson and the Decision to Use the Bomb Against Japan* (Cornell University Press, 2008), 93.
24. The President's Day, April 25, 1945, HSTL; Godfrey Hodgson, *The Colonel: The Life and Wars of Henry Stimson, 1867–1950* (Alfred A. Knopf, 1990), 316; "Memorandum Discussed with the President, April 25, 1945," National Security Archives, available at www2.gwu.edu/~nsarchiv/NSAEBB/NSAEBB162/3b.pdf.
25. Margaret E. Wagner, Linda Barrett Osborne, and Susan Reyburn, *The Library of Congress World War II Companion* (Simon & Schuster, 2007), 485.
26. Truman, *Memoirs,* 1:87.
27. McGeorge Bundy, *Danger and Survival: Choices About the Bomb in the First Fifty Years* (Random House, 1988), 59–62; Thomas F. Farrell, "Oppenheimer Scarcely Breathed," in *The Manhattan Project: The Birth of the Atomic Bomb in the Words of Its Creators, Eyewitnesses, and Historians,* ed. Cynthia C. Kelly (Atomic Heritage Foundation, 2007), 294–95.
28. This account relies on Bundy, *Danger and Survival;* Hamby, *Man of the People;* Richard Rhodes, *The Making of the Atomic Bomb* (Simon & Schuster, 1986); Ferrell, *Harry S. Truman;* Barton J. Bernstein, "The Atomic Bombings Reconsidered," *Foreign Affairs* 74 (1995); "The Effects of the Atomic Bombings of Hiroshima and Nagasaki," U.S. Strategic Bombing Survey, June 19, 1946, HSTL [hereafter Bombing Survey].
29. White House, press release, August 6, 1945, Ayers Papers, HSTL; Harry S. Truman, radio report to the American people on the Potsdam Conference, August 9, 1945, HSTL.
30. John Lewis Gaddis, *The United States and the Origins of the Cold War, 1941–1947* (Columbia University Press, 1972), 245; Robert J. Donovan, *Conflict and Crisis: The Presidency of Harry S. Truman, 1945–1948* (University of Missouri Press, 1996), 94; "The Manhattan Project: An Interactive History," U.S. Department of Energy, available at www.osti.gov/manhattan-project-history/index.htm.
31. Alexander Feinberg, "All City 'Lets Go': Hundreds of Thousands Roar Joy After Victory Flash Is Received," *New York Times,* August 15, 1945.
32. "Hiroshima Visitor Tells About Blast Aftermath," *New York Times,* October 8, 1945; Amy Goodman and David Goodman, "The Hiroshima Cover-Up," *Baltimore Sun,* August 5, 2005; Bombing Survey.
33. Boyer, *By the Bomb's Early Light,* 187–88; "Man of the Year, National Affairs," *Time,* December 31, 1945.

34. Donovan, *Conflict and Crisis,* 98.
35. "The 36-Hour War," *Life,* November 19, 1945.
36. Alonzo L. Hamby, "The Mind and Character of Harry S. Truman," in *The Truman Presidency,* ed. Michael J. Lacey (Cambridge University Press, 1989), 49.
37. Robert A. Pollard, "The National Security State Reconsidered: Truman and Economic Containment, 1945–1950," in *The Truman Presidency,* ed. Lacey, 208–9.
38. C. L. Sulzberger, "Big Three Try Again to Ease World Strains," *New York Times,* December 16, 1945; C. L. Sulzberger, "Unsolved Problems Cloud Europe's Horizons," *New York Times,* December 23, 1945; John Lewis Gaddis, *The Cold War: A New History* (Penguin, 2005), 253.
39. P. J. Philip, "4 Named in Ottawa: Report Asserts Agents Were Told to Get Atom and Radar Data," *New York Times,* March 5, 1946.
40. John Lewis Gaddis, "The Insecurities of Victory: The United States and the Perception of the Soviet Threat After World War II," in *The Truman Presidency,* ed. Lacey, 253–57.
41. Kennan, telegram to George Marshall ["Long Telegram"], February 22, 1946, Harry S. Truman Administration File, Elsey Papers, HSTL, also available at www.trumanlibrary.org; see John Lewis Gaddis, *George F. Kennan* (Penguin, 2011), 220–21; Dean Acheson, *Present at the Creation* (Norton, 1969), 151.
42. Gaddis, *The United States and the Origins of the Cold War,* 298.
43. Pollard, "National Security State Reconsidered," 211–12.
44. Colleen M. O'Connor, " 'Pink Right Down to Her Underwear,' " *Los Angeles Times,* April 9, 1990; "President's Order on Loyalty Hailed," *New York Times,* March 23, 1947.
45. Regarding Truman's explicit authorization, see, for example, Hayden B. Peake, "Harry S. Truman on CIA Covert Operations," Spring 1981, Center for the Study of Intelligence, National Archives and Records Administration, available at research.archives.gov/id/7283080.
46. Joseph and Stewart Alsop, "Truman and Foreign Affairs," *Los Angeles Times,* March 6, 1946.
47. This story is often repeated but of uncertain credibility. See Phillip S. Meilinger's biography of Vandenberg, *Hoyt S. Vandenberg: The Life of a General* (Indiana University Press, 1989), 85, 231 n. 2.
48. John Acacia, *Clark Clifford* (University Press of Kentucky, 2009), 61–62; Donovan, *Conflict and Crisis,* 305; Congressional Hearings, 80th Cong., 1st Sess., April 2, 1947–July 1, 1947; Sidney Shalett, "Army Intelligence Being Reorganized: Gen. H.S. Vandenberg Pushes Plan to Enable Us to Avert Any Other 'Pearl Harbor,' " *New York Times,* May 16, 1946.
49. "A Look Back . . . The National Security Council Helps Shape the CIA," October 14, 2010, Central Intelligence Agency, available at www.cia.gov; Church Committee, *Final Report, Book I: Foreign and Military Intelligence, United States Senate,* S. Rep. No. 94-755 (U.S. Government Printing Office, 1976), 508.
50. William Strand, "Truman at Mother's Bier: Told of Death While Flying to Her Side," *New York Times,* July 27, 1947.
51. Gaddis wrote, "Stalin's first priority after the war was to remove what he regarded as vulnerabilities in the south. . . . Three initiatives followed: Stalin delayed the withdrawal of Soviet troops from northern Iran, where they had been stationed since 1942 as part of

an Anglo-Soviet arrangement to keep that country's oil supplies out of German hands. He demanded territorial concessions from Turkey as well as bases that would have given the U.S.S.R. effective control of the Turkish Straits. And he requested a role in the administration of former Italian colonies in North Africa." Gaddis, *The Cold War,* ix–x, 28; see also Melvyn P. Leffler, *A Preponderance of Power: National Security, the Truman Administration, and the Cold War* (Stanford University Press, 1992), 103–4.

52. Quote in Gaddis, *Kennan,* 317–18, citing Kennan's National War College lecture, "Measures Short of War (Diplomatic)," September 16, 1946, in *Measures Short of War: The George F. Kennan Lectures at the National War College, 1946–1947,* ed. Giles D. Harlow and George C. Maerz (National Defense University Press, 1991), 17.

53. Kennan quoted in Gaddis, *Kennan,* 294–95; Rusk quoted in Gaddis, *Kennan,* 319.

54. Acheson, *Present at the Creation,* 214.

55. Leffler, *A Preponderance of Power,* 176; Daily Presidential Appointments, HSTL; Richard A. Best, Jr., "The National Security Council: An Organizational Assessment," Congressional Research Service, RL30840, December 28, 2011, available at fas.org/sgp/crs/natsec/RL30840.pdf.

56. Andrew, *For the President's Eyes Only,* 171–72. The minutes of the meeting do not refer explicitly to a covert action but to an initial directive to the CIA referenced in a separate memorandum, NSC 1/1 of November 14, 1947.

57. Quoted in Donovan, *Conflict and Crisis,* 358.

58. NSC minutes, 4th Meeting, RG 273, Records of the National Security Council, National Archives and Records Administration, Washington, D.C. NSC 4-A is not mentioned in the minutes. See note 1 in "Memorandum from the Executive Secretary of the National Security Council (Souers) to Director of Central Intelligence Hillenkoetter," *FRUS: Emergence of the Intelligence Establishment,* December 17, 1947, 649–51.

59. "National Security Council Directive on Office of Special Projects, NSC/2," June 18, 1948, *FRUS: Emergence of the Intelligence Establishment,* 713–15; Gaddis, *The United States and the Origins of the Cold War,* 162–64; Gaddis, *The Cold War,* 163, referencing Anne Karalekas, "History of the Central Intelligence Agency," in Church Committee, *Final Report, Book IV: Supplementary Detailed Staff Reports on Foreign and Military Intelligence,* S. Rep. 94-755 (U.S. Government Printing Office, 1976), 31.

60. "Policy Planning Staff Memorandum," May 4, 1948, *FRUS: Emergence of the Intelligence Establishment,* 668–72.

61. Gaddis, *George F. Kennan,* 317; Ludwell Lee Montague, *General Walter Bedell Smith as Director of Central Intelligence* (Pennsylvania State University Press, 1992), 78; Thomas Powers, *The Man Who Kept Secrets: Richard Helms and the CIA* (Knopf, 1979), 31–32.

62. Weiner, *Legacy of Ashes,* 27, 582; Evan Thomas, *The Very Best Men: Four Who Dared: The Early Years of the CIA* (Simon & Schuster, 1995), 40.

63. Church Committee, *Final Report, Book XVII: Testing and Use of Chemical and Biological Agents by the Intelligence Community,* S. Rep. No. 94-755 (U.S. Government Printing Office, 1976), 385, 387–88.

64. Allen W. Dulles, William H. Jackson, Mathias F. Correa, for the Intelligence Survey Group to the National Security Council, "The Central Intelligence Organization and National Organization for Intelligence," January 1, 1949, *FRUS: Emergence of the Intelligence Establishment,* 903–11.

65. Gaddis, *George F. Kennan*, 317–19; Kennan testimony quoted in Church Committee, *Final Report, Book IV,* 30–31.

66. "Bill Grants Entry to U.S. Spies' Aides," *New York Times,* February 24, 1949; "Full Committee Hearings on H.R. 1741, H.R. 2546, H.R. 2663," U.S. House of Representatives, February 23, 1949, 487–89.

67. Gaddis, *George F. Kennan,* 318–19.

68. "The Secret War in Korea: June 1950 to June 1952," Clandestine Services History, July 17, 1968, declassified July 2007, 19–21, 76–79, Federation of American Scientists, available at fas.org/irp/cia/product/korea.pdf.

69. Harry Truman, memorandum to the Secretary of State and Secretary of Defense, October 24, 1952, available from www.nsa.gov. Matthew M. Aid, *The Secret Sentry: The Untold History of the National Security Agency* (Bloomsbury, 2009), 44; "257. National Security Council Intelligence Directive No. 9, Revised," December 29, 1952, *Foreign Relations of the United States, 1950–1955: The Intelligence Community, 1950–1955,* 802.

70. George F. Howe, *The Early History of the NSA,* doc. no. 3217154, National Security Agency, available at www.nas.gov; Aid, *The Secret Sentry,* 25. For a discussion of the Brownell Committee Report, issued June 13, 1952, see the editorial note on p. 233 in Douglas Keane and Michael Warner, eds., *Foreign Relations of the United States, 1950–1955, The Intelligence Community, 1950–1955* (U.S. Government Printing Office, 2007). See also "The Creation of the NSA—Part 2 of 3: The Brownell Committee," *Cryptologic Almanac 50th Anniversary Series,* National Security Agency, available at www.nsa.gov.

71. Harry Truman, memorandum to the Secretary of State and Secretary of Defense, October 24, 1952, HSTL; see also Andrew, *For the President's Eyes Only,* 196–98.

72. Thomas Powers, *Intelligence Wars* (New York Review Books, 2002), 232–33; James Bamford, *The Puzzle Palace* (Houghton Mifflin, 1982), 12, 17; "The Many Lives of Herbert O. Yardley," National Security Agency, available at www.nsa.gov.

73. Nicholas Horrock, "Colby Says N.S.A. Tapped Phone Calls of Americans," *New York Times,* August 7, 1975; Church Committee, *Final Report, Book II: Supplementary Detailed Reports on Intelligence Activities and the Rights of Americans,* S. Rep. No. 94-755 (U.S. Government Printing Office, 1976), 740.

74. Church Committee, *Final Report, Book III: Supplementary Detailed Staff Reports on Intelligence Activities and the Rights of Americans,* S. Rep. 94-755 (U.S. Government Printing Office, 1976), 565–636; Aid, *The Secret Sentry,* 296.

75. Daniel Patrick Moynihan, *Secrecy: The American Experience* (Yale University Press, 1998), 142; Weiner, *Legacy of Ashes,* 969; Norman Polmar and Thomas B. Allen, *Spybook: The Encyclopedia of Espionage* (Random House, 1997), 107.

76. Moynihan, *Secrecy,* x, xvii, 70–71; Polmar and Allen, *Spybook,* 578; "Venona—Dated Documents," National Security Agency, Public Information, Declassification and Transparency, available at www.nsa.gov.

77. Exec. Order No. 9835 (March 21, 1947); Ralph S. Brown, Jr., *Loyalty and Security: Employment Tests in the United States* (Yale University Press, 1958), 487–88.

78. Brown, *Loyalty and Security,* 487–88; Moynihan, *Secrecy,* 161.

79. Truman, *Memoirs,* 2:269–89; Fred P. Graham, "J. Edgar Hoover, 77, Dies; Will Lie in State in Capitol," *New York Times,* May 3, 1972; "John Edgar Hoover," Federal Bureau of Investigation, available at www.fbi.gov.

80. Curt Gentry, *J. Edgar Hoover* (Norton, 1991), 322; The President's Day, April 23, 1945, HSTL.

81. Harry Truman, letter to Bess Truman, September 27, 1947, in *Dear Bess: The Letters from Harry to Bess Truman, 1910–1959,* ed. Robert H. Ferrell (University of Missouri Press, 1998), 550; Robert H. Ferrell, ed., *Off the Record: The Private Papers of Harry S. Truman* (Harper & Row, 1980), 22, citing Truman's note to himself, May 12, 1945.

82. *U.S. News and World Report,* December 19, 1983; Gentry, *J. Edgar Hoover,* 322–27.

83. Church Committee, *Final Report, Book III,* 301; Gentry, *J. Edgar Hoover,* 524.

84. Church Committee, *Final Report, Book III,* 636–40, 573; Gentry, *J. Edgar Hoover,* 228–30, 282, 353–54.

85. Truman issued Exec. Order No. 10290 (September 24, 1951); for detail, see also N. Cathy Maus, "History of Classification and Declassification," July 22, 1996, Office of Declassification, Department of Energy, available at fas.org/irp/doddir/doe/history.htm. FDR issued Exec. Order No. 8381, Defining Certain Vital Military and Naval Installations and Equipment (March 22, 1940); Harold C. Relyea, "Security Classified and Controlled Information: History, Status, and Emerging Management Issues," Congressional Research Service, RL33494, February 11, 2008, available at www.fas.org.

86. "Senate Urged to Void Truman News Gag Order," *Chicago Tribune,* September 29, 1951; Arthur Krock, "In the Nation: The New Checks on Government Information," *New York Times,* September 28, 1951; "U.S. Adds Controls on Security Data: Truman Says Order Is Aimed at 'Potential Enemies,' Must Not Bar Legitimate News," *New York Times,* September 26, 1951.

87. Harold C. Relyea, "Overview of 'Classified' and 'Sensitive but Unclassified' Information," Congressional Research Service, July 18, 2006; Maus, "History of Classification and Declassification," 6.

88. Richard G. Hewlett and Francis Duncan, *Atomic Shield, 1947–1952: A History of the United States Atomic Energy Commission,* vol. 2 (Pennsylvania State University Press, 1969), 366.

89. Gaddis, *The Cold War,* 34–36; Acheson, *Present at the Creation,* 345.

90. David Eli Lilienthal, *The Journals of David E. Lilienthal,* vol. 2: *The Atomic Energy Years* (Harper & Row, 1964), 571; Hewlett and Duncan, *Atomic Shield,* 366.

91. "Statement by the President on Announcing the First Atomic Explosion in the U.S.S.R.," September 23, 1949, HSTL.

92. "Explosion!" *New York Times,* September 25, 1949.

93. Richard Rhodes, *Dark Sun* (Simon & Schuster, 1995), 391, 645; Richard Polenberg, ed., *In the Matter of J. Robert Oppenheimer* (Cornell University Press, 2002), 105–6; Bundy, *Danger and Survival,* 202; General Advisory Committee [GAC], report of October 30, 1949, Historical Document Number 349, United States Atomic Energy Commission [hereafter GAC Report].

94. Sources for this account include GAC Report; Lilienthal, *Journals,* 2:581; Bundy, *Danger and Survival,* 207–8; Rhodes, *Dark Sun,* 392–403; Leffler, *A Preponderance of Power,* 329.

95. "Memorandum for the President by the United States Atomic Energy Commission," November 9, 1949, *Foreign Relations of the United States, 1949: Foreign Policy Aspects of the United States Development of Atomic Energy* [hereafter *FRUS, 1949: Atomic*

Energy], 576–99. Circumstances dealt these five men an awesome responsibility. Gordon Dean was a law professor and former law partner of Senator Brien McMahon. Lewis Strauss was a partner in a New York law firm with an interest in physics. Sumner Pike had served on the Securities and Exchange Commission and most recently directed the Office of Price Administration. Lilienthal was a Chicago lawyer who had chaired the Tennessee Valley Authority. Henry De Wolf Smyth, who had headed Princeton University's physics department, was the only scientist.

96. McMahon quoted in David McCullough, *Truman* (Simon & Schuster, 1993), 761; other quotes from Rhodes, *Dark Sun,* 404.

97. Quoted in Rhodes, *Dark Sun,* 404–5.

98. Lilienthal, *Journals,* 2:615–17; Rhodes, *Dark Sun,* 406; Keith D. McFarland and David L. Roll, *Louis Johnson and the Arming of America* (Indiana University Press, 2005), 220–21.

99. Quoted in Rhodes, *Dark Sun,* 406–7; "Memorandum of Telephone Conversation, by the Secretary of State," January 19, 1950, *FRUS, 1950: Atomic Energy.* A memo by Dean Acheson, regarding a phone conversation with Sidney Souers, said the president told Souers "he had a report from Sec. Johnson which to him made a lot of sense and he was inclined to think that was what we should do." *FRUS, 1950: Atomic Energy,* 511; see also "Memorandum by the Joint Chiefs of Staff to the Secretary of Defense (Johnson)," January 13, 1950, *FRUS, 1950: Atomic Energy,* 503; "The Chairman of the Joint Committee on Atomic Energy (McMahon) to President Truman," November 21, 1949, *FRUS, 1949: Atomic Energy,* 588.

100. Alfred Friendly, "New A-Bomb Has 6 Times Power of 1st," *Washington Post,* November 18, 1949; James Reston, "Atom Security a Dilemma to an Insistent Democracy: Lilienthal Envisions Policy to Permit People to Get Facts Without Aiding Potential Foes," *New York Times,* November 29, 1949; Joseph and Stewart Alsop, "Matter of Fact: It's Not So Funny, Really," *New York Herald Tribune,* December 2, 1949.

101. William L. Laurence, "Much Hydrogen Bomb Data Known; Process Involves Fusion of Atoms," *New York Times,* January 18, 1950.

102. The President's News Conference, January 19, 1950, HSTL; Bundy, *Danger and Survival,* 212.

103. "Report by the Special Committee of the National Security Council to the President," January 31, 1950, *FRUS, 1950: Atomic Energy,* 518.

104. Acheson, *Present at the Creation,* 349; Lilienthal, *Journals,* 2:632; Robert L. Beisner, *Dean Acheson: A Life in the Cold War* (Oxford University Press, 2006), 232–33. Other accounts differ slightly in Truman's words. See Bundy, *Danger and Survival,* 213; Rhodes, *Dark Sun,* 407.

105. Statement by the President on the Hydrogen Bomb, January 31, 1950, HSTL.

106. Anthony Leviero, "Historic Decision: Discussing Plans for Making Hydrogen Bomb," *New York Times,* February 1, 1950.

107. Bundy, *Danger and Survival,* 213.

108. "The Gravest Decision," *Wall Street Journal,* February 2, 1950.

109. Arthur Krock, "In the Nation: How the Super-Bomb Project Was Disclosed," *New York Times,* February 2, 1950.

110. Quoted in McCullough, *Truman,* 914.

111. "The Atomic Bomb," *Life,* February 27, 1950; "The Soul-Searchers Find No Answer," *Life,* February 27, 1950.

112. "Scientists Fear U.S. Strangles Defense," *Los Angeles Times,* March 24, 1950.

113. Rhodes, *Dark Sun,* 512.

114. John Lewis Gaddis, *We Now Know: Rethinking Cold War History* (Oxford University Press, 1997), 110–11.

115. "The President's Farewell Address to the American People," January 15, 1953, HSTL.

Chapter 5. Lyndon Johnson

1. George Kennedy, "Advocates of Openness: The Freedom of Information Movement" (Ph.D. diss., University of Missouri, 1978), 118, citing Samuel Archibald, speech, University of Missouri, April 7, 1978. Moss reported Johnson's words after meeting with Albert and McCormack, according to Archibald, Moss's chief of staff. Archibald appears to be the only source for this account that is widely quoted. Samuel J. Archibald, "The Freedom of Information Act Revisited," *Public Administration Review,* no. 39 (1979): 311–18; Michael Lemov, phone interview with author, December 13, 2013; Bruce Ladd, *Crisis in Credibility* (New American Library, 1968), 205–6. The likely date of leadership meeting was confirmed with Lyndon Baines Johnson Presidential Library and Museum (LBJL), Austin, Texas, and in the President's Daily Diary at LBJL.

2. Administrative Procedure Act, Pub. L. 79-404 (1946).

3. "Party Divisions of the House of Representatives, 1789–Present," United States House of Representatives, available at history.house.gov/Institution/Party-Divisions/Party-Divisions (accessed July 22, 2016); "Party Division in the Senate, 1789–Present," United States Senate, available at www.senate.gov/history/partydiv.htm (accessed July 22, 2016).

4. Robert Dallek, *Flawed Giant: Lyndon Johnson and His Times, 1961–1973* (Oxford, 1998), 299–300; Johnson quoted in Harry McPherson, *A Political Education* (Little, Brown, 1972), 268.

5. Michael Lemov, phone interview with author, December 13, 2013.

6. There are many sources of examples of information agencies withheld. Among them, House and Senate reports to accompany S. Rep. No. 813, 89th Cong., 1st Sess., Committee on the Judiciary, October 4, 1965; H. Rep. No. 1497, 89th Cong., 2nd Sess., Committee on Government Operations, May 9, 1966; Sam Archibald, "The Freedom of Information Act Revisited," 311–18; Sam Archibald, "The Early Years of the Freedom of Information Act—1955 to 1974," *Political Science and Politics* 26 (1993): 726–31; Jim Smith, "The Freedom of Information Act of 1966: A Legislative History Analysis," *Law Library Journal* 74 (1981): 231–80. The *Washington Post and Times-Herald,* November 2, 1957, recounts the story of Dulles's classified building.

7. Archibald, "The Freedom of Information Act Revisited," 312.

8. Kennedy, "Advocates of Openness," 64.

9. *The Nation* reported four months before the Bay of Pigs invasion that the CIA "has acquired a large tract of land" in Guatemala "that is being used as a training ground." "Are We Training Cuban Guerrillas?" *The Nation,* November 19, 1960. After the invasion, Kennedy denied CIA involvement. But by the last week of April both the *Los*

Angeles Times and the *New York Times* were reporting on the CIA's role. "Cuba Held Major Setback for U.S.," *New York Times,* April 22, 1961; Arthur Krock, "Lessons of Failure," *New York Times,* April 23, 1961.

10. Just two weeks after President Kennedy's assassination, a Gallup poll reported that 52 percent of Americans polled believed that "some group or element" other than Oswald alone was responsible for the assassination, and another 19 percent were uncertain that Oswald acted on his own. George Gallup, "Most Persons Doubt Oswald Acted on Own," *Los Angeles Times,* December 6, 1963; Anthony Lewis, "Panel Unanimous," *New York Times,* September 28, 1964.

11. Joint Resolution to Promote the Maintenance of International Peace and Security in Southeast Asia, Pub. L. 88-408 (1964).

12. "Lyndon B. Johnson: Foreign Affairs," Miller Center of Public Affairs, University of Virginia, available at millercenter.org.

13. Michael Beschloss, *Reaching for Glory: Lyndon Johnson's Secret White House Tapes, 1964–1965* (Simon & Schuster, 2001), 194; Lady Bird Johnson, *A White House Diary* (Holt, Rinehart and Winston, 1970), 248.

14. Nicholas deB. Katzenbach, *Some of It Was Fun: Working with RFK and LBJ* (W. W. Norton, 2008), 226–27.

15. Dallek, *Flawed Giant,* 269, 367–69, 475, 488; Roland Evans and Robert Novak, *Lyndon B. Johnson* (Signet, 1966), 412, 512.

16. Johnson knew that he was not the first president to engage in such secret surveillance. Johnson had learned from *Newsweek* editor Ben Bradlee and Associated Press reporter Joe Mohbat that Attorney General Robert Kennedy had ordered the FBI to bug Martin Luther King's hotel rooms. One of Hoover's lieutenants had offered to play tapes of King's sexual encounters for Bradlee when Bradlee went to interview Hoover in 1964. Katzenbach, *Some of It Was Fun,* 154; Benjamin C. Bradlee, *A Good Life* (Simon & Schuster, 1995), 272.

17. Select Committee to Study Governmental Operations with Respect to Intelligence Activities [Church Committee], *Final Report, Book II: Intelligence Activities and the Rights of Americans,* S. Rep. 94-755 (U.S. Government Printing Office, 1976), 98–102.

18. Church Committee, *Final Report, Book II,* 105.

19. National Security Act, Pub. L. 80-235 (1947).

20. The CIA conducted such surveillance "in response to . . . pressure from Presidents Johnson and Nixon." Church Committee, *Final Report, Book II,* 22, 98–108; note 462 cites a letter to Henry Kissinger, February 18, 1969.

21. David Wise, "Dilemma in 'Credibility Gap,' " *New York Herald Tribune,* May 23, 1965. Historian Michael Beschloss noted that this article may have been the first use of the phrase. Beschloss, *Reaching for Glory,* 310.

22. Dallek, *Flawed Giant,* 281–82.

23. Katzenbach, *Some of It Was Fun,* 201–2; James T. Patterson, *Grand Expectations: The United States, 1945–1974* (Oxford University Press, 1996), 529–35.

24. Garrison Nelson (University of Vermont), email communication with author, December 9, 2013.

25. Steven R. Weisman, "McCormack, Ex-Speaker, Is Dead," *New York Times,* November 23, 1980.

26. Kennedy, "Advocates of Openness," 115.

27. The law provided that all rules, opinions, policy statements, and guidelines be available to "persons properly and directly concerned except information held confidential for good cause found," and matters "requiring secrecy in the public interest," Administrative Procedure Act, Pub. L. 79-404 (1946); Library of Congress letter quoted in Cross, *The People's Right to Know,* 228.

28. Availability of Information from Federal Departments and Agencies, *Hearings, Subcommittee of the Committee on Government Operations, U.S. House of Representatives,* 84th Cong., 1st Sess. (November 7, 1956).

29. Democratic Party Platform of 1956, August 13, 1956, American Presidency Project, available at www.presidency.ucsb.edu [hereafter American Presidency Project].

30. S. 2148, 85th Cong., 1st Sess. (May 23, 1957).

31. Smith, "The Freedom of Information Act of 1966," 259–64.

32. Democratic Party Platform of 1960, July 11, 1960, American Presidency Project.

33. Quoted in Archibald, "The Early Years of the Freedom of Information Act," 726.

34. Kennedy, "Advocates of Openness," 117.

35. Tim Weiner, "C.I.A.'s Self-Critique in Bay of Pigs Fiasco," *New York Times,* February 22, 1998. Peter Kornbluh, "Top Secret CIA 'Official History' of the Bay of Pigs: Revelations," National Security Archive, available at nsarchive.gwu.edu.

36. Patterson, *Grand Expectations,* 494–95; Jim Rasenberger, *The Brilliant Disaster,* 325; "Cuban Prisoners Land in Florida: Ransom Is Paid," *New York Times,* December 24, 1962; Anthony Lewis, "Group Raised 3 Million in Cash in 24 Hours to Ransom Cubans," *New York Times,* December 26, 1962; Richard Eder, "Cubans Executive 5 April Invaders: 9 Get 30-Year Sentences," *New York Times,* September 9, 1961.

37. Address: "The President and the Press," Bureau of Advertising, American Newspaper Publishers Association, April 27, 1961, John F. Kennedy Presidential Library and Museum, Boston, Massachusetts; Herbert N. Foerstel, *Freedom of Information and the Right to Know: The Origins and Applications of the Freedom of Information Act* (Greenwood, 2009), 37–38.

38. Robert Dallek, "The Medical Ordeals of JFK," *Atlantic,* December 2002; Robert Dallek, *An Unfinished Life: John F. Kennedy, 1917–1961* (Little, Brown, 2003), 636; Patt Morrison, "Judith Exner and the End of Innocence," *Los Angeles Times,* March 1, 1998; Richard Pearson, "Judith Campbell Exner, Linked to JFK, Dies," *Washington Post,* September 26, 1999.

39. Archibald, "The Early Years of the Freedom of Information Act," 729.

40. Clark Mollenhoff, *Des Moines Register,* August 2, 1965.

41. *Hearings, Subcommittee of the Committee on Government Operations, U.S. House of Representatives,* 89th Cong., 1st Sess. (March 30, 1965).

42. Herbert N. Foerstel, *Freedom of Information and the Right to Know* (Greenwood, 1999), 44.

43. George Kennedy, *Freedom of Information: How Americans Got Their Right to Know,* available at www.johnemossfoundation.org.

44. Kenneth Culp Davis, a leading authority on administrative law, commented wryly soon after the law was approved, "The House committee ambitiously undertakes to change the meaning that appears in the Act's words." Kenneth Culp Davis, "The Information Act: A Preliminary Analysis," *University of Chicago Law Review* 34 (1967): 809 n. 130.

45. Ladd, *Crisis in Credibility,* 209; "Clarifying and Protecting the Right of the Public to Information," 89th Cong., 2nd Sess. (June 20, 1966), National Security Archive, available at nsarchive.gwu.edu.

46. Jerry Ford, "Your Washington Review," May 25, 1966, Gerald R. Ford Presidential Library and Museum, Grand Rapids, Michigan.

47. Smith, "The Freedom of Information Act of 1966," 277; Ladd, *Crisis in Credibility,* 208; Rumsfeld quotes in 88 Cong. Rec. 27,839–40 (October 21, 1965).

48. 89 Cong. Rec. 7,145–48 (1966); "Editors Told White House Seeks Secrecy," *Chicago Tribune,* February 22, 1966.

49. 89 Cong. Rec. 13,007 (1966).

50. Bill Moyers, "In the Kingdom of the Half-Blind," address delivered on December 9, 2005, for the twentieth anniversary of the National Security Archive, George Washington University, Washington, D.C., nsarchive.gwu.edu.

51. Robert E. Kintner, memorandum for the president, June 24, 1966, National Security Archive, nsarchive.gwu.edu; President's Daily Diary, July 4, 1966, LBJL; Claudia Anderson (LBJL), email communication with author, December 26, 2013; Moyers, "In the Kingdom of the Half-Blind."

52. "On This Day in History: July 4," LBJL. Johnson's signing statement foreshadowed what later became a common presidential practice of undermining unwanted legislation with contrary signing statements. President Ronald Reagan, signing a deficit reduction act in 1984, took issue with delegations in its provisions and instructed agencies to comply "in a manner consistent with the Constitution." Signing a balanced budget act in 1997, President Clinton objected to requirements for proposed new legislation and would construe the provision in light of his constitutional duties. Signing a law outlawing torture of detainees, President George W. Bush said he would interpret it "in a manner consistent with the constitutional authority of the President to supervise the unitary executive branch." Todd Garvey, "Presidential Signing Statements: Constitutional and Institutional Implications," January 4, 2012, RL33667, Congressional Research Service, available at www.fas.org.

53. Attorney General's Memorandum on the Public Information Section of the Administrative Procedure Act, U.S. Department of Justice, June 1967, available at www.justice.gov; Davis, "The Information Act," 785.

54. Archibald, "The Freedom of Information Act Revisited," 315.

55. S. Rep. 813, 3, 10.

56. Davis, "The Information Act," 762, 784–807.

57. Daniel Patrick Moynihan, *Secrecy: The American Experience* (Yale University Press, 1998), 173–74.

58. Ladd, *Crisis in Credibility,* 212.

59. Julie Thomas (California State University, Sacramento), email communication with author, December 17, 2013; Michael L. Lemov, *People's Warrior: John Moss and the Fight for Freedom of Information and Consumer Rights* (Fairleigh Dickinson University Press, 2011), 66–67, 201.

Chapter 6. Gerald Ford

1. Marjorie Hunter, "A Plea to Bind Up Watergate Wounds," *New York Times,* August 10, 1974; "Nixon Departure from White House," C-SPAN video from CBS footage, August 9, 1974; Bob Woodward and Carl Bernstein, *The Final Days* (Simon & Schuster, 1976), 437–38.

2. Gerald R. Ford, Swearing-in ceremony, August 9, 1974, Speeches and Statements, Gerald R. Ford Presidential Library and Museum (GRFL), Ann Arbor, Michigan.

3. White House Tapes, Watergate trial conversations, Oval Office 741-2, June 23, 1972, Richard Nixon Presidential Library and Museum (RNL), Yorba Linda, California.

4. *Hearings Before the Committee on Rules and Administration, United States Senate,* 93rd Cong., 1st Sess. (1973) (nomination of Gerald R. Ford of Michigan to be vice president of the United States, November 1, 5, 7, and 14), HRG-1973-RAS-0004, 38–40; James Cannon, *Gerald R. Ford* (University of Michigan Press, 2013), 144–45.

5. Gerald Ford, *A Time to Heal* (Harper & Row, 1979), 61, 71–77, 265; Thomas M. DeFrank, *Write It When I'm Gone* (G. P. Putnam's Sons, 2007), 11; James Cannon, *Time and Chance* (HarperCollins, 1994), 650.

6. Walter Cronkite, Eric Sevareid, and Bob Schieffer, interview with the president, White House Press Releases, April 21, 1975, GRFL; Cannon, *Gerald R. Ford,* 79–81.

7. William Colby, *Honorable Men: My Life in the CIA* (Simon & Schuster, 1978), 391, 402, 447.

8. Douglas Brinkley, *Gerald R. Ford* (Times, 2007), 156.

9. Ford, *A Time to Heal,* 181–82; Jerald F. terHorst, *Gerald Ford and the Future of the Presidency* (Third Press, 1974), 216–17.

10. Confirmed with Elizabeth Druga (GRFL), and Jon Fletcher (RNL), email communication with author, February 12, 2014, based on contemporary photographs.

11. Ford, *A Time to Heal,* 181.

12. Bob Woodward, *Shadow: Five Presidents and the Legacy of Watergate* (Simon & Schuster, 1999), 28; Barry M. Goldwater, with Jack Casserly, *Goldwater* (Doubleday, 1988), 356–57; Brinkley, *Gerald R. Ford,* 74, 81, 116.

13. Senate floor debate quoted in Freedom of Information Act and Amendments of 1974, Pub. L. 93-502 (1975), 285.

14. Freedom of Information Act and Amendments of 1974, Pub. L. 93-502 (1975), Section 552(b)(1).

15. Memorandum for the Record, Cabinet Meeting, August 10, 1974, National Security Adviser's Memoranda of Conversation Collection, GRFL; William B. Saxbe with Peter D. Franklin, *I've Seen the Elephant: An Autobiography* (Kent State University Press, 2000), 181.

16. Letters reproduced in 93 Cong. Rec., 33,159 (1974).

17. Gerald R. Ford, letter to Senator Edward M. Kennedy concerning the Freedom of Information Act (H.R. 12471), August 19, 1974, Box 1, White House Press Releases, GRFL. Also 93 Cong. Rec. 33,159 (1974).

18. Kennedy quoted in Conference Report, Freedom of Information Act and Amendments of 1974, Pub. L. 93-502 (1975), 367.

19. Harold Relyea and Sharon S. Gressle, "The Administration of the Freedom of Information Act," Congressional Research Service, inserted into 92 Cong. Rec. 9,949–55 (1972).

20. Samuel J. Archibald, "The Freedom of Information Act Revisited," *Public Administration Review* 39 (1979): 316; George Kennedy, "Advocates of Openness: The Freedom of Information Movement" (Ph.D. diss., University of Missouri, 1978), 162.

21. "Has the Press Gone Soft on Government Secrecy?" *Editor & Publisher* 100 (1967): 9, 53.

22. EPA v. Mink, 410 U.S. 73 (January 22, 1973).

23. Evan Hendricks, *Former Secrets: Government Records Made Public Through the Freedom of Information Act* (Campaign for Political Rights, 1982), 94–106.

24. Inserted in the Congressional Record by Kennedy during Senate floor debate, accessed from Conference Report, Freedom of Information Act and Amendments of 1974, Pub. L. 93-502 (1975), 304, 320; Exec. Order No. 11652 (March 8, 1972).

25. Walter Rugaber, "Critic of Auto Industry's Safety Standards Says He Was Trailed and Harassed; Charges Called Absurd," *New York Times,* March 6, 1966; Craig R. Whitney, "G.M. Settles Nader Suit On Privacy for $425,000," *New York Times,* August 14, 1970; Justin Martin, *Nader: Crusader, Spoiler, Icon* (Perseus, 2002), 43–53.

26. John D. Morris, "Nader Recruits 80 New Student 'Raiders' to Investigate the Operations of a Dozen Federal Agencies," *New York Times,* June 1, 1969; John D. Morris, "Nader's Raiders Sue for C.A.B. Data," *New York Times,* November 26, 1969; David Ignatius, "Stages of Nader," *New York Times,* January 18, 1976; Ralph Nader, "Freedom from Information: The Act and the Agencies," August 26, 1969, published in Subcommittee on Administrative Practice and Procedure of the Committee on the Judiciary, "Freedom of Information Act Source Book: Legislative Materials, Cases, Articles," S. Doc. No. 93-82, January 1, 1974, at 93-2, 411–25.

27. Newspaper articles inserted in 93 Cong. Rec. 36,593–94, 36,599 (1974).

28. It is unlikely that Rumsfeld played a role in Ford's decision whether to sign the information bill. In a 2010 interview he noted he was in Belgium part of the time finishing up NATO business and could not recall participating in Ford's decision. There is no evidence of Richard Cheney's role, although he wrote in his memoir about his admiration that Ford's extensive use of veto power had helped "lay to rest any assumptions on Capitol Hill that the executive branch had been cowed into submission by Richard Nixon's impeachment crisis." Michael L. Lemov, *People's Warrior* (Fairleigh Dickinson University Press, 2011), 184; Richard B. Cheney, *In My Time* (Simon & Schuster, 2011), 79; Bradley Graham, *By His Own Rules* (PublicAffairs, 2009), 107–8.

29. Elizabeth Druga (GRFL), email communication with author, February 12, 2014. Jules Witcover, "Freedom of Information Measure Vetoed by Ford as Peril to Nation," *Los Angeles Times,* October 18, 1974; Gerald R. Ford, "Veto of Freedom of Information Act Amendments," October 17, 1974, American Presidency Project, www.presidency.ucsb.edu.

30. The Senate had 58 Democrats and 42 Republicans before election day in 1974; the House, 248 Democrats, 187 Republicans.

31. Martin Arnold, "Ford Vetoes Effort to Improve Access to Government Data," *New York Times,* October 18, 1974.

32. "Vetoing Your Right to Know," *Chicago Tribune,* October 19, 1974.

33. "Federal Files: Freedom of Information," *Washington Post,* November 20, 1974, inserted in 93 Cong. Rec. 36,624 (1974).

34. 93 Cong. Rec. 36,593, 36,865 (1974); "Senate Defeats 2 Ford Vetoes, Matching House Action Bills," *New York Times,* November 22, 1974.

35. *Hearings Before the Subcommittee on Administrative Practice and Procedure of the Committee on the Judiciary United States Senate, 95-1,* September 15, 16; October 6; and November 10, 1977, 95th Cong., 1st sess.; Kennedy, "Advocates of Openness," 295–300; "Information—Please!," *Los Angeles Times,* May 4, 1982; Hendricks, *Former Secrets,* 6, 12.

36. Congress exempted CIA operational files and broadened the exemption for law enforcement files. Exec. Order No. 12356, National Security Information (April 2, 1982); President and Attorney General Memoranda, "New FOIA Policy," October 4, 1993, U.S. Department of Justice, available at www.justice.gov.

37. David S. Broder, "Truly Nixonian," *Washington Post,* August 19, 1998; Alison Mitchell, "Impeachment: The Overview—Clinton Impeached," *New York Times,* December 20, 1998; "A Deserved Fine for Mr. Clinton," *New York Times,* July 30, 1999; Neil A. Lewis, "Exiting Job, Clinton Accepts Immunity Deal," *New York Times,* January 20, 2001; James T. Patterson, *Restless Giant: The United States from Watergate to Bush v. Gore* (Oxford University Press, 2005), 388–98.

38. Seymour M. Hersh, "Huge C.I.A. Operation Reported in U.S Against Antiwar Forces, Other Dissidents in Nixon Years," *New York Times,* December 22, 1974; Pub. L. 80-253, 61 Stat. 495 (1947).

39. The memorandum, dated May 16, 1973, is available at www.foia.cia.gov/sites/default/files/document_conversions/89801/DOC_0001451843.pdf; Randall B. Woods, *Shadow Warrior: William Egan Colby and the CIA* (Basic, 2013), 356–60; Colby, *Honorable Men,* 340.

40. Church Committee, *Book II;* Hersh, "Huge C.I.A. Operation"; Laurence H. Silberman, memorandum to the president, January 3, 1975, Box 7, Folder "Intelligence—President's Meeting with Richard Helms," Richard B. Cheney Files, GRFL; Colby, *Honorable Men,* 394–405.

41. Ford, *A Time to Heal,* 229; Colby, *Honorable Men,* 392–93. It is likely that Ford was hearing these stories for the first time, as he said in his memoir, even though he had served as a member of the special House intelligence subcommittee during the late 1950s and early 1960s. The relationship of trust between intelligence leaders and congressional committees during those years meant that Congress received only general briefings and left intelligence agencies free to do their job.

42. National Security Adviser, Memoranda of Conversation Collection, January 3 and January 4 meetings, GRFL.

43. Ford, *A Time to Heal,* 265; "CIA—The Colby Report," "Intelligence—Colby Report," December 27, 1974, Richard B. Cheney Files, GRFL. In 2016, declassified documents showed that White House staff, including Cheney, edited the commission's report. The final report deleted a section on the CIA role in assassinations. "Gerald Ford White House Altered Rockefeller Commission Report," National Security Archive Briefing Book No. 543, posted February 29, 2016, National Security Archive, available at nsarchive.gwu.edu.

44. Gerald R. Ford, daily diary, January 16, 1975, GRFL; Cannon, *Gerald R. Ford,* 322–24; Colby, *Honorable Men,* 409–11.

45. "4/10/75—Foreign Policy Address, Joint Session of Congress," President's Speeches and Statements: Reading Copies, GRFL, 102.

46. Nicholas M. Horrock, "Ford Acts to Bar Death Plot Data: Asks Senators Not to Reveal Details," *New York Times,* November 3, 1975.

47. Select Committee to Study Governmental Operations with Respect to Intelligence Activities [Church Committee], *Alleged Assassination Plots Involving Foreign Leaders,* S. Rep. No. 94-465 (U.S. Government Printing Office, 1975), 255–56; Colby, *Honorable Men,* 404–7, 442.

48. Two Stanford University computer scientists testified that the NSA also tried to establish a uniform cipher for computer networks that would permit the agency to "raid data flowing into networks and penetrate personal-data files enciphered for security," NSA historian David Kahn wrote in the *New York Times* during the congressional investigations. David Kahn, "Big Ear or Big Brother," *New York Times,* May 16, 1976.

49. Transcripts, *Meet the Press,* August 17, 1975, and August 4, 2013.

50. Exec. Order No. 19905, February 18, 1976; U.S. Department of Justice, Office of the Inspector General, "The Federal Bureau of Investigation's Compliance with the Attorney General's Investigative Guidelines [Redacted]," Special Report, September 2005, available at oig.justice.gov; Philip Taubman, "An Attorney General Who Trusted the Law," *New York Times,* March 9, 2000; Remarks of the President to the Regulatory Committee for Intelligence, February 21, 1976, White House press releases, GRFL.

51. An Act to Amend the Foreign Assistance Act of 1961, and for Other Purposes, Pub. L. 93-559 (1974).

52. Foreign Intelligence Surveillance Act, Pub. L. 95-511, 92 Stat. 1783 (1978); National Security Act of 1947, Pub. L. 80-253, 61 Stat. 495 (1978), at § 505, 60.

53. S. Res. 400, 94 Cong. Rec. 14,673 (1976); H.R. Res. 658, 95 Cong. Rec. 22,949 (1977).

Chapter 7. George W. Bush

1. George W. Bush, *Decision Points* (Crown, 2010), 135; Bob Woodward, *Bush at War* (Simon & Schuster, 2002), 63.

2. Bush, *Decision Points,* 137.

3. George W. Bush, remarks at the National Day of Prayer and Remembrance Service, September 14, 2001, National Archives and Records Administration, American Presidency Project, available at www.presidency.ucsb.edu; George W. Bush, address to the Joint Session of the 107th Congress, September 20, 2001, available at www.americanrhetoric.com. National security adviser Condoleezza Rice confirmed to Bob Woodward of the *Washington Post* that Bush had already decided that the war would be "global in nature" in that first telephone conversation. National Commission on Terrorist Attacks Upon the United States, *9/11 Commission Report: Final Report of the National Commission on Terrorist Attacks Upon the United States* (Norton, 2004), 554 n. 5.

4. Donald Rumsfeld, *Known and Unknown: A Memoir* (Penguin, 2011), 353; Peter Baker, *Days of Fire: Bush and Cheney in the White House* (Doubleday, 2013), 134–35; Matthew M. Aid, *The Secret Sentry* (Bloomsbury, 2009), 219.

5. Richard A. Clarke, *Against All Enemies: Inside America's War on Terror* (Free Press, 2004), 24; Bush, *Decision Points,* 142, 154.

6. George W. Bush, address to the nation, September 11, 2001, available at archived George W. Bush White House website, available at georgewbush-whitehouse.archives.gov [hereafter George W. Bush website].

7. Bob Woodward, *Bush at War* (Simon & Schuster, 2002), 30; Condoleezza Rice, *No Higher Honor: A Memoir of My Years in Washington* (Crown, 2011), 77; Michael Morell, *The Great War of Our Time* (Twelve, 2015), 58 ("a major change in policy").

8. U.S. Department of Justice, Office of the Inspector General, *The September 11 Detainees: A Review of the Treatment of Aliens Held on Immigration Charges in Connection with the Investigation of the September 11 Attacks,* April 2003, 21, 37, 41, Office of the Inspector General, available at oig.justice.gov; Bush, *Decision Points,* 145.

9. *9/11 Commission Report,* 328; U.S. Department of Justice, *September 11 Detainees*; U.S. Department of Justice, Office of the Inspector General, *Supplemental Report on September 11 Detainees' Allegations of Abuse at the Metropolitan Detention Center in Brooklyn, New York,* December 2003, Office of the Inspector General, available at oig. justice.gov.

10. George Tenet, *At the Center of the Storm: My Years at the CIA* (HarperCollins, 2007), 170.

11. The president's order of September 17, 2001, remains secret in 2016; Woodward, *Bush at War,* 101; Larry Siems, "Document a Day: The Secret Beginning," American Civil Liberties Union, June 30, 2010, 4, 34–35, available at www.aclu.org/blog/speakeasy/ document-day-secret-beginning.

12. "Mad Cow Disease Suspected," *New York Times,* September 11, 2001; "Iran: Denial on Nuclear Weapons," *New York Times,* September 11, 2001; "Key Leaders Talk of Possible Deals to Revive Economy," *New York Times,* September 11, 2001.

13. William J. Clinton, "Address before a Joint Session of the Congress on the State of the Union," January 27, 2000, American Presidency Project, available at www.presidency. ucsb.edu.

14. Barack Obama, *The Audacity of Hope: Thoughts on Reclaiming the American Dream* (Crown, 2006), 344.

15. Bush, *Decision Points,* 134.

16. Tenet, *At the Center of the Storm,* 35–36; Rumsfeld, *Known and Unknown,* 286.

17. *9/11 Commission Report,* 262; Michael Morell, *The Great War of Our Time* (Twelve, 2015), 43.

18. *9/11 Commission Report,* 259 nn. 4–12; Rice, *No Higher Honor,* 68; Kurt Eichenwald, "The Deafness Before the Storm," *New York Times,* September 10, 2012.

19. Much of this history is well documented in Lawrence Wright, *The Looming Tower: Al-Qaeda and the Road to 9/11* (Vintage, 2006).

20. Bob Woodward, "CIA Told to Do 'Whatever Necessary' to Kill Bin Laden;" *Washington Post,* October 21, 2001; Daniel Patrick Moynihan, *Secrecy: The American Experience* (Yale University Press, 1998), 219.

21. *9/11 Commission Report,* 260–66; Michael V. Hayden, *Playing at the Edge* (Penguin, 2016), 11, 42.

22. Bush, *Decision Points,* 135.

23. *9/11 Commission Report,* 255–65, 366, quote at 265.

24. *9/11 Commission Report,* 1, 257.

25. *9/11 Commission Report,* 341. The focus of press coverage in 2001 was on terrorist attacks overseas. In early 2001, four Bin Laden associates were on trial for their alleged role in the bombing of American embassies in Kenya and Tanzania the year before, and the *New York Times* did publish a profile of Bin Laden and his organization in January 2001. Stephen Engelberg, "One Man and a Global Web of Violence," *New York Times,* January 14, 2001; Alan Feuer, "Varied Portraits of bin Laden Emerge in Embassy Bomb Case," *New York Times,* February 27, 2001.

26. Bob Woodward, *The War Within* (Simon & Schuster, 2008), 436.

27. Baker, *Days of Fire,* 147.

28. Bush, *Decision Points,* 135.

29. David Firestone, "Security Alerts Go into Effect Across Nation," *New York Times,* September 12, 2001.

30. Bush, *Decision Points,* 139; Baker, *Days of Fire,* 124, 132.

31. Bush, *Decision Points,* 135, 144.

32. "Bin Laden's Statement: 'The Sword Fell,'" *New York Times,* October 8, 2001.

33. Bush, *Decision Points,* 140–49.

34. Rumsfeld, *Known and Unknown,* 352.

35. Louis Fisher, "Military Tribunals: Historical Patterns and Lessons," Congressional Research Service, RL32458, July 9, 2004, available at www.fas.org.

36. The main Geneva Conventions, I–IV (1949), were signed by the United States in 1955, Afghanistan in 1956, Iraq in 1956, and Pakistan in 1951. International Committee of the Red Cross, *1949 Conventions and Additional Protocols, and Their Commentaries,* available at www.icrc.org.

37. Exec. Order No. 11905; Exec. Order No. 12333; 50 U.S.C. 1801; Select Committee to Study Governmental Operations with Respect to Intelligence Activities [Church Committee], *Final Report, Book II: Supplementary Detailed Reports on Intelligence Activities and the Rights of Americans,* S. Rep. No. 94-755 (U.S. Government Printing Office, 1976), 289, 292; Richard A. Clarke et al., *The NSA Report* (Princeton University Press, 2014), 12–14, 22–26.

38. New York Times Co. v. United States, 403 U.S. 713 (1971).

39. Pub. L. 103-286 (1994); Report of the Commission on Protecting and Reducing Government Secrecy [hereafter Moynihan Report], S. Doc. 105-2, December 31, 1997, 1.

40. Moynihan Report, xxxi–xlv.

41. William J. Clinton, statement on signing the electronic Freedom of Information Act amendments of 1996, October 2, 1996, available at www.gpo.gov/fdsys/pkg/PPP-1996-book2/pdf/PPP-1996-book2-doc-pg1743.pdf; The Freedom of Information Act Amendments, Pub. L. 104-231 (1996).

42. "U.S. Government Eavesdropping on Americans?" CNN, available at edition.cnn.com/TRANSCRIPTS/0512/16/acd.01.html.

43. Baker, *Days of Fire,* 29–30.

44. Richard B. Cheney, *In My Time* (Simon & Schuster, 2011), 308.

45. Barton Gellman, *Angler* (Penguin, 2008), 141–43, 162–67, 174–75.

46. Cheney had heart attacks in 1978, 1984, and 1988, a fourth one in November 2000 after the election, and a fifth one in February 2010.

47. Woodward, *Bush at War,* 137; Woodward, *The War Within,* 426–37.
48. Bush, *Decision Points,* 7, 26; "Transcript of George W. Bush's Acceptance Speech," ABC News, August 3, 2000, available at abcnews.go.com.
49. Bush, *Decision Points,* 34.
50. Bush, *Decision Points,* 473.
51. "Party Divisions of the House of Representatives," United States House of Representatives, available at history.house.gov/Institution/Party-Divisions/Party-Divisions (accessed July 22, 2016).
52. Quentin P. Taylor, ed., *The Essential Federalist: A New Reading of the Federalist Papers* (Madison House, 1998), 50, 70.
53. Baker, *Days of Fire,* 101.
54. The GAO's suit was later dismissed on technical grounds. National Resources Defense Council v. Department of Energy, 191 F.supp.2d 41 (2002); process used to develop the National Energy Policy, GAO-03-894, August 2003.
55. Gellman, *Angler,* 82–85.
56. Exec. Order No. 13233 (November 1, 2001), Further Implementation of the Presidential Records Act; Mary Graham, "The Information Wars," *The Atlantic,* September 2002.
57. Graham, "The Information Wars."
58. John Ashcroft, "Memorandum for Heads of All Federal Departments and Agencies," October 12, 2001, U.S. Department of Justice, available at www.justice.gov; Andrew H. Card, Jr., "Memorandum for the Heads of Executive Departments and Agencies; Action to Safeguard Information Regarding Weapons of Mass Destruction and Other Sensitive Documents Related to Homeland Security," March 19, 2002, Federation of American Scientists, available at www.fas.org.
59. Exec. Order No. 13292 (March 25, 2003); 66 Fed. Reg. 64347 (December 10, 2001); 67 Fed. Reg. 31109 (May 6, 2002); 67 Fed. Reg. 61465 (September 26, 2002); 68 Fed. Reg. 55257 (September 23, 2003).
60. Attorney General's Guidelines, May 30, 2002, U.S. Department of Justice, available at justice.gov/opa/docs/guidelines.pdf.
61. Quoted in Baker, *Days of Fire,* 164; Hayden, *Playing to the Edge,* 68–72.
62. "Latest Release of Documents on N.S.A. Includes 2004 Ruling on Email Surveillance," *New York Times,* November 19, 2013; Baker, *Days of Fire,* 164–65.
63. Baker, *Days of Fire,* 165; Bob Graham with Jeff Nussbaum, *Intelligence Matters* (University Press of Kansas, 2004), 263; Hayden, *Playing to the Edge,* 80.
64. James Risen and Eric Lichtblau, "Bush Lets U.S. Spy on Callers Without Courts," *New York Times,* December 16, 2005; Eric Lichtblau and James Risen, "Spy Agency Mined Vast Data Trove, Officials Report," *New York Times,* December 24, 2005.
65. Eric Lichtblau, *Bush's Law: The Remaking of the American Justice System* (Pantheon, 2008), 193–210; Bush, *Decision Points,* 176–77; Risen and Lichtblau, "Bush Lets U.S. Spy"; Report on email and Internet data collection under Stellar Wind, March 24, 2009, Office of the Inspector General, National Security Agency, Central Security Service, working draft, available at www.aclu.org.
66. Military Order—Detention, Treatment, and Trial of Certain Non-Citizens in the War Against Terrorism, 66 Fed. Reg. 222 (November 13, 2001).
67. Rice, *No Higher Honor,* 104–6; Baker, *Days of Fire,* 174–75.

68. Canadian Omar Khadr, fifteen, was captured in Afghanistan in July 2002. Khadr pled guilty in October 2010 to killing an American sergeant with a grenade during a 2002 battle (Khadr has since recanted his plea) and was sentenced to eight years, the first year to be served in American custody, the remainder to be served in Canada. Khadr was returned to Canada in September 2012. He was still serving his sentence as of August 2014. Ian Austen, "Sole Canadian Held at Guantánamo Bay Is Repatriated," *New York Times,* September 29, 2012; "Omar Khadr's Untold Story: Canada Should Let Media Interview Ex-Guantánamo Detainee," *New York Times,* August 3, 2014.

69. "Memorandum for Commander, United States Southern Command," Department of Defense, August 23, 2003, available at projects.nytimes.com/guantanamo/detainees/913-naqib-ullah; "Guantanamo: Ten Years On—Facts and Figures," Human Rights Watch, available at multimedia.hrw.org/dataviz/gitmo/main_dashboard.html#footnote_1.

70. Dana Priest, "CIA Holds Terror Suspects in Secret Prisons," *Washington Post,* November 2, 2005.

71. George W. Bush, Creation of Military Commissions, September 6, 2006, available at georgewbush-whitehouse.archives.gov; "Humane Treatment of al Qaeda and Taliban Detainees," February 7, 2002, available at George W. Bush website.

72. Select Committee on Intelligence, U.S. Senate, "Committee Study of the Central Intelligence Agency's Detention and Interrogation Program," December 2014, available at fas.org/irp/congress/2014_rpt/ssci-rdi.pdf; Dana Priest and R. Jeffrey Smith, "Memo Offered Justification for Use of Torture," *Washington Post,* June 8, 2004; Bush wrote later that "the foiled attack had a big impact on me. . . . By giving this terrorist the right to remain silent, we deprived ourselves of the opportunity to collect vital intelligence. Reid's case made clear we needed a new policy for dealing with captured terrorists." Bush, *Decision Points,* 165.

73. Baker, *Days of Fire,* 201–2.

74. Bob Woodward, *Plan of Attack* (Simon & Schuster, 2004), 249; George Tenet with Bill Harlow, *At the Center of the Storm* (HarperCollins, 2007), 362–66.

75. Select Committee on Intelligence, U.S. Senate, "Report on the U.S. Intelligence Community's Prewar Intelligence Assessments on Iraq," July 9, 2004, National Security Archive, nsarchive.gwu.edu; Gellman, *Angler,* 221–22; Bush, *Decision Points,* 252; Morell, *Great War of Our Time,* 77, 86, 89.

76. Hamdi v. Rumsfeld, 542 U.S. 507, 592.

77. I use "Patriot Act" as the more commonly known way to refer to the Uniting and Strengthening America by Providing Appropriate Tools Required to Intercept and Obstruct Terrorism Act (USA PATRIOT Act). For the charges of civil liberties violations, see U.S. Department of Justice, Office of the Inspector General, "The September 11 Detainees: A Review of the Treatment of Aliens Held on Immigration Charges in Connection with the Investigation of the September 11 Attacks," April 2003, available at permanent.access.gpo.gov.

78. Inspector General Act, Pub. L. 95-452 (1978).

79. U.S. Department of Justice, Office of the Inspector General, "The Federal Bureau of Investigation's Efforts to Improve the Sharing of Intelligence and Other Information," December 2003, available at oig.justice.gov; Central Intelligence Agency, Office of the

Inspector General, "Counterterrorism Detention and Interrogation Activities," May 7, 2004, available at www.fas.org; for a more general discussion, see Jack Goldsmith, *Power and Constraint* (Norton, 2012), 95–120.

80. Offices of Inspectors General, "Unclassified Report on the President's Surveillance Program," July 10, 2009, available at www.fas.org.

81. Lichtblau, *Bush's Law,* 62–64, 137–41.

82. Rice, *No Higher Honor,* 499–501; Baker, *Days of Fire,* 483.

83. Pub. L. 107-40 (2001).

84. USA PATRIOT Act, Pub. L. 107-56 (2001).

85. "Information provided voluntarily by non-Federal entities or individuals that relates to infrastructure vulnerabilities or other vulnerabilities to terrorism" was not subject to the Freedom of Information Act, with disclosure of some information a criminal offense. Gina Marie Stevens, "Homeland Security Act of 2002: Critical Infrastructure Information Act," Congressional Research Service, RL31762, February 28, 2003, available at www. fas.org; Homeland Security Act, Pub. L. 107-296 (2002).

86. *9/11 Commission Report,* 380–420.

87. Adam Clymer, "Congress Agrees to Bar Pentagon from Terror Watch of Americans," *New York Times,* February 12, 2003.

88. George W. Bush, "President's Statement on Signing of H.R. 2863," December 30, 2005, available at George W. Bush website.

89. Senate Select Committee on Intelligence, "Committee Study of the CIA's Detention and Interrogation Program" (Public Summary), December 9, 2014, available at fas.org; Matt Apuzzo and James Risen, "C.I.A. First Planned Jails Abiding by U.S. Standards," *New York Times,* December 11, 2014.

90. Stephen Breyer, *The Court and the World* (Knopf, 2015), 65–87.

91. Hamdi v. Rumsfeld, 542 U.S. 507 (2004); Rasul v. Bush 542 U.S. 466, 484 (2004).

92. Hamdan v. Rumsfeld, 548 U.S. 557 (2006).

93. Boumediene v. Bush, 553 U.S. 723, 732 (2008).

94. U.S. Const. art. III, § 2.

95. Priest and Arkin, *Top Secret America,* 32.

96. Woodward, "CIA Told to Do 'Whatever Necessary.' "

97. Seymour M. Hersh, "King's Ransom," *New Yorker,* October 22, 2001.

98. Priest and Arkin, *Top Secret America,* 33.

99. David Barstow, "How White House Embraced Suspect Iraq Arms Intelligence," *New York Times,* October 3, 2004; *"The Times and Iraq: From the Editors,"* New York Times, May 26, 2004.

100. Seymour M. Hersh, "The General's Report," *New Yorker,* June 25, 2007; James Dao and Eric Lichtblau, "Soldier's Family Set in Motion Chain of Events on Disclosure," *New York Times,* May 8, 2004; Thom Shanker and Eric Schmitt, "Rumsfeld Accepts Blame and Offers Apology in Abuse," *New York Times,* May 8, 2004.

101. Bill Keller, "The Leak Police," *New York Times,* August 5, 2012.

102. CBS News, "Bush's Final Approval Rating: 22 Percent," available at www.cbsnews. com; Bush, *Decision Points,* 259.

103. Priest and Arkin, *Top Secret America.*

Chapter 8. Barack Obama

1. Estimates of the crowd varied. Washington's mayor estimated 1.8 million, *Washington Post,* January 22, 2009; Nielsen put the number of U.S. television viewers at 37.8 million, about 25.5 percent of U.S. television households. "Nearly 37.8 Million Watch President Obama's Oath and Speech on TV," Nielsen Newswire, January 21, 2009.

2. The original documents are removed when the president visits the rotunda to protect them from the bright lights and equipment. Bruce Bustard (National Archives and Records Administration), phone interview with author, June 20, 2014.

3. Barack Obama, remarks on national security, May 21, 2009. Obama's speeches, statements, and papers are available at www.whitehouse.gov unless otherwise noted.

4. Robert M. Gates, *Duty* (Knopf, 2014), 323.

5. Barack Obama, remarks at George Mason University, January 8, 2009.

6. Mark Mazzetti, "Global Economy Top Threat to U.S., Spy Chief Says," *New York Times,* February 12, 2009.

7. Current Population Survey, Bureau of Labor Statistics, available at www.bls.gov/cps; *The Budget and Economic Outlook: Fiscal Years 2009 to 2019,* Congressional Budget Office, available at www.cbo.gov/sites/default/files/cbofiles. The *New York Times* estimate of $3.3 trillion reflects the full decade; Shan Carter and Amanda Cox, "One 9/11 Tally: $3.3 Trillion," *New York Times,* September 8, 2011.

8. Barack Obama, remarks on national security, May 21, 2009.

9. Peter Baker, "Obama's Path from Critic to Overseer of Spying," *New York Times,* January 16, 2014; Peter Baker, "Obama's War over Terror," *New York Times,* January 17, 2010.

10. David Remnick, *The Bridge* (Knopf, 2010), 217, 268.

11. Peter R. Orszag, memorandum for the Heads of Executive Departments and Agencies, Freedom of Information Act, January 21, 2009, White House, available at www.whitehouse.gov.

12. Barack Obama, memorandum for the Heads of Executive Departments and Agencies, "Transparency and Open Government," January 21, 2009; Peter R. Orszag, Memorandum for the Heads of Executive Departments and Agencies, "Open Government Directive," December 8, 2009, available at www.whitehouse.gov.

13. "President Obama Signs Executive Orders on Detention and Interrogation Policy," January 22, 2009.

14. Barack Obama, statement on release of OLC memos, April 16, 2009; Exec. Order No. 13526, Classified National Security Information (December 29, 2009).

15. Barack Obama, remarks on national security, May 21, 2009.

16. "The Guantánamo Docket," *New York Times,* projects.nytimes.com/guantanamo.

17. Baker, "Obama's War over Terror"; Senate Select Committee on Intelligence, Unclassified Executive Summary of the Committee Report on the Attempted Terrorist Attack on Northwest Airlines Flight 253, May 18, 2010, U.S. Senate Select Committee on Intelligence, available at www.intelligence.senate.gov/publications/report-attempted-terrorist-attack-northwest-airlines-flight-253-may-24-2010.

18. Barack Obama, statement on preliminary information from his ongoing consultation about the Detroit incident, December 29, 2009.

19. Peter Baker and Scott Shane, "Obama Seeks to Reassure U.S. After Bombing Attempt," *New York Times,* December 28, 2009; Peter Baker and Carl Hulse, "Obama Hears of Signs That Should Have Grounded Plot," *New York Times,* December 30, 2009.

20. Gates, *Duty,* 451.

21. "Russian Hackers Read Obama's Unclassified Emails," *New York Times,* April 25, 2015; "ISIS Is Cited in Hacking of Central Command's Twitter and YouTube Accounts," *New York Times,* January 12, 2015; "Hacking of Government Computers Exposed 21.5 Million People," *New York Times,* July 10, 2015; "The Panama Papers: Here's What We Know," *New York Times,* April 5, 2016.

22. "Authorities Cite Plan by 3 Men to Aid ISIS," *New York Times,* June 12, 2015, "Gunman in Texas Shooting Was F.B.I. Suspect," *New York Times,* May 4, 2015, "Attacker with Hatchett . . .," *New York Times,* October 24, 2014, "F.B.I. Treating San Bernardino Attack as Terrorism Case," *New York Times,* December 4, 2015; David E. Sanger, "U.S. Cyberattacks Target ISIS," *New York Times,* April 24, 2016.

23. "ISIS Is Cited in Hacking . . .," *New York Times,* January 12, 2015. Department of Homeland Security, "Cyber-Attack Against Ukrainian Critical Infrastructure," February 25, 2016, available at ics-cert.us-cert.gov.

24. Daniel Ellsberg, *Secrets: A Memoir of Vietnam and the Pentagon Papers* (Penguin, 2002), xii, 299–309.

25. New York Times Co. v. United States, 403 U.S. 713 (1971).

26. David Leigh, "How 250,000 U.S. Embassy Cables Were Leaked," *The Guardian,* November 28, 2010; Charlie Savage, "Soldier Admits Providing Files to WikiLeaks," *New York Times,* February 28, 2013.

27. Bill Keller, "Dealing with Assange and the Wikileaks Secrets," *New York Times,* November 26, 2011.

28. Eric Schmitt and Charlie Savage, "U.S. Military Scrutinizes Leaks for Risks to Afghans," *New York Times,* July 28, 2010.

29. "WikiLeaks: Unpluggable," *Economist,* December 2, 2010; "Reaction to Leak of U.S. Diplomatic Cables, Day 2," *New York Times,* The Lede blog, November 29, 2010.

30. David E. Sanger and Eric Schmitt, "Snowden Used Low-Cost Tool to Best N.S.A.," *New York Times,* February 8, 2014; Mark Mazzetti and Michael S. Schmidt, "Officials Say U.S. May Never Know Extent of Snowden's Leaks," *New York Times,* December 14, 2013. For "black budgets," see the *Washington Post* interactive feature at apps.washingtonpost.com/g/page/national/inside-the-2013-us-intelligence-black-budget/420/#document/p11/a117299.

31. Barton Gellman, Aaron Blake, and Greg Miller, "Edward Snowden Comes Forward as Source of NSA Leaks," *Washington Post,* June 9, 2013.

32. Presidential Policy Directive 19, October 10, 2012; "In the War on Leaks, Reporters Fight Back," *Washington Post,* October 6, 2013; "Too Many Secrets: What Washington Should Stop Hiding," *Foreign Affairs,* April 20, 2015. "Presidential Memorandum—National Insider Threat Policy and Minimum Standards for Executive Branch Insider Threat Programs," November 21, 2012, available at www.whitehouse.gov; "Executive Order 13587—Structural Reforms to Improve the Security of Classified Networks and the Responsible Sharing and Safeguarding of Classified Information," available at www.

whitehouse.gov; "Obama's Crackdown Views Leaks as Aiding Enemies of U.S.," *McClatchy,* June 20, 2013.

33. "Leak Inquiries Show How Wide a Net U.S. Cast," *New York Times,* May 25, 2013.

34. Barack Obama, remarks at National Defense University, May 23, 2013.

35. Matt Apuzzo, "Holder Fortifies Protection of News Media's Phone Records, Notes or Emails," *New York Times,* January 14, 2015; Charlie Savage, "Holder Hints Reporter May Be Spared Jail in Leak," *New York Times,* May 27, 2014; H.R. 2578, "Text of the Commerce, Justice, Science, and Related Agencies Appropriations Act, 2016."

36. For one summary of leak prosecutions, see Leonard Downie, Jr., "The Obama Administration and the Press," Committee to Protect Journalists, October 10, 2013, available at cpj.org.

37. See Steven Aftergood, "Report on Disclosures to the Media Is Classified," Federation of American Scientists, available at fas.org.

38. Christopher Drew, "Drones Are Weapons of Choice in Fighting Qaeda," *New York Times,* March 17, 2009; Simon Rogers, "U.S. Drone Strikes Listed . . .," *The Guardian,* August 2, 2012.

39. Mark Mazzetti, "A Secret Deal on Drones, Sealed in Blood," *New York Times,* April 6, 2013; New America Foundation drones database, available at securitydata.newamerica. net; "Covert Drone War," available at www.thebureauinvestigates.com/category/ projects/drones; Michael V. Hayden, *Playing to the Edge* (Penguin, 2016), 333.

40. Stimson Center, "Recommendations and Report of the Task Force on U.S. Drone Policy," June 30, 2014, available at www.stimson.org; New America Foundation drones database, available at securitydata.newamerica.net. The Stimson Report put the number of civilians killed in Pakistan in a range of 416 to 951, including 200 children.

41. Richard Haass, "The President Has Too Much Latitude to Order Drone Strikes," *Wall Street Journal,* February 18, 2013.

42. Gates, *Duty,* 591.

43. Rizzo, *Company Man,* 297.

44. Stimson Center, "Recommendations and Report of the Task Force on U.S. Drone Policy."

45. President Ford's Exec. Order No. 11905 (1976) was strengthened by Jimmy Carter's Exec. Order No. 12036 (1978).

46. Obama stated in a 2013 speech that "the targeting of any American raises constitutional issues that are not present in other strikes—which is why my administration submitted information about Awlaki to the Department of Justice months before Awlaki was killed, and briefed the Congress before this strike as well." Barack Obama, remarks at the National Defense University, May 23, 2013.

47. New America Foundation, "World of Drones: Military," available at securitydata.newamerica.net/world-drones.html.

48. Obama, remarks at the National Defense University, May 23, 2013.

49. Hayden, *Playing to the Edge,* 144, 147.

50. For a detailed account, see David E. Sanger, *Confront and Conceal* (Crown, 2012), 188–225; "Document Reveals Growth of Cyberwarfare Between the U.S. and Iran," *New York Times,* February 22, 2015; Hayden, *Playing to the Edge,* 152.

51. David E. Sanger and Steven Erlanger, "Suspicion Falls on Russia as 'Snake' Cyberattacks Target Ukraine's Government," *New York Times,* March 8, 2014; David E. Sanger, "Obama Lets N.S.A. Exploit Some Internet Flaws, Officials Say," *New York Times,* April

12, 2014; "The NSA Files," *The Guardian,* www.theguardian.com; Sanger, *Confront and Conceal,* 247.

52. Presidential Policy Directive 20, October 2012, available at www.whitehouse.gov; Sanger, "Obama Order Sped Up Wave of Cyberattacks Against Iran," *New York Times,* June 1, 2012.

53. Statement of Michael S. Rogers, USN, Hearing Transcripts, Transportation, Cyber Command Nominations, Committee on Senate Armed Services, March 11, 2014, available at services.senate.gov/imo/media/doc/Rogers_03-11-14.pdf; David E. Sanger and Nicole Perlroth, "N.S.A. Breached Chinese Servers Seen as Security Threat," *New York Times,* March 22, 2014; Barack Obama, remarks at the Federal Trade Commission, January 12, 2015; Department of Homeland Security, "Cyber-Attack Against Ukrainian Critical Infrastructure"; "Announcing the President's Commission on Enhancing National Cybersecurity," April 13, 2016, White House, available at www.whitehouse. gov.

54. See a summary of presidents' uses of secret surveillance in Charlie Savage, *Power Wars* (Little, Brown, 2015), 162–223.

55. *The 9/11 Commission Report* (W. W. Norton, 2004), 222, 518.

56. Hayden, *Playing to the Edge,* 30.

57. President's Review Group on Intelligence and Communications Technologies, *The NSA Report: Liberty and Security in a Changing World* (Princeton University Press, 2014) [hereafter *NSA Report*].

58. Barack Obama, "Remarks by the President on Review Intelligence," at the Department of Justice, January 17, 2014; Privacy and Civil Liberties Oversight Board, *Report on the Telephone Records Program,* January 23, 2014, available at www.pclob.gov.

59. ACLU v. Clapper (2d Cir. Court of Appeals, May 7, 2015).

60. Privacy and Civil Liberties Oversight Board, *Report on the Telephone Records Program,* 11, 16, 146, 168; *NSA Report.*

61. Obama, "Remarks on Review of Signals Intelligence"; USA FREEDOM Act, Pub. L. 114-23 (2015); Congressman Jim Sensenbrenner, "Author of Patriot Act: FBI's FISA Order Is Abuse of Patriot Act," Press Releases and Statements, June 6, 2013, available at sensenbrenner.house.gov.

62. Barton Gellman and Laura Poitras, "U.S., British Intelligence Mining Data from Nine U.S. Internet Companies in Broad Secret Program," *Washington Post,* June 7, 2013; Foreign Intelligence Surveillance Act (FISA) (50 U.S.C. § 1881a).

63. Barton Gellman and Ashkan Soltani, "NSA Infiltrates Links to Yahoo, Google Data Centers Worldwide, Snowden Documents Say," *Washington Post,* October 30, 2013.

64. Edward Wyatt and Claire Cain Miller, "Tech Giants Issue Call for Limits on Government Surveillance of Users," *New York Times,* December 9, 2013. ReformGovernment Surveillance.com is the website of a group partnership between Facebook, Google, Apple, Microsoft, and other tech companies to push for reforming current regulation on surveillance.

65. Eric Lichtblau and Katie Benner, "As Apple Resists, Encryption Fray Erupts in Battle," *New York Times,* February 18, 2016.

66. Scott Shane, "No Morsel Too Minuscule for All-Consuming N.S.A.," *New York Times,* November 2, 2013; James Glanz and Andrew W. Lehren, "N.S.A. Spied on Allies, Aid

Groups and Businesses," *New York Times,* December 20, 2013; James Risen and Laura Poitras, "Spying by N.S.A. Ally Entangled U.S. Law Firm," *New York Times,* February 15, 2014.

67. Siobhan Gorman and Adam Entous, "Obama Unaware as U.S. Spied on World Leaders: Officials," *Wall Street Journal,* October 28, 2013.

68. President Barack Obama, State of the Union Address, January 12, 2016.

Conclusion

1. Michael V. Hayden, *Playing to the Edge* (Penguin, 2016), 422.

2. New York Times Co. v. United States, 403 U.S. 713 (1971), 727.

INDEX

Abdulmutallab, Umar Farouk, 185,
    186, 193
Abu Ghraib, 176–77
Acheson, Dean, 97, 112, 114
Adams, Abigail, 47
Adams, John, 14, 37, 47, 48
Adams, John Quincy, 25, 28–29
Administrative Conference of the United
    States, 138
Afghanistan, 149, 156, 157, 167, 176, 182,
    188, 192
Agnew, Spiro, 134
Agriculture, U.S. Department of, 140, 164
Al-Awlaki, Anwar, 193
Albert, Carl, 118, 119, 121
Alexander, Keith B., 183, 195
Alien Enemy Bureau, 56, 105
Al Qaeda, 186; drone attacks on, 194; Iraq
    and, 169; operatives of, 156, 168, 182,
    193, 196; pre-9/11 activities, 152, 153;
    post-9/11 tactics to fight, 150, 163, 167,
    175, 176; September 11, 2001, attacks
    and, 149, 155
Alsop, Joseph, 113, 125
Alsop, Stewart, 113
Altman, Lawrence K., 78
American Civil Liberties Union (ACLU)
    (National Civil Liberties Board), 58, 70,
    75, 140

American colonies, 11, 42
American Daily Advertiser, 48
American Protective League, 56, 60, 61
American Society of Newspaper Editors,
    115, 124, 140
Annals of Congress, 36
Anthrax, 156
Anti-war movements: during Vietnam War,
    103, 118, 122, 145, 146, 205; during
    World War I, 53, 54, 55, 56, 57
Archibald, Sam, 130
Arkin, William M., 176
Arlington Hall, 103
Armey, Dick, 174
Articles of Confederation, 11, 12–13, 14,
    15, 16, 21, 24
Ashcroft, John, 150, 160, 163, 164, 165,
    167, 171, 174
Associated Press (AP), 123, 190
Atlantic, 7
Atomic Energy Commission (AEC), 109,
    110–114, 125
Aurora (General Advertiser), 40, 41, 45
Ayers, Eben, 80

Bache, Benjamin Franklin, 40, 41, 43, 44,
    45, 46
Baker, Peter, 162, 165, 168
Bank of the United States, 38–39, 42